THE HILDA JAMES STORY
LOST OLYMPICS
IAN HUGH McALLISTER

www.lostolympics.co.uk

To Sandra,
Best Wishes,
Ian McAllister

Published in March 2013 by emp3books Ltd
Norwood House, Elvetham Road, Fleet, GU51 4HL

ISBN-13: 978-1-907140-71-6

Dedicated to the memory of my
Father
Donald Hugh McAllister
24/5/1931 - 2/5/2011

We talked about this for years
In the end it just took too long
Sorry Dad

Notes:

1. Throughout the text I have included separate entries in **bold** detailing significant individual races where Hilda James either won, or broke records. **National** and **World** Records are underlined.

2. I have used a decimal standard for swim times. Although times in the 1910s and 1920s were recorded using 1/5ths of a second, I have used multiples of 0.20 seconds. Thus a time of 1 minute 53 3/5 seconds is noted as 1:53.60

3. Country and city names corresponding to the age are used throughout, with the corresponding modern names in brackets shown on their first use, e.g. Ceylon (Sri Lanka).

4. Dates are noted as day/month/year.

CONTENTS

CHAPTER 1
GARSTON

At the outbreak of the Great War in 1914, John James was living in a rented terraced house with his beloved wife Gertrude and their children. They had moved up from renting rooms over one of the shops in Garston High Street, or St. Mary's Road as it was properly known. 32 year old John worked on the early shift at the postal sorting office in South Liverpool. Even with a steady job money was tight, and he constantly found it hard to manage his family on postal wages.

John would appear later in the day on the streets of Garston with his ladders, cleaning windows to help make ends meet. He would also take on any other kind of casual work he could find. In fact John James had gradually built up a local reputation as an expert carpet beater and odd-jobber. He was also a bit of a rag and bone man into the bargain, recycling and selling on all sorts of used items. Three years younger than her husband, Gertie kept house and also took in sewing and dress-making to help boost their small income. She could make or knit anything, and her children were always turned out scrubbed clean and looking spotless.

It was a good thing John was a strong provider. There were four children, studious Elsie Mary, fun-loving Hilda Marjorie and two normally boisterous boys, Jack Paterson and Walter Edward. Elsie was a keen scholar and excelled at her lessons. The local school had already begun to suggest that she should be entered for grammar school examinations and attempt to win a coveted free place. Both under educated, John and Gertie doted on their clever eldest daughter and provision had been made for her to study. There was an attic which John had converted into a large bedroom with space for a homework desk, and he had carefully saved up to provide Elsie with a safety air heater.

Family life was pretty normal for the age; although money was always very tight there were plenty of traditional pastimes such as board and card games, and everybody had fun with an old piano in the front parlour. The boys preferred to play on the kitchen floor in the evenings and were often excused from family music sessions. They were usually allowed use of the kitchen for an hour after the evening meal, after which it was off to bed while Hilda sat by the kitchen table with her homework.

John came from Irish stock. His grandparents had been starved out of Ireland during the great potato famine of the mid 19th century, finally escaping across the Irish Sea to settle in Liverpool. They had lost their faith in the church, leaving tradition behind them as they fled from their native roots. Once settled in Liverpool, they were drawn in to Pastor Charles Taze Russell's Bible Study Movement. This was the organisation which would later be restyled as The Jehovah's Witnesses. Married to John James at just 17, Gertrude Acton was a strong, sure woman and deeply moralistic. Her family were actually Quakers, but to suit John she was happy to embrace Pastor Russell's teachings and joined the Movement, finding it a suitable vehicle for her fervent beliefs.

Alcohol was strictly prohibited, and the James' kept a dry house where Sundays were completely set aside for religious observance. There were no games allowed on a Sunday and the piano could only be used for hymns. After family Bible Study time, the two girls would be packed off to a suitable local Sunday group with their lunch. They would be joined by their parents and younger brothers for a Meeting later in the day.

Even though he worked for many hours in the day, John cherished a lifelong passion for growing fruit and vegetables. Somehow he managed to find the time to run his allotment, from which he fed the family. He had green fingers and always grew high quality produce. There was even some left spare to sell or trade on occasion. In the back yard there was a home-made coop where the children helped their father to look after the chickens which supplied eggs, and occasionally meat.

John was best described as a loving man turned hard by drudgery and fatigue. He was a disciplinarian and would start to unbuckle his belt as a warning to the children if they got out of line. At one time or another all four of them would get belted with the leather, quickly learning to avoid repeating the experience whenever possible. The James' children were always taught never to want or ask for luxuries because they had what they had, and that was good enough. Above all, they were allowed no self promotion and definitely no "airs or graces". Basically John and Gertie were poor but honest people, simple folk with little ambition. Poor as they were, for the James family life wasn't too hard by some reckoning. There were plenty of people around them who didn't have it so good.

Hilda Marjorie James was born on 27th April 1904, the second of John and Gertie's five children, of which four had survived. Just thirteen months younger than her sister Elsie, Hilda remained the youngest until she was four, Jack and Walter being born in 1908 and 1909. Finally, another baby boy arrived in 1912, although little Tommy was sadly lost after catching diphtheria during infancy. Elsie and Hilda shared chores and were at the same time close friends and fierce rivals for most of their lives. When sent on their normal walk to a local farm to collect supplies, Hilda was always required to carry the milk and Elsie the cheese. If Elsie had carried the milk and Hilda the cheese little of it would ever have arrived back at the house.

Elsie rarely played outside and always preferred the company of her books. On the other hand Hilda was skinny and athletic, exactly the opposite of her sister and quite the tomboy. She was usually to be found kicking a ball or engaged in some other form of street games, hopscotch and the like. She would often get into various scrapes with the other neighbourhood children. More often than not she had scabby knees, and she was always getting into trouble with her Ma over the state of her clothes. Gertie's younger daughter was a specialist at coming up with a novel excuse for having a torn pinafore, but in spite of having to wear the thing she could usually beat the local boys in any races they cared to run.

On one notable occasion the poor pinafore completely failed to make it home. Hilda was dared to climb over a large garden wall and throw fallers from an apple tree to her friends. She managed to complete the dare, but was then chased back over the wall by a huge dog which the house owner had let out when she was spotted. It was a good job the house had a very big garden, because she only just had time to scramble back up the wall before the dog caught up with her. There was a bit of a tug of war at the top and the dog ended up with most of her pinafore. Hilda dropped safely down on the outside and laughed with the others as they heard the dog's trophy being savaged in the garden. After examining the remains of the pinafore she quickly threw the rest of it back over the wall for the dog, because it really wasn't worth saving.

Arriving home later she tried to sneak in unnoticed, certain that there would be some sort of reckoning. Worse still, if she was caught telling lies it would definitely mean an appointment with Pa's belt and she knew that was best avoided. Hilda failed to make it to safety, and standing in the kitchen looking the worse for wear she had to tell her Ma that she didn't actually know where the pinafore was. After all the dog might have put it anywhere, so she reckoned it was as good as the truth. For a change Ma just sighed at her and she got away with it.

In spite of the general lack of funds, there were sometimes treats. If Elsie was dispatched after tea to fetch their Grandpa and Grandma James from a few streets away, the children knew they would be in for an evening of fun. Their grandparents would duly arrive with two of John's brothers to find the kitchen table cleared so that Ma and Grandma could spend the evening sewing or dressmaking together. The four men would sit in the front parlour and play cards until late into the night, but the adults would not settle down to their pastimes until there had been a proper show for the children.

Before they were finally sent off to bed, Elsie and Hilda would play the old piano and sing for the adults. Some sort of entertainment would follow as requested by the boys, usually a board game or a guessing game. After that, Grandpa James would solemnly produce his props from a large box and there would be a wonderful puppet show for the four excited youngsters to enjoy. The old man was apparently a dab hand at magic too. Grandpa was so clever that he could have someone choose a card and then correctly pick it out of a shuffled pack. He had even been known to make ha'pennies appear out of well behaved young people's ears.

By the spring of 1915 John had proudly supplied his family with transport. He had done a clearing job somewhere and rescued a couple of broken bicycles to restore for the girls. He and Gertie rode an old tandem he had acquired, and to that he attached a small home-made trailer that he had knocked together to pull the two boys along in style behind. John and Gertie must have both been pretty fit. The family would have made quite a sight as they rode out of South Liverpool into the countryside for picnics that summer.

CHAPTER 2
EARLY SWIMMING

At the start of the 1915 autumn school term Hilda started at Victoria School in Garston, a year behind her sister Elsie. As their strict religious doctrine conflicted sharply with the school's regular Church of England teaching, the James' girls were not allowed to participate in Religious Education (RE) lessons. Because Elsie had already been earmarked for an attempt at the Grammar School scholarship, she was allowed the time for extra maths study instead of RE, but that wouldn't suit Hilda.

The only other option available for avoiding the RE lessons was a twice weekly trip to Garston's Victorian Swimming Baths. Ma duly knitted her younger daughter a swimming costume, and the following Monday Hilda walked to the baths with the swimming class for the first time. Hilda was slow to get changed, mainly because the new costume was tight and scratchy. Even worse, it was horribly revealing and for that she instantly hated it. By the time she had fought her way into the beastly thing she could already hear the other children splashing about and shouting about how cold the water was. Hilda shivered at the thought, and her enthusiasm for swimming lessons faded fast. Maybe a dunk in the cold water wasn't going to be her thing after all.

Hilda could hear the swimming teacher working her way along the long line of changing cubicles banging all the doors open to check that everyone was changed and in the water. Cubicle inspection must have been fairly cursory because somehow, by thinking thin and keeping very still in the far corner she managed not to be noticed. At the end of the lesson and hidden among the crowd of children poolside, Hilda slipped into the girls toilets. By splashing some water on her hair and costume she was able to pass inspection and walk triumphantly back to school having survived the swimming trip.

By using the same dodge, Hilda successfully managed to hang out for another lesson before finally being discovered at locker inspection on her third attempt to hide. Just occasionally teachers don't do what you might expect. There was no real shouting or telling off, and she was not punished. Had she been, World sporting history might have turned out very differently. The teacher simply asked two of the older swimmers to walk the reluctant new girl to the shallow end and help her climb in. One of these was the school's Head Girl who Hilda knew her big sister Elsie admired.

Although Hilda cried until she had been taken down the steps and walked into the pool right up to her shoulders, the water actually wasn't too bad. She was then allowed back to the shallow end and left to stand holding the side bars until it was time to get out. Crucially during her first visit to the pool she was not forced to join in the lesson. Climbing out of the water at the end of the session, she did notice that to her great embarrassment the knitted costume weighed about three times as much when wet, sagged a lot and was positively indecent.

By the following Monday's visit to the baths Hilda had largely overcome her initial reluctance. The water had not actually been as cold as she had been led to believe, and both the swimming teacher and the Head Girl had earned her respect by being firm but fair because they had allowed her time enough to acclimatise at her own pace. She steeled herself to get in, get on with it and learn this new swimming thing. She said that at first it was just like playing about. She hadn't realised that almost immediately she had actually started to swim.

And so, on the 29th September 1915 and after just a couple of lessons, eleven year old Hilda Marjorie James joined many of her classmates in doggy paddling along the pool and back to earn her very first certificate from the Liverpool and District Teachers Association (L&DTA). All things considered it might have been a pretty inauspicious start, but ultimately it would prove to be the launch of an astronomical nine year amateur swimming career. Along the way Hilda would receive World acclaim as an ambassador for the sport.

29/9/15
L&DTA Swimming Certificate
3rd Class - 50 yards

1916 was a particularly difficult year in the James household. The postal sorting office closed, temporarily forcing John out of work. Because he was not prepared to go to war on account of his deeply held religious beliefs, there was immediately an urgent need to find an alternative course of action. Faced with the ever growing probability of conscription he might eventually have had to declare himself as a conscientious objector, a moral position during the Great War which brought stigma, revulsion and often even a jail sentence. However, John was a pragmatist. Not willing to jeopardise his family life he managed to tread a delicate balance between the practical reality of a country at war and the moral ideal of pacifism.

When John lost his job, Gertie had taken on lodgers in the form of two men from the countryside who came to find work in a local munitions factory. They rented the James' attic, and Elsie had to move down to share Hilda's bedroom. She was still able to study in peace because by this time water baby Hilda was usually out at the evening swimming session at the baths.

In the end the lodgers actually came to John's rescue when they found him a job as a middle manager at the factory. He was lucky, because although basically uneducated he had plenty of common sense to help him. He was only able to justify himself morally by the fact that he was not actually involved in making ammunition. In spite of all this he did fail to avoid local conscription, finding himself out on patrol most nights having being drafted in as a Special Constable on fire warning duty. He felt content to do that as he was seen to be doing his bit by helping to protect the neighbourhood.

In 1916, Hilda swam from strength to strength, gaining;

5/16
School Beginners Swimming Prize
A race across the pool - Won

5/16
The Lord Mayor of Liverpool's
Prize for Swimming
75 yards in 1:20.00

L&DTA Swimming Certificate 2nd Class
200 yards

L&DTA swimming Certificate 1st Class

For her 13th birthday in April 1917 Hilda asked her parents if they might be able to buy her a season contract for the baths. It was a big ask, but they did manage to scrape the money together from somewhere. After that she swam every evening between 6 & 7 PM. She was already gaining a reputation as a keen and dedicated swimmer, and she was soon granted special permission by the baths management to stay late until 8 PM with the senior swimmers. By this time she was already on the school swimming team, competing against other Liverpool schools at small local galas.

A visit to the baths in Garston cost a penny on a 1st class day when the water was crystal clear but freezing cold. Fresh water was supplied by Liverpool's revolutionary cold water system directly from the Lake Vyrnwy Dam some sixty miles to the south in Wales. On a 2nd class day it was only a ha'penny to swim, but the water could best be described as "pretty cloudy" from all the unwashed swimmers, as it didn't actually have a full filtration system. Like most Victorian baths Garston had hot bathtubs for hire, although many people didn't share Ma James' enthusiasm for washing properly with hot water and soap. A lot of the local folk simply visited the baths occasionally for a dip in the public pool, substituting that for a proper bath. Many of them were railway and factory workers with plenty of grime to wash off. On a 2nd class day the major compensation was that the water in the pool was actually warm, having been gradually heated by an ingenious system of pipes connected to Garston's waste incinerator which was situated next door.

Later in the year Elsie started at Aigburth Vale High School, having duly won the free scholarship as predicted. Gaining a good education was her dream, but achieving it would put an extra strain on the James' limited resources. John and Gertie were intensely proud that their clever daughter was going to get her education, but they soon discovered with some horror that the supposedly free scholarship only covered the basic school fees. Money would have to be found from somewhere for uniform, travel, books and so on. There were all manner of other extras to pay for.

Because Elsie had to leave home early and would get back later Hilda began to balance her swimming against extra chores, taking on many of Elsie's regular tasks as well as her own. The hardest thing she had to do was to make sure that two reluctant boys were washed and ready to their mother's high standard every day, before walking them to their school and hurrying to get to hers. Somehow she had also found the time and energy to begin earning her own contribution to the family coffers by taking a Saturday job at one of the greengrocery stores in Garston High Street.

The coach at Garston Swimming Club approached John James at the baths one evening. Mr. Howcroft wanted to ask Mr. James if he might allow his daughter to take up a club membership. John had been pleased to see Hilda's seemingly limitless energy and enthusiasm properly harnessed by her interest in swimming. Aware that Hilda would probably see club membership as an achievement equal to Elsie's school scholarship, he agreed to her becoming a Garston Swimming Club Junior.

More important recognition was soon to follow in the form of Liverpool and District Teachers Association certificates which were beginning to document the signs of a real emerging talent. Hilda was already returning some times which were significantly below the standards set for gaining the certificates.

12/9/17 - L&DTA Certificate
For Bettering Standard Time
(Set at 1:15.00)
75 yards Freestyle in 1.11.00

14/9/17 - L&DTA Certificate
For Bettering Standard Time
(Set at 1:20.00)
75 yards Breast Stroke in 1.11.60

As seems so often to be the case, just when things were looking rosy for the James family, disaster struck without warning. On Guy Fawkes Night, November 5th 1917, Jack and Walter were playing with some Bengal matches at a bonfire party. As 8 year old Walter tried to strike one of the matches the long head flew off and hit 9 year old Jack, still burning fiercely as it stuck to one of his woollen socks. His shorts caught fire and he was very seriously burned.

At the local hospital the distraught John and Gertie were simply told that Jack would not recover, and for many weeks the family kept a bedside vigil. As was so common then they had already lost one child during infancy, but they were not willing to give up another so easily. Once again the family re-organised to meet the changing circumstances and everyone pulled together. Reinforced by prayer, Ma stoically took up residence in the hospital ward and helped to look after her desperately sick child. She slept on a pallet alongside his bed and helped to tend him as best she could.

Common practice in those days would have meant having the eldest daughter automatically take over from her Mother at home. There was no way Pa would hear of Elsie leaving school, so it was suddenly delegated to Hilda to take up running the house. Fortunately, Ma had made sure that both her girls were properly trained, but it meant that at just 13½ years old, Hilda's formal education was effectively finished. She simply stopped attending school. To add to all her new household duties, she also managed to make twice daily hospital visits to Ma and Jack, bringing them her home-cooked food.

1917 – THE FIRST FEW SWIMMING BADGES ON A KNITTED COSTUME WHICH WAS "TIGHT, SCRATCHY AND HORRIBLY REVEALING, ESPECIALLY WHEN WET"

**1919 – MORE SUITABLY ATTIRED
AND ALREADY WINNING TROPHIES**

Jack was gravely ill for weeks on end, but did very gradually start to recover from the awful burns. Almost as soon as his recovery began he suffered a series of major setbacks and nearly died. The poor child was stricken with scarlet fever followed by a double mastoid abscess and bronchitis, all of which contrived to extend his hospital stay until well into the following spring. The lasting effects of the firework injuries and the series of infections left him very frail, with permanently damaged lungs, hearing and sight.

Like his sister Hilda, Jack James would never get to school again. The thin, pale child would be home schooled and eventually he would proudly become his religious family's bible study expert. Against all the odds Jack would eventually marry and become a father. As the years went by the long term damage became even more apparent, and by the time he reached middle age he was gradually losing both his sight and hearing. Often in great pain, he would somehow manage to struggle on as a delicate invalid until he was nearly seventy.

During this period Hilda demonstrated why she would later have the mental attitude for the competition circuit. She was absolutely determined to cope with the new arrangements and in fact she managed to run the house admirably through the winter of 1917. In a rare concession to his daughter and knowing that she had quite enough on her plate, Pa made the reluctant decision to let the two lodgers go. Although desperately tired most of the time Hilda still found the energy to swim, if not every single night then certainly every other. Whatever else she managed, Garston club nights on a Tuesday and Thursday were her "My Time", and even her father was not prepared to argue with her about that.

On Hilda's 14th birthday in April 1918, Liverpool City Council presented her with a complimentary year long swimming contract via the Schools Association. It was usual practice then for swimmers demonstrating better than the standard times to be rewarded in this way. Hilda had been told at a club night to expect the award. She was delighted, because with all the costs of Elsie's schooling she knew it would be difficult for the family to finance her hobby for another year. Even with all the extra tasks she had taken on, somehow she had managed to keep her Saturday job at the shop through the winter, carefully saving some of the few pennies she earned to try and help her father cover the cost of a new contract.

By the late spring of 1918 Ma was nursing Jack at home. He was still worryingly weak and listless, and his care took up most of her time. Hilda still ran the house and did most of the cooking. Once things settled down a bit at home, Hilda was offered a full time position as a shop assistant a the greengrocery. That helped compensate for the loss of the income from the lodgers which she mistakenly believed was somehow her fault. The shop owners knew how stoically she had coped and they were kind to Hilda. She was often sent home not only paid, but with a food parcel tucked under her arm containing "something to help out".

Also by then the club's coach had started to watch this particular young swimmer very carefully. Originally from Bury in Lancashire, 43 year old

William James "Bill" Howcroft was a moustachioed man of military bearing who was instrumental in the extraordinary success of the Garston Club swimmers. A straight talking man with an honest and direct approach, he was one of the country's leading coaches for many years, later developing into a swimming historian and author of some repute. At odds with his appearance, Howcroft delivered his rather refined Lancashire accent in a high pitched voice, which was ideal for getting his message across to swimmers from poolside. He was known to work his trainees hard, but with great results.

In the summer Mr. Howcroft wrote to Hilda's parents to ask them for a formal meeting. He and his wife were duly asked to tea one Sunday afternoon. Howcroft told Mr. and Mrs. James that their daughter was beginning to attract a lot of attention from within the swimming fraternity as a disciplined and fast swimmer. Her training was starting to come along in leaps and bounds at the club. More importantly, young Hilda was beginning to return some very fast times. It was his opinion that she might possibly even improve to a level where she may be able to challenge some English records in the future. He then asked John James if he would allow Hilda to travel around the country with the Garston Juniors team, giving demonstrations and competing at club level.

In fact, Howcroft had deliberately been holding back in his description of Hilda's swimming talent, lest he frighten her parents too much. At that time the Garston Swimming Club was one of the most prominent in the country, and to their coach it looked like they had the opportunity to develop a young swimmer that could do exceptionally well. Frankly, at this stage of her training he had never seen anyone quite like her. Even at that early stage Bill Howcroft genuinely believed he might have the makings of a major star on his hands.

After their visitors had left, there was quite a heated family discussion. Hilda was absolutely desperate to be given the chance to travel and compete but she was also mindful of her responsibilities to the family, both practical and financial. Her mother was harder to convince, as she worried about her younger daughter and the moral minefield of being away from the family. John said Hilda should be allowed the chance to compete if she was really that good, but Gertie was having none of it.

Elsie also wanted Hilda to be given her opportunity and was acutely aware of what her younger sister had given up to allow her the chance to grasp hers. She knew how difficult her Ma was going to be, so the next day she went out to the allotment to talk to Pa. Elsie begged him to let her take back some of

Hilda's many chores so that Hilda could deepen her involvement with the swimming club.

It was a very hard call for John, and it took him several days of serious thought in the peaceful surroundings of his allotment before he decided to seek approval from his wife. That was never going to be easy as his Gertie was strong willed to say the least, with fixed ideas about what was right. He would never lay down the law with her, either she would have to agree with him or he would not allow Hilda the chance to compete. In the end he did manage to persuade Gertie to concede her grudging approval, but only on the strict proviso that both the Club and Mr. Howcroft pledged to chaperone Hilda appropriately at all times.

Hilda had one other stroke of luck at that point, finding herself allowed by her employers at the greengrocery shop to take any time off she needed to attend competitions. The shop owners were already proud of their hard-working assistant, and were actually the very first people to openly associate themselves with Hilda's name and success as a swimmer.

The moment she started winning, Hilda's employers began to specifically market Fyffes brand bananas outside their shop with a board bearing the legend "Fyffes Bananas - As Used by the Garston Swimmer Hilda James to Aid in Her Training". Outwardly it was an innocent enough local advertising campaign, making their hard working assistant feel like a bit of a celebrity in the village, as everybody shopping In the High Street saw her name. A few years later she would be a proper celebrity and half the civilised World would know her name, but that first spot of local advertising would eventually come back to haunt her with dramatic results.

Permission for Hilda to join Bill Howcroft's travelling team was finally granted just in time for Garston Swimming Club to whisk their new junior team member away to the Northern Counties Amateur Swimming Association (NCASA) Championships. Hilda fully justified her place on the team, gaining 3rd places in both the 75 and 100 yards junior Freestyle races, plus an equal 3rd in the Ladies Breast Stroke. She then went straight on to compete at the 1918 Olympic Tests, winning a surprise medal in the 100 yards Freestyle race. Even though she was only just 14, Hilda then took the honours at Garston's own 100 yards championship.

1919 would be another year of very hard work for young Hilda James. At his request, the management at Garston baths had allowed Bill Howcroft to hold a set of keys, so he started to unlock at 6 AM on several mornings each week to allow Hilda exclusive access to the pool before work. Almost every evening she would be back at the baths training for at least another three hours. As she turned 15 Howcroft had his protégé on what would seem to be a normal training regime today, but a century ago it was nothing short of revolutionary.

Together they worked on different strokes and also on racing dives, turns, breathing methods, stroke timing and so on. He was starting to hone what he had correctly spotted as a rare natural talent. In addition to his own commitment, he had found a student who was willing to pay attention and work very hard. It has to be said that it wasn't only Hilda putting in all the extra time. Apart from organising her training, plus discharging all his normal club duties, Howcroft held down a full time job as a manager at the local gasworks.

Hilda might have been the club's new tool but Bill Howcroft was definitely the craftsman wielding it. On the one hand he was by all accounts a man as stern and demanding as her father, but on the other and quite unlike John James he had a well developed sense of humour which he brought to the club. Naturally, as a product of the age he was formal and proper most of the time, but he could relax and enjoy a proper laugh with his team when the circumstances permitted. Along with the rest of the Garston Juniors with whom she trained, Hilda liked and respected her coach, and she also began to get the best out of him by rewarding him with solid results.

Howcroft was also coaching several other very promising young swimmers, notably two girls called Charlotte Radcliffe and Grace McKenzie. They were a year older than Hilda and had both been under his tutelage longer. The pair also benefited from the new coaching routines and would often turn up at the pool early in the morning when they were not even scheduled to train. They did this partly to support Hilda but also on their own account. Usually she could out-swim the pair of them anyway, but competitively the friendly rivalry was good for them all. The three soon became great friends and close team mates, often travelling and rooming together at events. Although Howcroft was already renowned as a successful and respected coach, he was beginning to turn up the heat at competitions with a crack team of young swimmers.

The certificates kept rolling in too. In March 1919 Hilda was one of fifteen of Bill Howcroft's Garston Juniors awarded an unusual Certificate by the English Amateur Swimming Association (ASA). The exact wording read; "For honorary services rendered to the ASA in demonstrating the correct methods of swimming". This was in recognition of the wartime efforts of Howcroft and his young team in travelling and demonstrating to clubs all over the country.

In September Hilda bettered her NCASA Championship result of the previous year by winning the NCASA 75 yards junior Freestyle race at Westminster Road Baths in Liverpool. In fact she startled the meeting's officials with her performance, which was so good that she was immediately entered for the 100 yards senior race series later in the evening. Hilda gave the far more experienced senior field a proper fright in the 100 yards, returning an unprecedented second place.

This was probably the first event that made Garston's rival clubs really sit up and take notice. The year also saw her first recorded result in the English ASA Championships which were held at Garston, with a 6th place in the 100 yards senior race. She then managed to snatch a surprise medal at the 1919 Olympic Tests, when she recorded a time of 2.20.40 in the 150 yards back stroke.

24/9/19
NCASA Junior Ladies
75 yards Freestyle – Won
Time 53.60
Westminster Road, Liverpool

Following the end of the Great War, the munitions factory at Garston closed and John James returned to his odd-jobbing and window cleaning. He was always happier outdoors anyway and he felt morally relieved to be away from the arms business, which had served its purpose and seen him safely through the war. He would never return to the postal work, instead adding to his meagre income by taking on a second allotment which he began to run as a regular local market garden. As he was already a passionate and naturally talented gardener that suited him admirably, and in fact it did become quite a success. John was soon able to supply various shops with his high quality produce, including the one where his daughter worked.

**1918 - A CHILLY DAY OUTSIDE COVENTRY BATHS - BILL
HOWCROFT (RIGHT) ON TOUR WITH HIS GARSTON JUNIORS**
BACK ROW - ALAN MANN, WILLIE JOY, AUSTIN RAWLINSON, HARRY PHILLIPS,
WILLIE OWENS. MIDDLE ROW - MARGERY FINCH, MAY SPENCER, LILY BENNETT,
CHARLOTTE RADCLIFFE, HILDA JAMES. FRONT ROW – ROBERT McKENZIE, JAMES
EDWARDSON, JOE CROWTHER

CHAPTER 3
THE ANTWERP OLYMPICS

Hilda James was beginning to attract a lot of attention as a rapidly improving Northern Counties club swimmer. By early 1920 she was receiving some of the best coaching available in England from her mentor, the already highly respected Bill Howcroft of Liverpool's Garston Swimming Club. With that level of support she was beginning to nip at the heels of her contemporaries at both the Northern and English ASA competitions. Hilda was also working full time as a shop assistant in Garston and helping to support her family when she could. She was unaware that in the following four years she would be a household name both in England and across the globe, as she became one of the first true sports celebrities.

The year started with her usual round of solid performances in the main ASA Championships. Hilda was placed 4th in the 220 yards and 3rd in the 100 yards Freestyle races, which were both won by a lady from Nottingham called Connie Jeans. Hilda added a respectable 2nd place in the 150 yards backstroke event.

Constance Mabel Jeans was five years older than Hilda and already long established as one of England's top female swimmers. The two would subsequently share a fierce and occasionally unpleasant rivalry over the following five years, with Connie often swimming better but young Hilda sometimes better still. Several record times would change hands between the pair more than once, sometimes in rapid succession. From the outset Connie undoubtedly had the youngster marked down as a threat. For her part, Hilda could never resist a challenge. It is not exactly clear why, but after just one meeting the pair apparently took an instant and lasting dislike to each other.

Hilda had also begun to develop her gala performance beyond mere racing. When warming up at the pool she had gradually taught herself to swim a lot of unusual strokes and trick routines. At first this was all just for her own amusement. Why bother warming up for racing by, well, racing? Howcroft and the other Garston swimmers became involved, mostly because she started to make them laugh by doing imitations of them and also of swimmers and divers they knew from other clubs. There was no shortage of material, with plenty of interesting characters on the swimming circuit to impersonate.

She was so cheeky that she even contrived to add a regular poolside turn as "Mr. WJ 'Owcroft, the World's Strictest Trainer", exaggerating his loud and high pitched Lancashire accent which famously echoed off the tiles and the ceiling. She would puff out her chest and strut up and down the side of the pool armed with a pool hook, ordering the other swimmers about. Egged on by her team mates one evening, she finally dared to perform it in front of him. Bill Howcroft watched dumbfounded for a few seconds before helplessly roaring with laughter. The Garston coach could see his team becoming a close unit and enjoying themselves while they worked. He appreciated the joke.

Eventually Hilda developed all these high jinks into a much more structured 20 minute routine, which quickly became a crowd favourite and a staple request whenever she was invited to open a gala programme. She would swim feet first or dive like a duck at the pond, float under water with one leg sticking up pretending to be a submarine with a periscope, emerging from the water upside down and legs first. There were tricks known as "Rolling home", "Monkey up a Stick", "Porpoise", "The Nervous Diver" and many others. She had a personal favourite called "The Crab", which involved swimming sideways along the pool using just her legs while remaining vertical, waving her hands in the air to make pincer movements.

She didn't realise it then, but independently she was starting to develop some of the manoeuvres we enjoy watching today in Synchronised Swimming. If Hilda had lived until 1984 she would undoubtedly have been delighted to see the American Synchro Swimmer Tracie Ruiz lifting that sport's first Olympic Gold Medal in Los Angeles. In fact, so successful was the trick performance that for a while Hilda even mulled over the idea of developing a professional swimming act. Maybe she could join a travelling circus or a carnival? Thinking about the reaction she might get from her parents, she wisely let that idea slip away for the meantime.

The next big event on the 1920 swimming calendar was the Olympic Trials in Southport. The difference between Olympic Tests and Trials was in name only; Trials events were held in an Olympic year and Tests in other years. With Hilda's steadily improving results and support from her club she was invited to enter the competition at the last minute. Bill Howcroft reckoned that she might just snatch a medal in the backstroke, as she was rapidly improving on her performance with it.

Ladies backstroke in those days was a double arm stroke i.e. with both arms rotating together. Howcroft was also busy helping another of his other promising youngsters, a childhood pal of Hilda's called Austin Rawlinson, to develop as a backstroke contender. Austin was already using the then revolutionary single arm rotations which would later become the standard back crawl method. Using it, Austin would dominate English competition for several years hence, but generally the ladies weren't using the new back crawl by that stage.

In the event, Hilda astounded the selectors by taking not one but three gold test medals in the 100 and 220 yards Freestyle, plus the 150 yards backstroke which she completed using the traditional method. The Garston Coach was justifiably delighted with his confidence in her ability to rise to the great occasion.

23/7/20 Olympic Tests
100 yards Freestyle
Won - Gold Test Medal
Time 1:11.00
Southport, Lancashire

23/7/20 Olympic Tests
220 yards Freestyle
Won – Gold Test Medal
At Southport, Lancashire

23/7/20 Olympic Tests
150 yards Backstroke
Won – Gold Test Medal
At Southport, Lancashire

Following that series of performances Hilda James was suddenly dynamite, and the 16 year old was immediately selected for a place on the Great Britain Olympic team for the VIIth Olympiad in Antwerp later in the year. Hilda's Garston team mates Grace McKenzie and Charlotte Radcliffe had already been selected; in fact even the reserve member of the relay team was another of Howcroft's young swimmers from Garston called Lillian Birkenhead.

Pressure was therefore put on the James family by the club, to allow Hilda to travel with her friends. The Olympic Committee already had suitable chaperonage arranged and although her mother was none too pleased about it, the precedent had already been set.

There was the usual round of objections from Ma and the subsequent series of rows between her parents. Pa won the round again this time, and Hilda suddenly found that her family's permission to travel for British competitions had been extended to cover the Olympic Games in Belgium. Together with the four Garston girls the Olympic swimming relay team would also include

Hilda's great rival, Nottingham's Connie Jeans. It looked like a dream team to the selectors.

All their travel and accommodation would be paid for, but the swimmers were required to purchase their own silk costumes for the Games. They were highly expensive items by the standards of the time, and as usual there was simply no spare money available in the incredibly tight James budget. In fact, none of the Garston girls came from well off families and the problem of outfitting was shared by the whole team.

If Hilda thought that the cost of a swimming costume might stop her going, she need not have worried. It quickly became known in and around Garston that their swimmers were going to Antwerp en masse. In a spontaneous act of support, the town got right behind their team. In just a few days the required money was raised with small donations from local businesses and collection tins in various shops.

The decision to stage the 1920 Olympic Games anywhere in Europe was incredibly brave. It was only 18 months after the end of the Great War, and the entire continent was still in a state of chaos. In fact the Games had only been switched to Antwerp from the planned city of Budapest in 1919, so preparation time had been very limited as had been the available resources.

The city of Antwerp had suffered severe damage by sustained cannon fire during a major battle following a German siege in 1914, and post-war repairs had only just been properly started. The hastily prepared Olympic swimming and diving venue, officially known rather grandly as the Stade Nautique d'Antwerp, was in fact nothing better than a roped off canal basin surrounded by temporary seating. Even at the height of the summer the water was cold and dirty. To their profound disgust the diving competitors suffered the worst of it, emerging from the water covered in mud and slime from the bottom. Frankly, it stank.

The competitors' accommodation in Antwerp was also probably best described as basic. In fact some of the American team had taken one look at their allocated billets and promptly decided to stay on their nice cosy ship tied up in the harbour. Under the circumstances that was an odd and yet very telling move, as they had done nothing but complain about third class conditions all the way across the Atlantic Ocean.

Their ship, the U.S. Army troop carrier "Princess Matoika", had arrived in New York on one of a series of repatriation runs bringing home not only the wounded, but also the remains of many soldiers killed during the war in

Europe. The better part of two years on from the end of the conflict, that operation was still not complete. The second-hand ship was old and rusty, with very few amenities for athletes and only the most basic accommodation. There was apparently a serious rat problem aboard, and the male competitors were housed below the waterline where one of the major complaints was that it still stank of death and decay.

To add to the misery, their Atlantic crossing had taken well over two weeks instead of one because they had sailed far to the south of the normal routes to avoid icebergs, making conditions even worse in the stifling heat below decks. Conditions failed to improve, even after a sit-in protest aboard. In fact after the games and in spite of having tried to deal with the interior of the ship themselves, they flatly refused to travel back to New York aboard her. Everything considered, if the accommodation on the ship was actually considered better than what was on offer in town, conditions in Antwerp itself must have been pretty dire.

The Olympic Games were staged throughout the summer in those days, with each sport having almost completely separate events at different times. The swimming competitions were held over an eight day period, starting on 22nd August. Across the entire Games, 29 countries were represented by about 2,700 competitors, but in all just 64 of these were women. The British Ladies' Swimming Team only had three events to contest, the 100m and 300m Freestyle and the 4x100m Freestyle Relay.

The USA completely dominated the solo events with their rising star Ethelda "Thelda" Bleibtrey taking both Gold Medals. In the 4x100m final the American team won by an unprecedented 29 seconds over Great Britain, thereby comprehensively destroying the World Record by a vast margin of over 40 seconds with a time of 5:11.60. Backed by her team mates, Thelda had completed a clean sweep by lifting her third Gold Medal of the week. All in all not a bad performance for a girl who had only taken up swimming in the first place to help her recover from the effects of childhood polio.

The other relay teams might as well have been in a different race, but the British girls managed to arrive at the finish line three seconds ahead of third placed Sweden. In spite of the almost unbelievable time set by the Americans, they had managed to break the 1912 English Record (and previous World Record) by some twelve seconds. Hilda James, Connie Jeans, Grace McKenzie and Charlotte Radcliffe were now Olympic Silver Medal holders, and they instantly became National Stars.

29/8/20
Olympic Final
4x100m Freestyle Relay
Won Silver Medal
Team – Hilda James, Constance Jeans,
Grace McKenzie, Charlotte Radcliffe
Time 5:40.80
Stade Nautique d'Antwerp, Belgium
English Record

Despite the creditable Silver Medal performance, it was patently obviously that there was a serious problem with British ladies' swimming. The British team had swum all their races using a stroke called the Trudgen. Named after its English progenitor John Trudgen, it was a hybrid stroke consisting of a basic front crawl movement with a scissor kick something like that of a side stroke.

The Americans had comprehensively beaten them using a new kind of Freestyle stroke. Known as the American Crawl, this had actually been imported to the USA late in the previous century. Bringing together different elements from various strokes found among the indigenous Pacific cultures, it had first been used at the Olympics in 1904 by Charles Daniels and with dramatic effect too. Daniels had worked hard on modifying an early version of the stroke known as the Australian Crawl, finally refining the leg strokes to evolve a new six-beat kick for every pair of arm rotations. He had then unleashed the new weapon on an unsuspecting Olympics, causing an absolute sensation with his fast new stroke and taking two gold medals by huge distances.

Just days before, Hilda had been thrilled to see the great American swimmer from Hawaii, Duke Kahanamoku, also using the American Crawl to good effect. An old boy by competition standards and actually swimming on his 30th birthday, Duke had powered to the line and retained his Olympic 100m title in a new World Record time. Even so, she had been surprised to see the same stroke being used by the ladies. For some strange reason the idea never seemed to have occurred to anybody else except the Americans.

Of course, ever since those Olympic Games in 1920 the American Crawl has been considered the fastest and most efficient racing stroke and is now synonymous with the term Freestyle. There could be no accusation of unfairness as it had been a Freestyle event, but Hilda felt that the British Team had simply been outwitted by clever coaching. She was sorely hurt that her team had been beaten, no, in fact the proper term was thrashed, by half a minute. Her eyes were opened to the possibilities. It just would not do! There had already been some fraternising between the various swimming teams. When they were not competing, the Americans had been busy at the quay cleaning up parts of the "Matoika". The American Swimming Team hosted a reception aboard for swimmers and coaches from all the other competing countries. Although she had been invited, Connie Jeans failed to turn up. After their first exchange at a race meeting against Hilda she had refused to associate with any of the Garston swimmers, as she considered them to be lower class. The Garston girls couldn't care less. It was a fact beyond dispute as they were from a relatively industrial corner of South Liverpool.

The Manager of the American swimming team proved to be much more inclusive. Charlotte Epstein was delighted to meet Bill Howcroft and the British Swimming Team including all four of the girls from Garston. They all hit it off really well, and Hilda was about to capitalise on that opening. Seeking out Miss Epstein on the morning after the relay final, Hilda enquired if she could possibly beg the Americans for some lessons in the rapid new stroke. She found the Team Manger more than happy to oblige, just as long as Hilda dispensed with the stiff British formality and call her "Eppie" like everyone else did.

Born a native of New York City in 1884, Charlotte Epstein was a legal secretary and court stenographer by profession. A keen campaigner for Women's Rights, she would later be acclaimed as one of the most important Jewish women of the era. While never a serious competitor herself, she was a keen leisure swimmer and a founder member of the recently formed Women's Swimming Association of New York (WSA), dedicated to publicising and encouraging swimming for women. Her considerable organisational skills had naturally propelled her into the role of Olympic Swimming Team Manager for the United States. If Hilda was going to spread the WSA message in England, that was well and good with Eppie. She told Hilda she would ask the coach.

In Coach Louis de Breda Handley, Eppie had a real asset. Ten years older than his Team Manager, the handsome Italian American was himself a double Olympic Gold Medallist, as part of the teams that had won both the 4x50 yards Freestyle Relay and Water Polo finals in 1904. He had spent years helping to refine and develop Charles Daniels' American Crawl, with considerable success. Having just witnessed his 1920 American Olympic Team lift 11 out of the 15 Gold Medals in the swimming and diving events at Antwerp was a fitting testament to Handley's work.

Handley was also a keen teacher and an advocate of new sports for women. He had worked wonders for American swimming, both as a recreational activity and as a sport. All things considered he was probably the most influential swimming instructor in the World at that time. Together he and Eppie were a formidable force for their team and country, and indeed the sport of swimming at large.

The new American star, triple Gold Medallist Thelda Bleibtrey volunteered to help her coach with the task of teaching Hilda. Mindful of the British way of doing business Handley observed the proper protocols, first checking with Bill Howcroft that the British Team Coach was happy for him to offer the team some lessons. With Howcroft's approval, Handley was then able to give Hilda the news that that he and Thelda were willing to take her back into that ghastly canal and start teaching her the new stroke. Naturally, he also enquired if the rest of the British girls would like to join in.

Hilda also wanted to involve Bill Howcroft in the actual training process. He was also busy as the British Team Coach, but he did of course make time to meet her and the Americans for some of their sessions. Handley welcomed and encouraged his involvement just as Eppie did with Hilda. In fact the two coaches quickly found that they had a lot in common. Their basic teaching methods were very similar, and they ended up having several useful meetings on the subject. However, their personalities were literally worlds apart. Louis Handley's open and relaxed style contrasted sharply with the naturally rather reserved and stiff demeanour of his English counterpart. In spite of this, or perhaps it was even because of it, the two men instantly took a strong liking to each other.

It was to be the beginning of a long association and friendship which would later develop into a successful writing partnership. The pair would later collaborate in a publishing venture resulting in a series of books on the subject of swimming techniques. In 1932 Bill Howcroft and his wife would even travel to the USA to visit Louis Handley. While in New York Howcroft would be surprised to find himself participating in the filming of a series of training films, commentating on performances and techniques as demonstrated by Handley's swimmers and divers.

Coach Handley and Thelda explained the basics of the new stroke to Hilda. It was much smoother in the water than the Trudgen and wasted less energy, featuring the six leg beats during each stroke cycle rather than the side stroke scissor kick of the older stroke. It wasn't particularly easy to get all the elements correct and there was very little time available. Resisting the Stade Nautique for as long as possible, they began by having their new pupil lie face down on a bench to learn the movements and coordination sequence for the stroke, before taking it into the horrible canal.

In spite of the freezing water and meagre facilities, they managed to hone Hilda's technique on and off over the next couple of days. Coach Handley had told them he was a keen pupil and as expected, she quickly got to grips with the basics. Handley made her work hard although he had a much more laid back approach than Howcroft. Right from the outset he resisted any possible temptation to call her Miss James, or even just Hilda. It was "Kiddo", and she liked the informality with which he delivered it. His team all called him "Coach", and in her turn Hilda immediately joined in with that, finding it thrilling to use the daring familiarity with such an important adult. With her own coach she was still strictly on "Mr. Howcroft" terms.

Although each lesson had to be brief because of the conditions Hilda was absolutely determined to stick at it. From the very first attempt she could tell that they really were on to something big. It was simply a faster and far more economical stroke than any she had learned before. As soon as she got the arm and leg co-ordination right, the streamlining of the legs and the way they were used more like fins immediately felt far more natural and efficient than the stilted, stop-start motion of the scissor kick. She told Bill Howcroft afterwards that it was like trying to compare fish with frogs. She did begin to wonder if she might ever feel warm again, but she wasn't about to give up trying until she could manage the tricky breathing manoeuvre correctly.

Like Howcroft, the charismatic Handley was a patient but exacting teacher whose mere presence easily inspired those in his charge. By the end of their training sessions and with a little patience all round, manage it correctly she had. It seems odd that the other English girls were not involved in most of these activities. Charlotte, Grace and the relay reserve Lillian had definitely been invited and did actually join in as far as doing the bench training, but not one of them could be persuaded back into that canal under any circumstances.

Both Handley and Howcroft admired Hilda for her perseverance, but the coaches quite understood the other girls' reservations. In one of his more humorous moments, Howcroft told his team that even the inspirational Louis de Breda Handley himself would not have persuaded him to get in the water. Not entirely unexpectedly Connie Jeans was nowhere to be seen.

Hilda's principal thought was that Thelda was very plucky for repeatedly pitching herself into Antwerp's disgusting Stade Nautique just to help coach her. It was indeed a very generous gesture for the new triple Champion to make. Thelda was a couple of years older than Hilda, taller than the English girl and built considerably more solidly. She was friendly and very relaxed, easily making fun of herself while teasing Hilda. She told Hilda that she didn't feel the cold too badly, the main problem was that their pupil was far too skinny for the cold water and she should eat more to help her put on some proper insulation.

Thelda Bleibtrey was definitely one of the more interesting swimming characters of the 1920s. A staunch campaigner for women's rights, she would eventually be able to claim two arrests over her swimming antics. Never mind the Stade Nautique, Thelda really wasn't frightened of anything, or anybody for that matter. Her first brush with the law had been during the previous year, when she had been charged with "Nude Swimming". Not quite as lewd as the charge may suggest, Thelda had daringly removing her stockings before entering the water at Manhattan Beach. In 1919 this heinous crime constituted nudity in the eyes of the law, although she had modestly left on all the other cover-up attire required to protect moral decency at the time. After a publicity campaign and various protests the charges were soon dropped, and in fact the requirement to wear stockings while swimming was soon rescinded.

Ethelda Bleibtrey 1 – Authorities 0.

On the second occasion, she would spearhead the campaign to allow swimming in New York's Central Park Reservoir. Paid the huge sum of $1,000 to stage a 1928 publicity stunt for the campaign, she duly dived into the reservoir for the assembled press. The police were also well aware of the event and were watching from the large crowd. Emerging from the water Thelda was promptly arrested by the waiting cops and spent the night in jail. The event caused a publicity splash far bigger than the one in the actual water, with The City's Mayor, Jimmy Walker becoming personally involved. Once again Thelda got her way and the Reservoir was soon opened for public swimming.

Ethelda Bleibtrey 2 – Authorities 0.

Even though she had many other duties to contend with, Charlotte Epstein also considered it important that she spend some time with Hilda. She told the English girl all about the WSA and its work. She described the ongoing revolution in ladies' swimming that she and her coach were staging in America. She added that Hilda ought to think about coming over and visiting them, just to see what she was talking about. Hilda was under no illusions as to the likelihood of that ever happening.

Looking back across all those years it seems that almost everyone in the swimming world Hilda James came into contact with could feel her potential and tried to find ways to feed her obvious enthusiasm. Although they all worked together over such a short period of time, Hilda struck up lasting friendships with Charlotte Epstein and Louis de Breda Handley, friendships from which they were all to reap huge and unexpected benefits in the future. She also became very close friends with the American team swimmers Helen Wainwright and Aileen Riggin, but especially with their triple Gold Medallist, Thelda Bleibtrey.

On the Olympic Swimming Team's return to England there was considerable press attention about the Silver Medal winning ladies and also the men's team who had beaten long odds to snatch Bronze Medals in the 4x200m Freestyle Relay. Along with the others Hilda was now catapulted straight onto the circuit of major competitions and demonstrations.

The press started to take a much keener personal interest in the new swimming sensation which largely seemed to be emanating from the Garston club and its remarkable coach. The Daily Express was especially supportive of Hilda, with their weekly swimming columnist "Leander" often having something to say about her exploits. It was apparently Leander who awarded her the nickname, starting a trend which many of the other papers quickly followed. Almost overnight, Hilda James became known as "The English Comet".

Hilda's English swimming revolution was about to begin. There was practically a whitewash as she dominated most of the 1920 ASA competitions with her newly acquired weapon, the 6-beat American Crawl. To the absolute delight of the ASA and audiences all over the country she turned in a round of astonishing results as she introduced England to the new stroke by smashing records left, right and centre. If the Americans had seen this coming, might they have thought twice about taking the pains they did to teach her how to do it?

8/9/20
Liverpool & District Championships
100 yards Freestyle - Won
Wigan, Lancashire

15/9/20 ASA Cert. 1991
300 yards Freestyle - Won
Time 4:20.00
Manchester
English Record
World Record

29/9/20 ASA Cert. 1993
440 yards Freestyle - Won
Time 6:30.60
Seacombe, Wirral
English Record

6/10/20
NCASA 4x100 yards Freestyle
Squadron Championship – Won
Moss Side, Manchester

By the time the Garston Team reached the Northern Counties Squadron Championship, Hilda and Bill Howcroft had both been busy doing some coaching. The team were now unassailable as they were all swimming the American Crawl.

9/10/20 ASA Cert. 1994
500 yards Freestyle - Won
Time 7:25.80
Northwich, Cheshire
English Record
Unofficial World Record
Due to timekeeping discipline

15/10/20 ASA Cert. 1996
220 yards Freestyle – Won
Time 2:59.00
Seacombe, Wirral
English Record

8/12/20 ASA Cert. 1997
100 yards Freestyle – Won
Time 1:10.00
Seacombe, Wirral
English Record

8/12/20 ASA Cert, 1998
150 yards Freestyle – Won
Time 1:53.60
Seacombe, Wirral
English Record
World Record

AUGUST 1920 - ANTWERP
THE BREASTPLATE FROM HILDA'S OLYMPIC SWIMMING COSTUME
TOGETHER WITH THE BRONZE COMPETITOR'S MEDAL AND SILVER
OLYMPIC MEDAL

CHAPTER 4
BANANAGATE

Connie Jeans became particularly upset with her rival's performances, quickly labelling the whole Garston team as cheats and dismissing their new technique as nothing more than a gimmick. There still seemed to be a difference of opinion about whether she had been invited to be coached by the Americans on the new stroke. Apart from Hilda, the other three Garston swimmers certainly had, but none of them could bear the thought of diving back into the awful canal.

Connie apparently insisted that she hadn't even been asked, but the fact remains that even if she had been it was unlikely that she would have taken part. They may have won their Olympic Silver Medals as a team, but it certainly didn't mean that she had to party with the other team members, especially if they were the lower class lot from Garston.

Whether it suited the Nottingham swimmer or not, at the age of just sixteen a star had indeed been born. Whenever Hilda was swimming within reasonable range of home, her Ma and Pa were being invited to sit with the local dignitaries and enjoy the fun. Hilda almost always enjoyed good press, with the papers often making much of the fact that The English Comet was a diminutive competitor standing just 5'3" tall (1.60m). She was wiry rather than muscled and, as her American friend Thelda Bleibtrey had noted, much more slightly built than most other swimmers of the time. She would gradually develop broader shoulders as she got stronger, but invariably she would indeed be one of the smaller competitors lining up to race.

By this time, Hilda had also started on a personal mission to give free coaching to younger children everywhere she swam, and that contributed greatly to her popularity with both local as well as national papers. Whenever possible she would arrange to turn up in the afternoon at gala venues to invest some of her time coaching and encouraging others before racing in the evenings.

The press were certainly in raptures after the 1920 results, but uncannily like the tabloids of a later age, just as the new star hit the big time it looked like a scandal was starting to brew. Questions were apparently being asked about the new record holder's amateur status.

Somebody, mentioning no names but generally assumed to be a rival with a grudge and a reputation to protect, was obviously trying to cause trouble. Several anonymous letters had been received by certain newspapers, including one addressed personally to Leander at the Daily Express. Somebody was saying that Hilda was being given Fyffes brand bananas, and that she was selling her name to that company for advertising.

In the 1920s, amateur competitors were strictly bound to receive no remuneration for their efforts. A club was allowed to pay for some travel and accommodation costs, or was allowed to accept the same for their members to compete elsewhere. Under no circumstances were the competitors to be paid for their services, or allowed to receive anything that could be deemed to have any monetary value. For a race win the norm was to accept a small badge or maybe a token trophy. If a major cup was won, the swimmer's club would usually be allowed to hold it for a year on their behalf.

Could Hilda James prove that she had not been receiving any money for advertising bananas, either from Fyffes or her employers? In fact, for most of her life Hilda was very nearly vegetarian and loved all kinds of fruit. Of course it did nobody any harm to say that she ate bananas and found them to be a good training food; the fact is that she was probably the first sports competitor anywhere to use them specifically as such. It just wasn't allowable to say that they were Fyffes bananas, or worse still to advertise where she had acquired them.

1921 opened with Hilda swimming at a gala or giving a demonstration almost every week. On 22nd January she was invited to give a demonstration of the radical new American Crawl at a meeting of the Midlands Counties ASA at Nottingham, Connie Jeans' home club. As usual she was asked to open the evening with her crowd pleasing 20 minute trick routine. Unknown to her coach, on this particular occasion she had inserted a surprise opening item into her regular programme. Hilda had something to say for herself, and because bananas were not available in a can, she had apparently taken it upon herself to open a can of worms instead.

The packed Nottingham audience were delighted when the evening opened with Hilda James appearing from the changing rooms. The English Comet was greeted with the usual warm applause, which rapidly turned to laughter as she strolled slowly along the poolside to the racing blocks. The Garston girl was casually finishing off a large banana, before handing the skin to a surprised official. She then announced to the packed house that she would like to show them all how to swim like a monkey, and dived in for a demonstration length of the newly obsolete Trudgen stroke.

Realising the joke immediately, the crowd roared with mirth but it was apparently all too much for Connie. She had got the joke alright, but absolutely incensed with the open taunt she failed to appear for her own race. In fact for the better part of the next two years Connie Jeans would flatly refuse to swim at any event where Hilda James was booked.

Hilda's usually tolerant coach could not believe what he was witnessing and suffered what for him was a rare sense of humour failure. He sat aghast as the scene unfolded. Utterly furious with Hilda, after the gala he marched his team smartly back to the station in complete silence. Once safely on the train he lost his temper and berated his star loudly in front of her team mates. Startled, she did something she would never have dared to do in front of her father and shouted straight back. For the only time in her career mentor and pupil had a blazing row.

Hilda may have overstepped the bounds of good taste, but in that little pantomime she had psychologically put the banana affair neatly behind her. She had also discovered that she could successfully play to a bigger audience than her coach and team, or even a packed swimming pool. Ever afterwards she would often modify her gala performance slightly, mischievously opening the show with something new or topical just to keep Bill Howcroft guessing.

Luckily the public's perception of "Bananagate", as it would undoubtedly have been called today, soon died down. The ASA became seriously concerned on receiving reports from the Nottingham gala debacle. The governing body were not about to let their young star or their new swimming revolution get into trouble on account of a piece of fruit. They certainly didn't want to create any further sensation and decided on a pragmatic but low key approach. Contacting Fyffes, their officials were pleased to learn that Hilda was not receiving any money from the company. The ASA then went swiftly to work to repair the damage and quietly lay the matter to rest once and for all.

Firm steps were taken with certain newspapers and individuals, plus a shop in Garston. To his profound embarrassment Howcroft was one of those summoned to a rather awkward meeting with officialdom at the ASA. The ASA accepted his plea of innocence on the Nottingham debacle, but he left the meeting having been issued with a firm set of instructions. Coach Howcroft was to make sure that henceforth his young protégé was made aware, in no uncertain terms, of exactly what she could and could not say and do.

The rivalry between the Garston and Nottingham star swimmers immediately became something of a challenge for the press, raising the profile of swimming even further as sports pages got involved. Any publicity is good publicity as the saying goes, and possibly more column inches were devoted to the story than any previous British swimming topic. Various clubs and associations spent the rest of that year and most of the next trying to host a race featuring the two swimmers, but for the meantime at least they were all made to wait.

Having quickly regained his composure following the fallout from the Nottingham meeting, Bill Howcroft simply couldn't believe that Connie was refusing to swim against Hilda. Working carefully to avoid the wrong sort of attention from the ASA, he and Hilda even hatched a cunning plan between them to test her rival.

They managed to sneak up on a meeting one evening in Leeds where they knew the Nottingham girl was due to race. On being invited to the meeting they had originally made their excuses, saying that they were reluctantly forced to decline the invitation and offering their apologies. On the day of the meeting Howcroft had sent a telegram late in the afternoon, to the effect that their plans had changed and they would in fact be able to attend after all.

After arriving at the baths as late as they could possibly contrive, Hilda quickly changed for racing. As she stepped out poolside (mercifully without a banana this time) there was a surprise announcement detailing the last minute programme change. The club was delighted to be able to report that unexpectedly Miss Hilda James would be competing, a fact which was received with delighted applause.

Following Hilda's first race a subsequent announcement was made, to inform the audience that with regret Miss Constance Jeans had been forced to withdraw from the evening's racing due to sudden illness. That brought forth an unprecedented round of booing and a slow hand clap. Bill Howcroft was horrified at this clear demonstration of displeasure from the audience. He had not expected such an overt reaction and remained worried about it for several weeks afterwards in case the ASA might get to hear. Even if they did, nothing was ever said.

1921 saw an ever increasing list of races won and records smashed.

6/4/21
Scottish ASA
200 yards Freestyle – Won
Time 2:49.60
Glasgow, Scotland
Scottish Record

Hilda held an extensive series of Scottish Records broadly in line with her English ones. There are very few for which there is material proof in the form of surviving certificates or relevant newspaper cuttings. Unfortunately the historical swimming records of the Scottish ASA were accidentally destroyed during an office move in the 1960s.

5/7/21
English ASA Championships
100 yards Freestyle - Won
Time 1:11.00
Garston, Liverpool

15/7/21 ASA Cert. 140
300 yards Freestyle - Won
Time 4:13.80
Garston, Liverpool
English Record
Unofficial World Record
Due to timekeeping discipline

Recording times was a problem at all swimming competitions until digital electronic timekeeping was introduced. For a record attempt in 1920s Britain, each competitor was timed by three dedicated officials who had to manually start their official stopwatches at the gun. The watches also had to be stopped manually and all three were required to record a finishing time showing the same $1/5^{th}$ of a second (0.20). Stopwatches were generally only accurate to one fifth of a second anyway. If one official recorded a time slower or faster by just $1/5^{th}$, the ASA would award an English Record based on the slower time.

Under the same timing rules, the World governing body FINA (Fédération Internationale de Natation) would not ratify a World Record. Along with everyone else competing in the sport, these inaccuracies dogged Hilda James throughout her career. In Hilda's case it resulted in her officially breaking just six World Records. Try counting the unofficial World Records throughout the text, many of which were several seconds below the target times but were never officially ratified, at least by FINA. In the example above, the time of 4:13.80 could stand for an English Record and was in fact a massive 6.20 seconds inside her own World Record with an accuracy of 0.20 seconds. Paradoxically, the English Record would therefore stand at an official mark 6.20 seconds lower than the World Record. In both Britain and America, the national swimming authorities were challenging FINA.

29/7/21 ASA Cert. 141
440 yards Freestyle - Won
Time 6:16.60
Leeds, Yorkshire
English Record
World Record
Time also allowed for 400m
English Record
World Record

Four records in one swim! Common practice was to aim for separate records by touching a hanging marker at the shorter distance and then swimming on to complete the longer distance. It required great discipline by separate timekeeping teams. In this case only one team was used, but as 440 yards is equal to 402.37m, FINA did allow the finishing time to stand for a 400m record. In this particular race Hilda had lowered her own 440 yards English Record by an unprecedented 14.00 seconds to break the World Record.

17/8/21 ASA cert. 142
500 yards Freestyle - Won
Time 7:13.00
Garston, Liverpool
English Record

13/9/21 ASA Cert. 137
100 yards Freestyle - Won
Time 1:09.80
Southport, Lancashire
English Record

22/9/21
English ASA Championships
220 yards Freestyle - Won
Time 3:05.20
Nottingham, Derbyshire

5/10 21
NCASA Championships
100 yards Freestyle - Won
Time 1:12.60
Bolton, Lancashire

10/10/21
NCASA 4x100 yards Freestyle
Squadron Championship – Won
Retained by Garston for 2nd year running
Chadderton, Lancashire

26/10/21 ASA Cert. 139
220 yards Freestyle – Won
Time 2:56.80
Seacombe, Wirral
English Record

31/10/21 ASA Cert. 138
150 yards Freestyle – Won
Time 1:51.00
Seacombe, Wirral
English Record

21/12/21
Scottish ASA
200 yards Freestyle - Won
Time 2:49.00
Leith, Scotland
Scottish Record

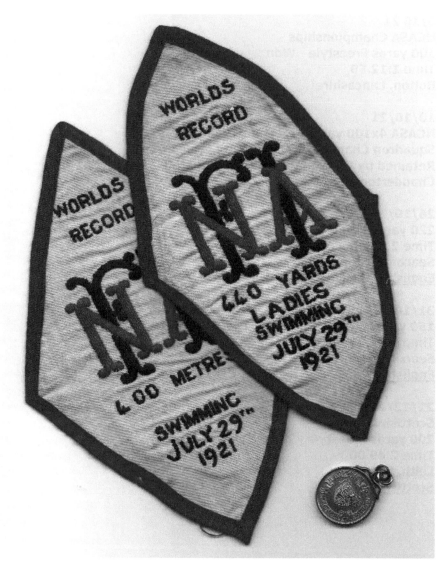

29/7/21 – TWO FINA WORLD RECORD PENNANTS FROM ONE RACE AT LEEDS PLUS ONE OF THE SMALL GOLD WORLD RECORD MEDALS AWARDED BY THE ENGLISH ASA

CHAPTER 5
CUNARD

1922 would undoubtedly be remembered as the vintage year for both Hilda James and Bill Howcroft. Since returning from the Olympic Games she had kept up a regular correspondence with her friend, the American triple Olympic Gold Medallist Thelda Bleibtrey. However it was a letter from the Women's Swimming Association of New York (WSA) which would cause the most excitement when it arrived at the Garston Swimming Club.

The letter contained an official invitation from Club Captain Charlotte Epstein for Hilda James to visit the United States for the summer racing season. The WSA wanted Hilda to participate in a series of high-publicity staged invitation races in the New York area, plus various other galas and exhibitions. Following that the plan was for her to join a major amateur swimming tour, travelling as far west as Chicago on the Great Lakes.

When Bill Howcroft unexpectedly called at the James' home to break the news, it caused the first really serious family row about her swimming career. Eppie had alluded to a possible visit during their meetings at the Antwerp Olympics two years previously, but Hilda never imagined it would actually be discussed.

Naturally Hilda was beside herself with excitement, but nobody was really surprised to find that her mother was less than enthusiastic about the prospect, to say the least. Absolutely horrified at the thought of having her younger daughter away from home for over two months touring the USA, she simply refused to hear anything said about it. After Howcroft left, Gertie and her John had a loud and prolonged disagreement. They were at odds again because John was well aware that Hilda needed to keep progressing and how much she would benefit from the stimulation and challenge of the tour.

As Hilda was still an amateur, her swimming could not bring any money in of course. In spite of the Garston Club and Liverpool Council largely covering the costs, the family often had to dig deep into their already limited resources to support their increasingly famous daughter. When Hilda was away swimming she didn't get paid at work, although her employers were still happy to support her in their own way by allowing the time off. To Gertie James it just didn't seem fair, but she was just being obtuse because the proprietors of the shop did a lot more than pay Hilda a wage.

Whether she was an amateur or not, with Hilda James as their employee they continued to quietly reap the benefits of their association with her, something that even the ASA could not fully stifle. Gertie benefited hugely from this along with her whole family. Out of gratitude the shop was quietly supplying the family with all the bananas they could eat, along with a lot of other goods.

Bill Howcroft refused to be deterred by Gertie James' latest tantrum, which had frankly been in line with his expectations. He and John James had developed a good working relationship over the years and he knew the best thing to do was to leave that problem for John to deal with. He was a methodical man and relished his own kind of challenge, so he resolved to plan the trip anyway as an exercise in logistics and see what transpired.

He was faced with two problems; travel and chaperonage. The WSA was very generously offering to cover the entire cost of the tour once Hilda arrived in America, but there was simply no money available anywhere for Hilda to travel to New York. Equally, there was absolutely no chance that either of her parents would be able to accompany her. John had to earn a living and Gertie had a house to run, plus her family and the crippled Jack to look after.

Ever resourceful, the pragmatic Bill Howcroft had other ideas. His years of running the Garston Club and organising swimming events had furnished him with a long contact list and a great deal of determination to go with it. He was not afraid to ask for the apparently impossible and knew the correct ways to go about it. He wrote a carefully worded letter to a contact in Liverpool called Ernie Jones, who worked in the Cunard offices at the Pier Head and was also the Chairman of the Company's own swimming club located at the Adelphi Hotel.

Howcroft explained the basic problem and detailed some of the ongoing difficulties with Hilda's difficult family. He wanted to know if Ernie could suggest who at Cunard might be the right person to ask for a spot of financial help, or possibly even some kind of practical support for their local swimming champion. Ernie duly pushed the letter up his chain of command, along with a suggestion to his superiors that even if nothing else could be done, the Cunard Swimming Club might do well to associate their name with that of Miss James.

By that time the name Hilda James was synonymous with Liverpool, as of course was the name of the Cunard Line. Someone at the Company quickly had the bright idea that if they played their cards right, they might be able to do even better than Ernie suggested. Cunard could take the opportunity to aim high and actually make the name Hilda James synonymous with Cunard itself rather than merely the Company's swimming club.

To achieve that, they could possibly attempt to forge a connection between the star and the club as a starting point, a means to an end. As history would demonstrate, Cunard took the long view and was willing to do whatever it took to achieve the idea. That would include waiting patiently for as long as necessary, but for the meantime they were not in a hurry. Cunard duly wrote back via Ernie Jones. Bill Howcroft was told that, on the assumption that money would be no object, he was to detail exactly what he needed.

The only remaining barrier was the weird and unpredictable James family. By this time, the James' and the Howcrofts were, if not actually friends, at least very well acquainted. John and Gertie James had tentatively put their complete trust in Howcroft to look after their daughter from the age of just 14. True to his word, the Garston Club had indeed chaperoned her correctly and they had all been rewarded by having her become a major star by the time she was 16.

Whether her parents, especially her mother, actually felt rewarded is a different matter. Whenever Hilda arrived home after a big win or record swim, Ma would still always emphasise her dislike of her daughter's activities, often by having some extra and usually onerous task waiting especially for her. Hilda did actually consider giving up competing sometimes, but when she was tired of the constant travelling the very idea of playing into her Ma's hands by giving in to her wishes always kept her going. Equally as stubborn as her parents, Hilda James would not be a quitter for anybody.

Howcroft had a series of meetings with Cunard, and the tour was all organised in principle before he dared to consult the James' again. When he did call on them he arrived while Hilda was at work, accompanied by his wife Agnes. He told the James' that against all the odds he had managed to secure a sponsor for the American trip. Passage would be arranged and paid for by Cunard if her parents would give Hilda their permission to visit America. To protect Hilda as an amateur competitor, accepting the offer would mean having her change swimming clubs so that it could be the Cunard Club that was seen to be paying for the venture.

Noting the by now expected darkening look on Gertie's face he quickly unveiled his master stroke and offered to have his wife act as Hilda's personal chaperone for the tour. In the end it took some more argument from John, but Gertie apparently got along well with Agnes Howcroft, who often accompanied her husband and the Garston girls when they were travelling. She still didn't like it one bit, but once again she had found herself backed into a corner and was obviously furious that she couldn't find any flaws in the plan. Finally she was forced to relent and grudgingly (as usual) allowed John to tell the Howcrofts that Hilda would have permission to travel to New York with them.

Bill Howcroft left the James' house as pleased as Punch! There is no doubt that it was entirely due to the calm and measured nature of the coach's forward planning, plus his and John's careful handling of her mother that Hilda was eventually allowed to tour America.

Excited as he was, thus far Howcroft had somehow managed to keep all these negotiations secret from Hilda. He was pleasantly surprised that on his request even John James had agreed that he and his wife would keep it quiet, to allow the coach his moment of triumph.

Cunard had invited him to bring his champion to an afternoon tea meeting at their fabulous neo-gothic Headquarters building at Liverpool's famous Pier Head. Opened in 1917, the Cunard Building still stands majestically alongside the Port of Liverpool and Royal Liver Buildings, overlooking the Mersey. Today they are known fondly as "The Three Graces". When viewed from the Wirral side of the river at Birkenhead they form one of the best known port skylines in the World.

As she walked into the Cunard Building, Hilda was under the impression from her coach that she might be asked to appear at a Cunard club swimming gala. She was well used to that kind of request, but at this particular meeting she was being lined up for the surprise of her life.

To start with, planning meetings didn't usually involve a sumptuous tea. Once she had been served, Hilda was astonished to hear that Cunard were taking an active interest in the development of their local swimming champion. They had recently become aware of her outstanding and frankly unprecedented invitation to visit New York. The Company had considered at length the difficulty her club might have in funding the necessary travel. As fellow Liverpudlians, Cunard had been busy asking themselves how they might be able to help.

As a company, Cunard thought that the opportunity was simply too good to miss. They were therefore delighted to find themselves in a position where they were able to offer Miss James a free return passage to New York on board one of their liners, in order that she may be able to accept the invitation. Naturally her entourage, which would consist of her coach Mr.

Howcroft and, crucially, her chaperone Mrs. Howcroft, would also be accommodated.

Just like that! Hilda turned to look at her coach in disbelief and found him grinning back at her like a lunatic. Unable to contain the excitement any longer and knowing that his young champion would already be fretting about her parents' reaction, he quickly owned up to his subterfuge. He told her not to worry because they already knew all about it at home. And what was more incredible, after some very careful negotiation and to his eternal amazement, her mother had already granted the necessary permission.

If the Garston coach and his champion were to accept, Cunard wanted to ask for something from Hilda in return; specifically permission for the Company to start using her name. If she wanted to avail herself of their free travel offer, Hilda would also be required to accept an immediate complementary life membership and agree to a move from Garston to become a Cunard Club swimmer. This would mean her officially being based at their swimming club at the Adelphi Hotel in central Liverpool.

At virtually no cost, the Cunard name would therefore become associated with one of England's top sports stars and hopefully would also start to appear in record listings and newspaper articles. As a Cunard Club swimmer, the travel costs of her voyage to New York and any subsequent publicity would also fall comfortably within her amateur status. The deal on offer would involve her being seen regularly at the hotel and possibly making herself available to Cunard on request, for occasional publicity events an so forth, thus raising her own profile in associating with the company.

Hilda knew that they did have much better facilities at the Adelphi than at the old Garston baths. Long considered one of the best hotels in England, for many years the Adelphi had been the launching point for Cunard's wealthier and better known transatlantic passengers. A stay at the Adelphi before setting off across the Atlantic Ocean was simply de rigueur. The hotel also boasted of the finest swimming pools in the country.

In spite of all the luxury on offer, the Cunard Swimming Club's actual competitions had to be held across the Mersey at the Guinea Gap baths in Seacombe, because the Adelphi pool wasn't a regulation size for racing. Hilda James and Bill Howcroft didn't hesitate in accepting Cunard's offer. Hilda instantly became a Cunard member, but Howcroft requested that she be allowed to compete for Garston until the end of the season and a transfer date of October 1st was agreed. Hilda James didn't know it, but The English Comet was finally about to break out from her status as an English Champion and burst onto the World Stage.

Rather than just using their great liners as part of the transport system, albeit in the finest style possible, leisure cruising was fast becoming the next big thing. Cunard already had the right tools in its collection of fine and respected ships, and the Company was beginning to explore the possibilities of the new market.

Deputy Chairman and Chief Ship Designer Sir Percy Bates was busy working on modifying the interiors on some of the series of 20,000 ton ships already on order. To cater for the emerging ocean cruising market, various changes were being introduced incrementally as more ships were brought into service. The program would finally culminate in a one-off, completely redesigned World Cruise Liner to be introduced to the market when the time was right. If Sir Percy Bates had his way, his baby was going to be an absolute stunner.

It was probably during the planning for Hilda and the Howcrofts' visit to New York that the Company and its forward thinking Deputy Chairman had begun to wonder if they might be able to tempt the swimming star into turning professional. What if they were to use her star profile as an added attraction to draw in custom, by offering her a kind of celebrity crew posting? He soon began to dream about the possibility of tempting her aboard the unique new cruise ship. Working through the very astute Sir Percy, it would take the Company considerable time and persuasion to achieve, but with patience and some very personal encouragement from him that day would eventually come.

In the meantime, normal swimming duties carried on. Before travelling to America two more records fell;

26/5/22
ASA Championships
300 yards Freestyle - Won
Time 4:08.40
Garston, Liverpool
English Record
Unofficial World Record
Due to timekeeping discipline

4/7/22
English ASA Championships
220 yards Freestyle - Won
Time 3:10.00
Hyde, Manchester
20/7/22
NCASA Championships
100 yards Freestyle - Won
Time 1:09.40
Burslem, Stoke
English Record

When the 300 yards World Record once again remained unratified, Hilda had begun to feel increasingly frustrated with the whole timekeeping system. She told her coach that she would break the 100 yards World Record by a whole second in the upcoming NCASA race at Burslem. Unusually, Hilda was disappointed with her performance on the night, because she somehow caught her foot on the pool's end rail during one of the turns and missed a stroke.

CHAPTER 6
DECK ORNAMENT

Adam Hay McAllister was born in Sunderland during 1868. At the beginning of the 20th Century he was working for the railways and had settled at Cullercoats, near Newcastle on England's north east coast. Adam had married Isabel Parker in 1890 and their family expanded slowly. Evie was born in 1891 followed by Alison in 1892, but sadly their second daughter was lost in 1895. Isabel gave birth to another daughter in 1897 who they also christened Isabel. A son followed, William Hugh arriving on 15th February 1900. They lost another baby boy in 1902.

Having already lost two of his five children, Adam's wife sadly died in 1905 leaving him with the two girls aged 14 and 8, and five year old Hugh. After that the children were brought up with the help of their father's sisters Jessie and Minnie. When his father remarried in 1914, Hugh decided that he wasn't at all keen on his stepmother and went to live with his Aunt Minnie. Adam and his second wife Ethel went on to have two more children, Douglas Hay in 1919 and finally Gordon in 1926. When Gordon was born, Adam was already 58 and his eldest daughter Evie 35.

Hugh McAllister was a pretty normal kid, bright and high spirited. As a young teenager he would get into the usual kind of trouble, often with his best friend Algy Belcher. When operating together they were apparently considered a pair of regular renegades. On one particular occasion they managed to paralyse the entire local railway system. After climbing up the outside stonework of one of the local railway bridges, Algy fell head first over the parapet landing on the track and knocking himself clean out. Hugh followed his friend over safely but knew that he shouldn't move the injured Algy who was lying across the rails.

Hugh quickly ran along the line to the station signal box, just in time to stop a train which was preparing to pull out. Without stopping to fully explain himself, he then sprinted off along the station platform hotly pursued by the train's guard who thought the pesky youngster was just trying to get away. Far from thinking of escape, Hugh was actually on his way to the Belcher house round the corner to fetch Algy's mother. Ma Belcher apparently opened her front door, took one look at Hugh's expression and slapped him sharply round the head without so much as waiting for an explanation, to the amusement of the guard.

It wasn't just railway bridges either. Apparently Hugh was always a great climber, and would attempt to scale any obstacle. He once attracted an audience after the local Policeman spotted him climbing up the crumbling sea cliffs along the coast. The poor Bobby didn't dare shout at the lad to come down for fear of scaring him into falling, so he was forced to stand and watch. This created enough interest that gradually a small crowd gathered with him to enjoy the entertainment. On reaching the top, Hugh gave a cheery wave and disappeared, in spite of being sternly told to come down for a few words with the law.

Hugh studied at Tynemouth Grammar School, leaving at the age of 15. He was a keen student with a mind agile enough to frighten some of his teachers; he was fascinated by mathematics and technology. In his final year at school he handed in an essay on the development of aircraft and the future of flying. He was awarded top marks, because nobody really had a clue what he was talking about but trusted that he probably did.

Feeling somewhat misunderstood he left school in disgust to seek out a more practical education. If the whole country was going to war, then so was Hugh McAllister. Like so many other youngsters around him he lied about his age to the Army recruiters and proudly joined up in October 1915. How he managed that is a complete mystery because he apparently looked about twelve at the time, but during basic training he was lucky enough to be found out and packed safely off home.

Hugh kicked around for a few months at his Aunt's house while trying out a few local jobs, but none of them lasted for more than a week or two. His father was having none of that. With all the young men away at war, Adam eventually collected his son from Aunt Minnie's and marched him on down to Palmer's shipyard where there was proper work available.

It was October 1916, and Hugh McAllister suddenly found himself apprenticed as a riveter. He liked the work even less than some of the other things he had tried. In fact Hugh reckoned that all it was good for was as practice for going to Hell. The sheer noise was painful and it was viciously hot as a heater boy for the riveting teams. He had always considered himself reasonably fit, but being a slight and skinny teenager he found the work physically exhausting. Hugh rapidly came to the conclusion that riveting was just not his kind of technology, in fact he thought that if he stayed for any length of time it would probably kill him sooner rather than later. There had to be a better way forward.

Already deeply interested in ships, Hugh had always enjoyed watching and noting down details of the shipping on the busy River Tyne. If building them was not to be his vocation, maybe a more subtle technology would open a door into the world of seafaring. He had been following the developments of the recent science of wireless ever since becoming fascinated with it following the tragic sinking of the White Star liner RMS Titanic in 1912. Apart from reading about the developments, he already knew the Morse code inside out. In fact he had most of his friends trained to use it, and they would exchange secret notes in lines of dots and dashes.

After less than a year of riveting, Hugh found the opportunity to speak to a group of Marconi Wireless Company engineers who were fitting some equipment aboard one of the new ships being completed at Palmer's. They were impressed with the skinny teenager, who did seem to know what he was talking about. Hugh was quickly sent for an interview with Marconi, during which he was set a practical test. To their surprise, the Company discovered that they were dealing with a youngster who was able to receive and transmit Morse code fluently; in fact he could work the equipment much faster than some of their more experienced operators. In October 1917, he was offered a Junior Wireless Officer posting, working for Marconi aboard one of the Royal Navy's requisitioned wartime hospital ships.

So after all, Hugh McAllister finally went to war. Junior Wireless Officer was a grand title indeed. In fact as a 17 year old he still only looked about twelve and was usually referred to irreverently by the regular seafarers as the "deck ornament", rather than by the correct title of Mr. McAllister. It wasn't much fun.

The small wireless team both worked and slept in very cramped conditions. They were housed inside a tiny shack perched on the foredeck, where they suffered the very worst of the weather. In the North Sea that often meant being battered by waves coming solidly over the bow of the ship. As the junior, Hugh naturally drew most of the night shifts and got very little sleep. He also suffered terribly from bouts of sea-sickness which rendered him less than useful for much of the time. Apparently smoking helped, so starting him on a lifetime habit.

There was a certain amount of cruelty dealt out for junior officers who suffered badly on the sea, especially those in the deck ornament classes. On one occasion poor Hugh was prescribed a patent "cure" involving a piece of raw bacon attached to a length of string. The treatment involved swallowing the bacon while retaining a hold of the other end of the string. Enough said! Suffice to say that even aboard the hospital ships some of the doctors enjoyed their bit of fun, but Hugh was utterly miserable and sick most of the time. Not surprisingly he was also left with a life-long mistrust of the medical profession.

In the end he was at sea for less than a year, but to Hugh it felt like a lifetime. No, several miserable lifetimes. Occasionally it did make him seriously consider backing down and begging to resume his career as a riveter where at least he could die in the comparative luxury of mere Hell. At least there he would die warm; in fact when he did die there would even be the possibility that he might still be holding onto his breakfast. It seemed for a while that he was literally caught between the Devil and the deep blue sea.

In later years Hugh would come to the opinion that the hospital ship posting may have been part of a greater test, which he had somehow managed to pass. Marconi Wireless had an extensive headquarters and factory complex located safely on dry land at Chelmsford in Essex, and he was extremely relieved to be unexpectedly reassigned to work with the scientists there. At the time Marconi was one of several companies vying for supremacy at the forefront of early wireless development, and there was definitely plenty to keep an agile young head occupied.

Hugh had finally found himself thrown in amongst engineers and technicians of similar mind. They fed off each others' ideas, and he enjoyed long sessions talking about and even helping to design new pieces of hardware in the various forums and workshops. It was cutting edge stuff and much more suited to his original idea of technology. Apart from the ongoing development projects he was kept busy building and testing regular transmitters and receivers, often staying on long after regular hours to work on his own ideas and refinements.

With excellent mathematical skills but no formal training on the technical side of wireless, Hugh immediately realised that he had landed squarely in the college of his dreams. He willingly set about completing the most advanced scientific education he could contrive, soaking up information from the much more highly qualified people around him. Whenever he wasn't at work he would be busy reading the latest papers on technology and developments. Many of the scientists around him had never been to sea, and Hugh was surprised to find that quite quickly some of them actually began to turn to the new boy for opinions and ideas.

Time passed quickly as Hugh got to grips with advanced wireless theory and technology. He was developing into an original thinker and somebody that the company was beginning to rely on for ideas. In 1920 he was asked if he fancied doing a tour of duty aboard the Cunard superliner RMS Aquitania. The liner had been one of the hospital ships in the war and during her extensive post-war refit Marconi had been contracted to equip her with some new pieces of wireless gear. Somebody with a soldering iron and plenty of initiative was permanently stationed aboard just in case anything went wrong.

Both Cunard and Marconi were always looking for ways to improve their service delivery, and they wanted Hugh to see if he could spot any possible refinements for the shipboard systems. Remembering his desperate battles with sea-sickness, he had to be reassured that Aquitania would be a lot more comfortable than his last ship. After all, she weighed over 45,000 tons and was equipped with the latest anti-rolling devices. Following a day visit aboard her at Southampton Hugh finally agreed to go.

Although there was competition from several other shipping companies, the World's great and good generally tended to travel on the Cunard Line. Aquitania, known affectionately in the trade as "The Ship Beautiful", was one of their three mighty flagships. Together with the smaller RMS Mauretania and larger RMS Berengaria they maintained a tight schedule running the Company's weekly express service between Southampton and New York. As a Marconi contractor aboard a Cunard ship Hugh was once again given the rank of Junior Wireless Officer, although the title was only a courtesy one as he was still being paid by Marconi.

Hugh liked being stationed aboard the enormous liner. The wireless crew had proper cabins adjoining their transmitting office, usually known as the radio shack, high up on the boat deck. While they did have to share, it was usually organised so that bunk-mates would be on opposite duties. There were properly rostered watches too, and usually everybody managed to get plenty of sleep. Situated at the aft end of the ship they were also comfortably located above the spray line and safely out of most of the elements. It certainly knocked the meagre accommodation aboard his first ship into a cocked hat.

As an officer, even just a courtesy one, Hugh was well looked after. The work consisted largely of manning the telegraphy office situated in the public area, for the purpose of transmitting and receiving telegrams on behalf of the passengers. Up in the radio shack there was a constant stream of messages and regular weather reports, plus greetings to and from other shipping to transmit and receive. His favourite watch was in the evenings when ship's time corresponded with midnight in London, as he enjoyed receiving the daily news for transcription to the on-board newspaper printing office. He always liked to be the first to know what was happening in the World.

Apart from being provided with his uniform and dress whites, Hugh was allowed privileges such as being invited to appear at formal dinners and dances as if he were a regular officer. There were often chances to see and speak to some of the World's more interesting and important people, as well as the many celebrities who regularly chose the Cunard liners as their preferred method of transatlantic travel.

On one particular westbound voyage during the summer of 1922 he remembered patiently waiting his turn to ask the young English Swimming Star Hilda James for a dance. He found her very pleasant and they chatted easily for a while before he safely returned Miss James to her chaperones. She was being taken to New York free of charge by Cunard to participate in a demonstration swimming tour in the United States, accompanied by her coach and his wife. As Miss James was one of the first true sports celebrities, she was considered a bit of an interesting novelty at the time. A dance with her was something to write home about indeed.

Marconi had made a good choice in sending Hugh McAllister to look over Aquitania's wireless setup. He did manage to suggest some improvements to the system during his time aboard, modifying the external aerial rigging and partially reorganising the radio shack itself to make the task easier and more efficient. He must have made a big impression with Cunard, because in October 1922 the Company successfully poached him from Marconi with the offer of a shipboard position within Cunard itself.

Hugh retained the rank of Junior Wireless Officer, making several transatlantic crossings to the United States and Canada aboard the new post war mid-size liners RMS Samaria and RMS Laconia. The winter of 1922 was spent working on various scheduled sailings from both Hamburg and Liverpool. Even crossing the Atlantic in the depths of the winter weather Hugh was surprised to find that he didn't suffer from sea-sickness. They might be less than half the size of Aquitania, but to his mind these new 20,000 tonners were good solid ships.

**1922 - CUNARD WIRELESS OFFICER
WILLIAM HUGH McALLISTER**

52

CHAPTER 7
CONQUERING AMERICA

Rather than have Hilda James travel to New York directly from Liverpool, Cunard decided to send her on their flagship express service from Southampton. That way, they could make her as highly visible as possible in her new role as a Cunard Club swimmer. On Friday 21st July 1922, accompanied by Bill and Agnes Howcroft she departed by train from Liverpool's famous Lime Street station for Southampton. Cunard's publicity department had been busy, and the travellers had arrived at the station to find a surprise waving off party assembled. The Lord Mayor of Liverpool was also present, along with various Cunard dignitaries and members of Garston Council.

The City of Liverpool had been delighted to hear that Cunard were in the business of lending their support to one of the city's favourite daughters, Hilda James. As a gesture from the city, special arrangements had been made for the party to travel in a private first class compartment aboard the train. Following a short address, Hilda was presented with a bouquet and a large basket of fruit from Garston council. She decided that it had probably come from the greengrocers where she worked, as it contained a prominently displayed bunch of bananas.

By now even Bill Howcroft had recovered enough from the notorious banana incident to laugh about that, and already in high spirits they shared the joke. Finally the train set off to "Three Cheers" from the amassed crowds of swimmers and well-wishers with the star and her coach rebelliously waving bananas at them all from the compartment window.

Bill and Agnes Howcroft were equally as excited as Hilda. What an extraordinary adventure the coach had managed to concoct. Hilda was going to show America just what she was capable of, participating in some World class competitions and helping to raise the profile of her sport as a whole. Howcroft was planning to find time on the tour to develop his own association with the likeable American coach Louis Handley, with whom he had been exchanging letters since meeting at the Olympics. What made the whole affair even better was the fact that they were travelling for free, and in considerable style too. In many ways even he couldn't believe that they had got away with it.

The three travellers sailed from Southampton the following day aboard RMS Aquitania, Cunard's fondly nicknamed "Ship Beautiful". The Company had put a lot of thought into the planning of their sponsorship for Hilda's tour. They wanted to gauge the reaction of their more influential passengers to the English star and, although they were accommodated in second class cabins due to availability, the party were allocated places in the first class Louis XVI dining room in order to maximise Hilda's exposure with the customers that mattered.

Exactly as Cunard had hoped, the star immediately attracted a great deal of attention from both passengers and crew alike. All the ship's officers apparently queued up patiently to ask her to dance in the evenings. One of them was a keen young wireless officer with piercing grey eyes who she talked to for a while after their dance. She would later describe him as "Quite dashing, really".

Hilda and the Howcrofts received a surprise invitation to dine with Aquitania's Captain. They were taken to visit the bridge, and also offered an extensive below decks tour of the ship. In return, Hilda was delighted to be asked if she would mind giving a series of swimming demonstrations at the fabulous indoor pool. Both she and Howcroft also spent several afternoons coaching swimmers, a task she always relished.

On the final night of the cruise Hilda had yet another surprise. During the usual final evening ball, the Captain made an announcement that Cunard wanted to make a presentation to their honoured guest. Hilda was delighted when she then received a small silver cup from him as a token of Cunard's appreciation for the time she had given up for coaching and the displays she had put on. Hilda thought that somehow it was all wrong – in her opinion she really ought to have been presenting them with something.

Aquitania arrived in New York on 28th July 1922, and the great tour of the North Eastern USA began with a flourish. After a press call for publicity photographs aboard the ship, Hilda and the Howcrofts were met by her old friend Thelda Bleibtrey together with a rising young star, sixteen year old Gertrude "Trudy" Ederle, who had been desperate to meet the English champion. Thelda would be joining the tour in a support capacity and also to participate in demonstration events, but she would not be allowed to compete in the racing as she had recently turned professional and become a WSA instructor.

The visitors were taken for dinner at a top restaurant before being checked in at their hotel. The WSA had made arrangements for all the accommodation and, although they would obviously not be as spoiled as aboard the ship, they were to be kept in comfortable enough surroundings. Apart from some hotel stays, they were entertained by, and invited to stay with various swimmers' families during the tour. Naturally many of the WSA members wanted to meet their distinguished visitors face to face.

The following evening there was an official invitation to meet Charlotte Epstein and several other top people from the WSA for a more formal dinner at none other than the high altar of New York society itself, the Waldorf-Astoria Hotel. As WSA Team Captain, Eppie was acting as the official sponsor of Hilda's American visit. To the Howcrofts' surprise she greeted Hilda like a long lost relative, shrieking with delight and hugging her. The ever charismatic Louis Handley also greeted Howcroft loudly, vigorously shaking his hand and clapping the Englishman on the shoulder. For the rather stiff and proper Howcrofts such demonstrative public displays were a bit over the top; these brash Americans were going to take some getting used to.

Hilda was even more amazed when Eppie told her that at the conclusion of the tour there was actually going to be a huge gala dinner and dance in her honour. Not only that, but it was to be held at Madison Square Garden. At that time the 19th Century building bearing the name, and which incidentally would be demolished just a few years later, held the largest indoor arena in the World.

There was time for a couple of sightseeing days before the serious business of swimming was due to start. Eppie had organised one or other of the swimmers Hilda already knew to be on hand as escorts each day. Even before the familiar skyline we know today and which is dominated by the great art deco skyscrapers of the 1930s, New York City was home to the tallest and most impressive buildings to be seen anywhere. Hilda was transfixed by the strangely shaped Flatiron Building at the junction of 5th Avenue and Broadway.

The party was also taken to the top of the World's tallest structure of the day, the Woolworth Building, much further south along Broadway. There, they marvelled at the panoramic views from the 57th floor. The express elevator had whisked the visitors up from street level to the 54th floor in just a minute, after which there were still three storeys to climb to the observation deck. When the elevator operator released the brake for the descent back to street level, Hilda suffered a momentary attack of the horrors when she felt the car plunge towards the ground, stranding her poor stomach in limbo somewhere near the top.

They received an invitation to tour Liberty Island. At the usual vantage point in the statue's crown they were able to look out at the view of New York Harbour from the tiny windows all the way round. The visitors were also afforded the most unusual honour of being encouraged to continue their climb all the way up to reach the inside of Liberty's torch. The ascent to the torch itself had been closed to the public since a terrorist attack in 1916, and incidentally has never been re-opened since. Consequently, very few people have ever made the complete climb. They visited Central Park and rode on the Staten Island Ferry. In fact, during a few whirlwind days they managed to take in all the major tourist sights the city had to offer in the 1920s.

The American girls had been excitedly following Hilda's progress in England with their swimming stroke. Those she had not met before were delighted to be introduced, and everybody treated her like an old friend. They were all looking forward to competing against their visitor. In many ways Hilda felt a kinship with them, and she immediately liked their open and friendly style as hosts. It was obvious to her right from the outset that nobody was about to start any personal rivalries, although they were all looking forward to some fierce competition in the pool. Eppie had managed to drive the WSA motto "Good sportsmanship is greater than victory" right to the very core of the sport. Hilda understood and identified with them. In many ways they were demonstrating the kind of attitude that largely persists in American sports to this day.

Swimming was due to begin in earnest on 1st August 1922 with an unusual ocean event. The Joseph P. Day Cup race would test a large field of swimmers over a 3½ mile open water course from Breeze Point to Brighton Beach off the Brooklyn coast. Anticipation was high, and the day before the race a cartoon appeared in the New York papers. Around a fine drawing of Hilda poised in diving position for a race there was a series of small sketches depicting episodes from her life.

One was entitled "Mr. James has a carpet cleaning establishment – It's the "Clean Up" family of England", and showed Hilda supposedly talking to her father. John James was depicted as a chubby seaside postcard character with a moustache, and holding a carpet beater. Hilda told her hosts it was all highly amusing because in her opinion the cartoonist had mistakenly drawn her coach, Mr. Howcroft. Her father was actually a short, thin and wiry man – and clean shaven to boot! In the cartoon, which parodied the English accent for Americans, her father is saying "I'll beat all the carpets in Europe – You clean up all the swimming records – Wot Sye Hilda?" She replies "Jolly well agreed old thing". Her reputation as a reluctant learner was a cause for mirth as well. Another of the drawings featured her sitting on the side of a swimming pool, while the coach begs her "For Hold Hingland's syke come in Hilda"

31/7/22 - LINING UP TO COMPETE IN AMERICA AND THE CARTOONISTS HAD A FIELD DAY

Hilda had never swum a race in open water (unless of course you wanted to count the filthy canal basin that the City of Antwerp had used as a makeshift Olympic venue). In fact she had never been in any kind of race longer than a mile. At the starting line of the Day Cup she found herself drawn on the very outside of the 52 swimmers present, noting that all her serious American rivals had drawn starting positions a lot closer to the beach.

It seemed to take forever to marshal the swimmers and their support teams in rowing boats into position for the start. Conditions were pretty poor, it was raining hard and the water was quite choppy when the gun went off. The swimmers had to fight against the ocean swell, plus an oncoming breeze. Small wonder it was called Breeze Point, she thought, more like half a gale! For a competitor used to a flat calm pool it was hard work indeed. Eventually the rain got much heavier, leaving many of the girls struggling to even see their support teams clinging on for dear life in the small boats.

Bravely battling along, Hilda reckoned she was swallowing half the ocean and thought that the conditions were becoming far too extreme to even allow the race to finish. She actually switched to the old fashioned Trudgen stroke for

57

a while, keeping her head a bit higher in an effort to swallow less water. Trying to find something positive to hang onto, at least she was pleased to have found that the water was actually not as cold as that Antwerp canal. It felt like small comfort under the circumstances, but true to form she simply refused to quit.

Finally the sea state did get the better of her, along with many of the others. Fighting against an unpleasant bout of sea-sickness, she was forced to stop and tread water while simultaneously trying to vomit and avoid drowning. In spite of it all, Hilda somehow managed to get going again, although she knew that her usual near-perfect strokes were a bit more ragged than she liked. Her first attempt at open water racing eventually came to a miserable conclusion as she frankly struggled across the line to claim what felt like a valiant third place behind Trudy Ederle and Helen Wainwright just as it began to thunder.

Eighteen months younger than Hilda, the sensational Trudy Ederle was swimming in her first significant race and had simply dominated the ocean from the gun to the finish. A few years later she would go on to spectacular Olympic Gold Medal success. She would also become World famous as the first woman to successfully swim the English Channel on her second attempt in 1926, an achievement made even more incredible by recording a time faster than any man had yet managed.

Hilda James' third prize was a beautiful art deco bronze and silver cup, one of the few real trophies she was ever allowed to keep. Immediately after receiving it the visitor was interviewed by an eager young reporter from the New York Times. Freezing cold and still tending to be sick, Hilda managed to be magnanimous in defeat, telling him that "The best girl won, of that there can be no doubt".

Privately she reckoned that apart from not actually drowning, her finest achievements of the day were twofold. She claimed joint triumphs for getting through the interview without complaining about the conditions, and just managing to move far enough to one side afterwards so as not to spoil the reporter's nice shoes.

Trudy Ederle was actually a non-starter at the next event on 5th August, a 300m invitation race during a major WSA gala at the 75 yard long Brighton Beach salt water lido. Also tired and seasick following her supreme effort in the Day Cup, Trudy had been given scant time to recover from her win before being taken by train to compete in another major race meeting at Indianapolis. Fatigued she may have been, but at Indianapolis on the day before the Brighton Beach Invitational she had actually managed to break the 400m World Record in 5:53.20. However on returning to New York feeling exhausted and very unwell, she was forced to withdraw from competing at the Brighton Beach event.

The fact was that, whether the swimmers were having the time of their lives or not the pace on the summer tour was hard. Apart from the actual swimming there were publicity events and long hours of travel to accomplish. Trudy's off day came right at the start, but later in the busy schedule, both Helen Wainwright and Hilda James would be forced to sit out and watch at meetings through fatigue and illness. It is very likely that ocean and river events probably contributed to this, the risk of infections generally being that much higher than in the swimming pools.

Hilda hadn't competed since the Day Cup. After an inauspicious start to her tour she felt that she had something to prove to these people for teaching her the stroke that had brought her such spectacular success. Pumped up with sheer excitement, she was on fire as she dived into the water. Willing herself to be at her very best, she contrived to put on a breathtaking display over four lengths of the big pool, beating the all-star line up and winning the 300m race in spectacular style. She also comprehensively demolished two American Records.

The 300 yards record holder Aileen Riggin had actually paced Hilda for most of the race, swimming right alongside her and therefore several seconds inside her own personal best, but eventually fading in the last half length to finish just three yards adrift. Another of the in-form Americans, Ethel McGary, had positively hounded Aileen all the way and finally finished third by less than a yard.

In the stands, Eppie was beside herself with delight and had shouted until she was completely hoarse. In a single race lasting just 4½ minutes, her crack swimmers had found themselves tested to the limit, and her decision to bring young Hilda James from England had been fully justified.

5/8/22
WSA Invitation Race
300m Freestyle – Won
Time 4:33.80
Brighton Beach, NY.
American Record
English Record
Unofficial World Record
Due to timekeeping restrictions
Race also timed for 300 yards
Time 4:08.80
American Record

Hilda had sliced a massive 8.40 seconds off Aileen Riggin's 300 yards American Record and her time of 4:33.80 for the 300m was inside the previous World Record. After being widely hailed as a new World Record by the Americans, Eppie was openly furious when FINA refused to ratify that particular time. Ever afterwards, she would fiercely maintain that Hilda had in fact broken the World Record.

It was symptomatic of the long running battle between swimming management and its governing body. Eppie had been fighting FINA on the subject of what she saw as their indifferent attitude to ratification for a long time. This time, for a short while it was an American Record that Hilda was left holding with a time lower that of the World Record.

In spite of all the records and successes she had managed to date, Hilda knew from that moment that she had contrived to achieve something really special. That swim, and more especially the series of photographs documenting it, caused an absolute press sensation across America. It neatly gave Eppie exactly what she wanted by launching the 1922 WSA summer tour into the public consciousness. Hilda James was already a major star in the UK and Europe, but after the Brighton Beach race she became an instant star in the New World.

Frankly, the press had been left a mite mystified as to Hilda's possible potential after the Day Cup. After all, the visitor had arrived in New York on the back of a major hype from Charlotte Epstein, following which she had promptly turned in what they perceived at the time to be a rather dull third place. No matter, because now they couldn't get enough of Hilda James.

The American swimming fraternity already knew it of course, but to the American public it looked like The British suddenly had a serious contender. What was more; they had just dropped her like a bomb among the American swimming royalty. The English Comet indeed; Hilda James had arrived.

The WSA tour had been organised to raise the public's awareness of swimming as a recreational pastime and sport for women. In fact there was quite a circus as the show rolled through the Eastern States. Various clubs held galas and invitation events in each different city, with the swimmers usually spending part of every day coaching and demonstrating followed by racing events in the evenings. Many well known American swimmers, both male and female, participated as their schedules allowed but apart from having to miss one gala due to illness, Hilda was there competing against them at every event.

In fact, during all the years she competed as an amateur, the 1922 American Summer Tour was probably one of the best times Hilda would ever have. She never lost her enthusiasm for being in the water. Happy to coach every day, she would sometimes demonstrate her trick strokes and comedy dives several times during an afternoon as they hosted different school parties, before competing in the evenings. She would cheerfully race absolutely anybody whenever she was asked.

On 8th August there was a gala in Chicago. The tour then moved on to Indianapolis for a major three day event at the Broad Ripple pool. Following the usual mornings spent coaching there was a major gala on each of the three afternoons, stretching on into the evenings. For laughs one evening, she even found herself pitted against a group of local male club swimmers and still managed to come first.

The Indianapolis visit would turn out to be the highlight of highlights for Hilda. Little did she know it, but she was about to witness an almost unbelievable performance, and meet a swimmer who would leave a deep and lasting impression upon her for the rest of her life.

CHAPTER 8
JOHNNY

On the first day at Indianapolis, the evening's racing finale was a Men's 100 yards Invitation Freestyle event. Eppie had made sure that the scheduling for Hilda's appearance in the gala that evening allowed her to finish early. She wanted her English guest to be out of the water and dressed in time to join the audience for what she had promised Hilda and her coach would be a real treat, because the top local boy was swimming.

Hilda sat with Eppie and the Howcrofts, and they watched in awe as an astonishing young man won the race by a huge margin. Just watching him perform gave Hilda the chills. At the end of his short race, she found herself standing up, completely transfixed at his performance and almost unable to even draw a breath.

From that moment on she was adamant that he swam the most perfect Freestyle stroke she would ever witness. He was effortless and economical in the pool, and Hilda told Eppie afterwards that it had been like watching a torpedo. She was amazed that for all the speed he attained there was hardly a splash, he simply wasted no energy. It wasn't only his swimming that she admired either, because out of the water she thought he was the most beautiful man she would ever see.

The object of all this breathless attention was indeed an extraordinary character. A month previously, the young Johnny Weissmuller had blasted himself into the record books as the first swimmer in history to cover 100m in less than a minute. Completing the swimming equivalent of the four minute mile in just 58.60 seconds, Johnny had taken almost two seconds off the long standing World Record held by an old friend of Hilda's from the Antwerp Olympics, the Hawaiian born champion and Gold Medallist Duke Kahanamoku.

On this particular occasion at Indianapolis Johnny had requested that there be two timekeeping teams present, as he was going to attempt to break World Records at both 80 and 100 yards during the 100 yard swim. In fact he took the 80 yards record easily in 40.60 seconds, but just failed to get below his own recent 100 yard record of 52.60. Eppie had apparently told him that their English star guest would be watching, and afterwards she reckoned that he had probably just been showing off.

Hilda didn't have it all her own way during the tour, nor had she expected to. The honours would generally be split evenly around the competitors, which contributed to the friendly atmosphere among the touring party. As Eppie had hoped, all the swimmers were acting like a proper touring team, with any personal rivalries saved strictly for when they were in the water. They were a WSA team, so it was all "Good Sportsmanship" and so on.

Hilda loved the whole affair because she simply didn't usually get the quality of competition that she was offered in America. Back home in England Connie Jeans wouldn't even swim against her, but in America all the stars lined up for their turn. Although she wasn't keen on the Nottingham girl, Hilda did think it was a real shame that Connie had never put herself in a position where she might have been invited on the tour. Hilda knew that if her main English rival had been along she would undoubtedly have found herself right in the mix, winning some of the honours with the best of them.

Every event in every city was over-subscribed, with every venue sold out in advance. The Americans had a magnificent arsenal at their disposal, with specialists and all-rounders available to challenge at every distance. Aileen Riggin and Helen Wainwright were no exceptions of course. Hilda had met and become good friends with these two in Antwerp during the Olympic Games. Aileen held the record as America's youngest Olympic Gold Medallist after having created a surprise by winning the 3 metre springboard diving event. She had a wonderful fizzing personality and was apparently a complete natural comedienne, loved by her team for her quick sense of humour. For her part she though Hilda's trick swimming and clowning about were great fun, especially when the English girl started working on a daring new impression of Coach Handley. Working together for a while, Aileen and Hilda entertained the entire company. Helen had been the runner up to Aileen in Antwerp and so was an Olympic Silver Medal winner just like Hilda.

On 11th August, the second day of the Indianapolis gala, there was another clash of the titans in a 300m race. On this occasion, after swimming neck and neck for almost the entire distance, Helen just managed to beat Hilda to the line. In doing so she snatched back Hilda's 300m World Record for the home country after the visitor had held it for just six days.

Swimming alongside each other had spurred them both on to a stellar performance. Helen had actually lowered Hilda's record time by yet another amazing four seconds to 4:29.80. In second place, Hilda finished just 0.40 seconds behind having sliced nearly four seconds off her own personal best, the Brighton Beach swim of the previous week. Once again poor Eppie had shouted herself hoarse, and could revel in the publicity her tour was creating.

Hilda put in a strong 100 yard backstroke performance the following afternoon, finishing third behind Helen and Aileen in spite of swimming with her usual stylish double-arm backstroke against their obviously more progressive back crawl. Later the same evening the visitor was scheduled to compete in the annual USA 300 yards championship medley race, consisting of 100 yards each of breast stroke, back stroke and Freestyle. But this time, Hilda James had a surprise up her sleeve for the hosts.

After one quick session in the training pool with Bill Howcroft, she took a huge gamble by daringly changing her tactics for the race and swimming the back crawl for the first time. It successfully kept her in contention during what she and Howcroft had identified as her weaker leg in the race. There was therefore some surprise at the pool when she unleashed the new weapon, beat the field and become the 1922 USA 300 yards Ladies Medley Champion. The Americans hadn't bargained for the rapid change of tactics, but they were beginning to get used to sharing the honours and were happy to do so.

She knew that Johnny was watching the proceedings this time, and Hilda had decided that she too could afford to show off a little. She had neatly reversed the old saying to read "What's sauce for the Gander is also sauce for the Goose!" At the end of a very exciting evening she left the pool as the proud holder of a small, suitably low value octagonal Indianapolis Athletic Club medal.

Whereas Hilda James is remembered principally as a pioneer of the modern Freestyle stroke she was actually an accomplished all-rounder, often demonstrating the other strokes to good advantage. Some of her contemporaries may have remained amateur for longer, some may eventually have broken far more records, but years later Bill Howcroft would say there was no doubt in his mind that Hilda was the best and most stylish all-round female stroke swimmer he ever saw.

12/8/22
USA Annual Championship
300 yards Individual Medley – Won
Indianapolis

On the back of the magnificent Brighton Beach result and the subsequent news frenzy it caused, Hilda was the centre of attention everywhere they went. However much fuss was created, the American girls remained very tolerant. They knew they had a new star in their midst, and her record swim had brightened the shine from that star enormously in the eyes of the American public, reflecting its light on all of them. Charlotte Epstein was beside herself with excitement. Publicity was the whole point, and with Hilda James gracing her summer tour Eppie had found it in spades.

Taken to heart by the public as well as the other swimmers, the visitor was showered with gifts wherever they went, although Howcroft was always there to make sure her amateur status was kept intact. A few small items must have escaped his attention as one or two still survive in the collection, including an engraved plaque which actually had to be removed from an enormous silver cup she won at a gala at Riverton on 26th August.

Even Eppie was kept busy deflecting some of the more generous offers of gifts from all manner of Hilda's fans including organisations, clubs and individuals. Many of these could most definitely be filed in the non-amateur category, but the WSA Captain did manage to negotiate some of the offers into more practical and lasting support for the good of swimming in general. After all, that was the whole purpose of the exercise. She did begin to wonder if she might be able to find a suitable gesture or a fitting gift for her guest to take home.

Back in New York City there was a major swimming event at Madison Square Garden on August 17th. Over 10,000 people packed the stadium, an audience which managed to break its own World Record as the largest for any swimming event at the time. True to form, they were treated to yet another spectacular race. Hilda delighted the huge crowd as she outpaced a 400m all-star invitation field. This time she won by an even more emphatic margin of over ten metres, once again claiming herself a place in the American record books.

On August 19th, Hilda made her second attempt at ocean racing. This time it was a long course 1500m event off Manhattan Beach, a distance over which she was considered to be improving by Bill Howcroft. With sea conditions much more conducive than the race at Brighton Beach just a few weeks earlier, she came a very close second to Helen Wainwright. With her English friend in hot pursuit, Helen had been spurred on to her own stellar performance, breaking yet another World Record in 25:06.60, a figure which would subsequently stand for over three years.

There was another significant gala at Woodmere, Long Island where the visitor won invitation races at both 220 yards Freestyle and 110 yards breast stroke. Next she appeared at a benefit event at Princeton University, NJ, wowing a large student crowd with the trick swimming routine. Riverton, NJ, and Bridgeport, CT, both held galas. Hilda then appeared in the Rariton River gala at New Brunswick, NJ, and finally back at Brighton Beach where the tour had kicked off some six weeks before. It had been nothing short of a spectacular success for Eppie, and her visitors were due to be leaving for home in a few days aboard the Cunard liner Mauretania.

The Connecticut meeting was significant for a different reason. After her first major appearance in the Day Cup and the amazing result it produced, Trudy Ederle beat Hilda by a large margin in a 220 yards race. It marked the start of Trudy's phenomenal rise to prominence which would simply eclipse every previous women's swimming achievement and re-write all the record books. Trudy was simply unstoppable, and would remain so for many years. The last significant race of the tour was another example of the same talent. At an Invitational over 500 yards, Trudy destroyed both Helen and Hilda with consummate ease.

Hilda was lucky that she had visited New York at exactly the right time. In fact the real revolution in American swimming was starting all around her during Charlotte Epstein's WSA summer tour of 1922. Over the following few months a string of phenomenal performances would be recorded, with Trudy Ederle and Johnny Weissmuller rising to prominence as the superstars swimmers of the age. If the WSA tour had been planned for the following year Hilda would have found women's swimming totally dominated by Trudy Ederle, who by then was breaking almost every record available. It has to be said that with the state of the competition on a 1923 tour, Hilda James would have been extremely unlikely to create the kind of impression that she did in 1922.

After appearing in Connecticut, a visit to Niagara Falls was arranged for the English guests. They were treated to a river trip aboard the "Maid of The Mist". Even after all her later travels Hilda would hail the experience of looking up into the falls from the boat as one of the more spectacular sights she ever saw.

17/8/22
WSA Invitation Race
400m Freestyle – Won
Time 6:19.40
Madison Square garden, NY
English Record
American Record

20/8/22
WSA Invitation Race
220 yards Freestyle - Won
Time 2:55.20
Woodmere, Long Island, NY

20/8/22
WSA Invitation Race
110 yards Breast Stroke – Won
Time 1:44.00
Woodmere, Long Island, NY

There was just one more major event left on the tour calendar, and it didn't even involve swimming costumes. The final spectacular was the long-awaited Madison Square Garden dinner dance that Hilda had been promised in her honour. It involved a lot of planning. Hilda and Agnes Howcroft's outfits had both been checked by Thelda and Trudy and subsequently deemed unsuitable for the event. Eppie was quickly enlisted to help out.

As Bill Howcroft was meeting Louis Handley for lunch before the event she quickly organised a girls shopping trip to Bloomingdales, managing to make it look like it had been planned all along. Eppie had decided that she would contrive an informal atmosphere, and there was soon some light hearted behaviour as she teased the visitors about their reserved demeanour. After weeks of cajoling, she finally managed to coax Hilda into calling Mrs. Howcroft by her first name of Agnes.

In the vast Bloomindales dress department both the visitors found themselves being encouraged to try on some fabulous but, if the truth be told, horribly expensive dresses. There was great fun as they all admired themselves modelling the various styles they liked and some hilarity about how Agnes' husband might react to a few of the more modern outfits.

For Hilda all the humour struck a bit of a hollow chord. She knew exactly how her parents would react to her appearing at home with expensive and modern clothes. She and Agnes were also both worried about the sheer cost of some of the items they were trying on. Finally Agnes asked Eppie where in New York City they might find outfits in their (significantly lower) price range, or even some nice cheap material so that they might run something up for themselves.

Suddenly the pair found themselves being presented with heaps of shopping bags in which their favourite dresses had been packed along with shoes and handbags, in fact all the required accessories. They were both shocked to find that what to them felt like an astronomical bill was casually being signed for against somebody's account. When they started to protest Eppie cut them off sharply, insisting that some of the items were personal gifts from a hugely grateful sponsor and she was certainly not going to allow anyone to spoil their shopping day with an argument. She would therefore hear no more about it!

Eppie was always firm, but apparently she wasn't really fierce unless properly cornered. Hilda made them all laugh by telling Agnes in a loud stage whisper that she wouldn't ever want to really fall out with the WSA Team Captain.

Leaving Bloomingdales, the Americans did allow some face saving by suggesting that their visitors might like to treat them to lunch at a restaurant. And if the party didn't choose the most expensive eatery in the city, well nobody cared to comment.

Over lunch Eppie finally relented a bit and offered the visitors some explanation. She owned up that during the tour, various individuals and organisations had approached her with offers of gifts, some of which were simply far too lavish to be acceptable. She had been trying to find a suitable idea that would be consistent with Hilda's amateur status.

With the gala dinner coming up, Thelda and Trudy had sounded her out on the subject of suitable dresses. She had immediately decided it would be a grand idea to go shopping, and following a few quick enquiries certain individuals had readily offered to quietly make contributions towards the cost. Eppie was at pains to explain that amateurism came in many guises, fortunately not all of them quite as stiff as the Howcroft vision. Therefore, not having Agnes' husband out shopping with them had even been part of the greater plan.

She then looked at Agnes and started laughing again as she pointed out that it was a girls' conspiracy; whatever else happened they all had to stay out of trouble with Coach Howcroft. Agnes certainly had the measure of him, so the lunch party finished in high spirits after agreeing that it would be far better to simply leave the coach out of the explanation. After lunch there was an extra treat planned as they all spent some time at a hair salon, another new luxury Hilda had never experienced before.

Late in the afternoon Agnes and Hilda arrived back at the hotel, with the Americans joining them to get ready for the evening together. The humble James children had always had it drilled into them from early in their lives that they were very ordinary and that they should never get ideas above their station. On no account were any airs and graces permitted. Good as her mother's dressmaking was, Hilda had spent most of her life in various altered hand-me-downs and home made clothes. Now she was experiencing something completely new. She had been dressed and attended like a princess by her friends, even submitting to having some make up applied to her face. There was simply no way her Ma would ever have allowed that.

And never mind the price of the absolutely gorgeous outfit, her hair-do alone had cost what would have been most of a year's clothes budget at home. Although still uneasy about the sheer cost of it all, when she finally caught sight of the slight, unfamiliar figure looking back at her from the full length mirror Hilda had to admit to herself that frankly she did look like a million dollars. For the first time in her eighteen years, deep down Hilda James knew that she actually deserved it.

Hilda had already been entertained at some fine gala dinners during her time swimming and not least during the past few weeks on the tour, but nothing she saw would ever be like that evening's event. The Women's Swimming Association was congratulating itself on the spectacular success of their summer tour while seeing their new favourite English cousin off home with a bang. She simply could not believe the lavish splendour of the huge hall, and the vast party that had been organised for her as one of the Guests of Honour.

Before the event Eppie had politely asked Hilda if she would mind sharing that honour with Johnny Weissmuller. Frankly, Hilda had been astounded at the thought that she could possibly object to sharing anything with that one! Hilda and Johnny sat together at the top table accompanied by Bill and Agnes Howcroft. The Women's Swimming Association was represented by their Captain Charlotte Epstein and their Triple Olympic Gold Medallist and new trainer Thelda Bleibtrey. The City of New York was represented too, by its Mayor John F. Hylan. Hilda's sponsors Cunard were there in the person of their Director of American Operations Sir Ashley Sparks.

After dinner there were various speeches. Mayor Hylan spoke about the excitement of American swimming and its new stars. As their special guest, Hilda James found herself singled out for individual praise, along with many of her friends, both old and new. The Mayor also congratulated Johnny Weissmuller on his recent successes, not least of which was the spectacular string of World Records he had turned in over the summer.

Charlotte Epstein then addressed the hall on the subject of the triumph of the amateur summer tour as a whole, and the massive contribution that their visitor had made to it. She explained that by that she meant a contribution both in the practical sense, and also by creating the dramatic publicity right at the start of the tour with the astounding swim at Brighton Beach. As usual she then dispensed with formality and managed to embarrass Bill Howcroft, asking him to stand and receive applause as Hilda's mentor and coach. Eppie also raised a laugh by adding that Hilda's comedy impression of Mr. Howcroft's unique coaching style would be long remembered as one of the highlights of the entertainment at many of the galas over the past weeks.

Finally she formally wished their distinguished visitors God Speed home, before springing her last surprise. Hilda was presented with a beautiful gold ring as a token of the Women's Swimming Association conferring a Life Membership upon her. During the obligatory standing ovation and in one of her by now familiar spontaneous gestures, Eppie duly abandoned ceremony to walk down in tears and hug an astonished Hilda. In the final crescendo of applause Hilda also suddenly found herself completely choked with emotion by all the fuss. Keeping tight hold of Eppie for as long as she could, Hilda realised that she had seen through the hard shell of determination and grown to love the American woman.

During the tour Hilda had been introduced to dozens of America's top swimmers both male and female, and most of them were at the party. After the excitement died down a bit she spent a long time surrounded by the members of her new club, accepting their congratulations and best wishes.

She was going to miss the competitiveness and friendship she had found, everyone from the eager young rising star Trudy Ederle to the impish cheerfulness of Aileen Riggin; from her closest rival in the pool, Helen Wainwright to her first American friend, the stoic Thelda Bleibtrey. She would miss too the enthusiasm and informality of Coach Handley, who still insisted on calling her "Kiddo" as he clapped her on the back, and of course the thrill of watching the beautiful Johnny Weissmuller swim. Most of all, she was going to miss her sponsor and possibly her greatest ever supporter, Charlotte Epstein.

The English Comet had also made a massive impression with the Americans, and every one of them, plus many others wanted to tell her so. They were going to miss her too, from every gritty and determined performance she had turned in to the fun and laughter. In spite of all the hard work there had been a lot of high jinks during the summer. That evening for the first time, this poor window cleaner's daughter from south Liverpool was finally beginning to feel like the celebrity that everybody else knew she had already become.

Finally, towards the end of the long evening there was the dancing. Because Johnny Weissmuller was the American star of the moment and joint Honoured Guest at the event, Hilda was thrilled to find herself being invited to the first dance by him. The major difficulty she had with Johnny was her complete inability to breathe properly when she was anywhere within twenty feet of him. She could time her breaths in the pool, stroke, kick, rotate and inhaling to a pattern, but when Johnny was nearby she jolly well just about suffocated. Hilda was both delighted and embarrassed when everybody stood to watch and applaud as the two World Champions took to the floor.

Later still, Johnny managed to catch her attention again and they quietly slipped outside the hall where they could find some peace. She already knew that somebody must have prodded him into asking her to dance, because socially he was awkward, and painfully shy outside his comfort zone. She might have suddenly lost the power to draw breath once again, but he couldn't seem to speak at all. What a comedy act they would make. She smiled up at him, willing them both to relax enough for conversation.

Johnny stammered and paused, then stammered once again and stopped completely. Taking a deep breath and gathering himself for another attempt, he bravely tried to string a sentence together. She waited patiently while he struggled with the words, and eventually he won the battle against shyness and haltingly managed to ask Hilda to accept a gift. Instantly relieved with himself, Johnny grinned widely down at her and she felt her heart perform its own racing dive.

He reached out and caught her hand, quickly pressing something into it before simply turning on his heel and just walking away. For a moment Hilda had dared to fancy that he might actually be about kiss her but in the event she was suddenly left standing alone, still completely breathless and tightly gripping what felt like a coin.

Hilda opened her fingers and had a closer look. Lying in the palm of her hand was one of the small octagonal medals from the Indianapolis Athletic Club meeting, bearing the engraved inscription "100YDS FREESTYLE MEN 1922". Hilda knew that whether he had been pushed into it or not, she had just witnessed Johnny Weissmuller climb a personal mountain.

She might not have received the kiss to go with it, but no matter. Hilda would forever admire Johnny Weissmuller for that simple gesture. Of all the many souvenirs and mementos Hilda collected along the way; together with the Olympic Silver Medal she would always treasure that unremarkable little trophy most of all. Talking about the events over fifty years later, she would say that emotionally she considered the Madison Square Garden gala evening to have been the pinnacle of her entire amateur career.

Before finally leaving New York City for Liverpool, another most unusual event occurred. Hilda actually managed to spend a whole day out of town with the other swimmers. It was the first and only time that she would be out of sight of one or other of the Howcrofts since they had left Liverpool over eight weeks before. After the Madison Square event, Hilda had asked the American girls if they could possibly arrange for her to meet Johnny Weissmuller just one more time, but she certainly hadn't banked on being secretly whisked away from Manhattan for a whole day.

The American swimmers all appreciated Hilda, but they just couldn't get to grips with the Howcrofts' attitude. Bill Howcroft might be able to enjoy a laugh at home in Garston Baths with his team, but in America he and his wife were both perceived as being very stuffy. In fact, for weeks there had already been some secret plotting going on behind the scenes, quietly working against what they perceived as an old-fashioned chaperoning tyranny guarding Hilda. She was a swimmer, she was one of their own and for goodness' sake, now she even belonged to their club. They wanted her to themselves for a while without being overshadowed by her dull coach and his wife.

Of course Eppie had used Louis Handley to keep Howcroft out of her way during the girls' shopping trip, but Hilda never managed to find out how both her chaperones were kept off the scent for a whole day. However they achieved it, between them Hilda's friends did manage to successfully hoodwink the Howcrofts.

After sneaking into the hotel and waking her very early with the news that they were going out to meet Johnny, Thelda quietly spirited Hilda away. They met up with some of the other girls, and after stopping at a diner for breakfast they took their English friend out to Brooklyn with an exciting underground train ride on the Sea Beach Subway line. They were on their way for a visit to the World famous amusement park at Coney Island. When they arrived in Brooklyn, Johnny and a group of the other young guys were already waiting to meet them. They had a ball, not arriving back in Manhattan until very late and putting the day-long chaperoning subterfuge under great strain. Suffice to say that on this occasion they all managed to get away with it.

It turned out that Johnny was a lot of fun in a group; it was in any one to one situation that he struggled so badly to communicate. Just before they finally parted company at the end of their big day out, Hilda managed to arrange things with the girls so that she could snatch a few private minutes with him away from the crowds.

Before being hustled out of the hotel in the morning she had just had time to pocket something that she wanted to give him. After all, fair exchange is no robbery. Wherever the great Johnny Weissmuller's trophy collection resides now, it should contain a small octagonal medal from the Indianapolis Athletic Club, bearing the engraved legend "300YDS MEDLEY WOMEN 1922". Oh yes, and she had managed to get her kiss.

It has to be said that in spite of all that these remarkable young people had achieved, they were mostly still just teenagers. Hilda James and Johnny

Weissmuller were 18, Trudy Ederle and Helen Wainwright just 16. In fact at the advanced age of 20, Thelda Bleibtrey was actually the old lady of the group.

Johnny Weissmuller would, of course, go on to become one of the most loved and respected figures of the entire 20th century, sporting or otherwise. He would revel in Olympic success, eventually winning an astounding five gold medals (One of them in the 100m backstroke at Paris in 1924 where Austin Rawlinson would be placed 5th). Hilda held just six World Records, but Johnny would eventually retire after breaking nearly seventy. That would include lowering his 100m time by another astounding 1.20 seconds in 1924, a figure which would then stand unbroken for an unprecedented ten years.

Although never a great conversationalist, Johnny did successfully overcome much of the early shyness that so held him back socially. From 1929 onwards, he would go on to develop a lucrative career as a model and later a major movie star, best remembered as the original screen Tarzan in a dozen movies. Not many people realise that before all that, he was one of America's premiere swimming stars in the 1920s, and a pioneer of the sport.

Eppie had warned Hilda that the WSA would be turning out in force when she departed for home, so she wasn't entirely surprised when there was a spectacular and very loud waving off party at Manhattan's Chelsea Piers on 5th September. It looked like every swimmer in America was there to wave the visitors off as Mauretania slowly backed away from the quay for another voyage home to Southampton.

On arrival at the terminal Hilda and the Howcrofts had been treated to one final surprise when they were received aboard the ship by none other than Cunard's American Director, Sir Ashley Sparks. They discovered that he had personally made arrangements for them to travel home as first class guests. Having made such an impression on their Cunard hosts along with the ongoing American publicity, the Company had seen fit to raise their profile even further. Cunard had even been a major contributor to the cost of the Madison Square gala dinner.

The travelling party waved for as long as they could see their friends at the pier and Hilda finally had time to reflect on the tour. She had grown to feel like she belonged in New York and was genuinely sad to be leaving the city. Anyway, now she was a life member of the WSA she would always think of Eppie as her Team Captain.

She was determined to take inspiration from the way Eppie operated and to always be firm, decisive and fair but with fun and laughter always readily available when suitable. What a great outlook, she though. As her mind drifted back to the reality she would face in a week or so she worried about reaching home and wondered how her life might have turned out if her Ma had been even half as enthusiastic and supportive as the American woman.

During the voyage home, Hilda told Bill and Agnes Howcroft that she would probably be going to live in New York City when she was 21 and allowed to make her own decisions. Eppie had said that she would always be welcome as an instructor at the WSA and that anyway, suitable work would be easy to find. In the meantime the three of them reminisced about the spectacular success of the tour. Hilda was once again happy to continue giving shows, and to spend the afternoons coaching with Howcroft in Mauretania's pool. She felt that she owed it to Cunard to give back as much as she could for their kindness. After all, without the Company's offer of free passage, she would not have seen America, or been feted like she had.

Seated at the Captain's table one evening, Hilda was asked if she had any plans to turn professional, as Cunard might well have some ideas for her to consider. She was told that the Company was busy planning a series of new ships that would be dedicated to ocean cruising and they might well be looking for swimming instructors and the like. Not just instructors mind, but multi-skilled high profile people, possibly even those with good sporting pedigrees.

Of course Hilda had actually considered the thought of turning professional some time before, when she first began to develop all the trick swimming. The idea of a travelling circus or carnival act seemed to keep floating back to her in different guises, but right now the next major challenge on her mind would be the 1924 Olympic Games in Paris. If she could keep up the form she had found on the American tour she would be sure to strike gold, but for that to happen she would need to remain strictly amateur for two more years. There was no point discussing turning professional for the meantime and Hilda politely turned the conversation away.

Just as they had done aboard Aquitania, the officers on the ship all wanted to dance with her. She realised that although she had been too busy to give it much though, she had been half hoping to meet that young wireless chap again, the one with the piercing eyes. She hadn't realised that they might end up on a different ship altogether. Now what was his name again? She had quite liked him. No, it had gone. Oh, well, she mused, ships in the night.

**5/8/22 – GIVING NO QUARTER AT BRIGHTON BEACH, NEW YORK
THE PICTURE THAT HERALDED A PUBLICITY SENSATION ACROSS
THE USA**

CHAPTER 9
HOMECOMING

Hilda was involved in a very interesting race meeting on 15th September 1922. On arrival at Southampton and before even taking the train home to Liverpool, she had travelled straight to London for a planned appearance in the ASA Championships at Hampstead over the weekend. Bill Howcroft didn't think it was a good idea, and for the first time in their association he had actually asked her to give the meeting a miss. He thought Hilda was unwise to insist on racing because she had spent over a week with no serious practice aboard Mauretania, but Hilda had told her coach that although it was a tough challenge she needed to go and race.

The Nottingham star Connie Jeans had finally come down off her high horse and learned the American Crawl. Hilda was wise enough to know that she would be seen as churlish if she failed to appear against her rival. After all, she had been waiting for the opportunity to race Connie for the better part of two years. Nobody could have foreseen the momentous swimming drama that would unfold during the following week.

The travelling party was met at Southampton by Gertie James so that she could escort Hilda to London. The Howcrofts had to travel straight to Liverpool, so the other Garston swimmers met Hilda at the championships accompanied by the Club Secretary Mrs. Gallagher. Amazingly, all four Garston girls from the 1920 Olympic team were drawn in the same heat of the 100 yards event, so Hilda swam against her old friends Charlotte Radcliffe, Grace McKenzie and Lillian Birkenhead to claim her place in the final.

Connie Jeans had always been a seriously good swimmer; there was never any doubt on that score. Hilda had always known that she would be a real contender again once she learned the crawl. She also knew that Connie was a fierce competitor and always put in a determined performance. Hilda was correct to be expecting a difficult race.

In the event though, Bill Howcroft proved to be right. Flushed by the new turn of speed she had found after learning to swim the crawl, Connie Jeans was indeed on sparkling form. She beat Hilda comprehensively in the final, taking another 0.20 seconds off Hilda's 100 yards record time set in July and therefore lowering the Ladies English Record to 1:09.20. The press had finally got their grudge race, fortunately under the stern eye of the ASA itself whose representatives had been watching with great interest. It has to be said that the result went against all their expectations. Although the actual record margin was small, after a decidedly lacklustre performance the now former record holder Hilda James had finished over three seconds adrift and right at the back of the field.

Connie's obvious delight would soon be shaken. Hilda would unexpectedly clock a faster time just three days later, but fortunately for the Nottingham swimmer it would be an unofficial one. Not surprisingly, Hilda had been extremely irritated with herself for swimming such a dull race at the championships. She accepted the fact that she should have paid more attention to her coach and travelled home in low spirits prepared to eat humble pie. She was also upset that she had let her team down by beating them all in the heats, denying them places in the final only to swim like a complete donkey herself and give it away cheaply. What a way to end a triumphant summer, with such a miserable homecoming.

Hilda would be cheered up as soon as she arrived in Liverpool. The Garston swimmers arrived in Liverpool on the Sunday afternoon to be met at Lime Street by yet another noisy party, as a crowd of over 250 stood on the platform to cheer and wave at her. The Garston faithful were not about to accept any suggestion of misery. After the reports from her American tour, the home crowd obviously didn't think one poor swim was such a big deal. Stepping off the train amid all the excitement, she could already feel the mood lifting.

Hilda actually had to spend some time at the station signing autographs before she could finally get away and return home to Garston courtesy of one of the town councillors, a Mr. Atkin, who for a rare treat took her and Mrs. James home in his car.

The following day there was a proper Garston homecoming gala planned, which was to be hosted by the Lord Mayor of Liverpool. Hilda spent the day lightly training in her home pool. By 6 PM there was a queue stretching right around the corner from the baths for a meeting that wasn't even scheduled to start until 7.30. Once inside the pool there was a carnival atmosphere and a great deal of noise, with chanting and cheering for Hilda to appear. She was busy behind the scenes offering her apologies to Bill Howcroft, who said there was really no need. For goodness' sake, anyone could turn in the odd duffer! He just told her to get out there and enjoy her moment.

Once she had made her entrance and order was restored, Bill Howcroft announced to the audience that Hilda had brought back a surprise for them all. He told the story of her learning the back crawl in a single afternoon, and how it had helped to gain her an American title in the annual 300 yards medley race. She then demonstrated the new stroke in a mixed event, losing to local back crawl specialist Austin Rawlinson in a 100 yard fun challenge amid a lot of good humoured heckling. She and her friend Austin were happy to take a bow, both grinning widely at the loud banter which was still being delivered by their team mates. The Garston Club liked to put on a bit of a show for His Honour, The Lord Mayor.

Hilda did her usual entertainment turn of course, having been busy refining the new impression to open her part of the show while she was away. She strode out equipped with the familiar pool hook for what initially appeared to be her regular "Mr. 'Owcroft" act. Instead, she set the hook down and strolled gently around casually taking in the scene, before starting to drawl at her "class", formed from a few members of the team who were waiting in the water. Hooking her thumbs into an imaginary pair of braces, she announced her new character and "The Relaxed American Coach, Mr. Handley" was born.

"Here, you're lookin' good there Kiddo. Work awhile on that ol' leg kick there fella. Oh yeah, smooth as silk with those arms missy, an' no splashin' now. Darn right on the dive, boys! Hey, where's that Limey Howcrawft gotten to? You workin' those purdy gals a' yours reeeel hard, Howcrawft? Know what? You slay me, Man!"

The Garston audience howled with laughter. Poor Bill Howcroft was left as pink as a rose, shaking with mirth and completely helpless as his team all pointed at him in delight. Yes, Hilda might exasperate him sometimes, but what a character she had turned out to be. It wasn't only her racing performances either; she had brought real entertainment to the sport. To borrow an expression from her new victim, his friend Louis de Breda Handley, "Man! what a gal!"

After an evening of cheerful competition, the final swimming event was the one serious item on the bill, the ladies 220 yards. For that there was an official ASA timekeeping team present. As she walked to the blocks, Hilda deliberately allowed herself to reflect on the recent Hampstead disaster and felt herself getting angry.

Spurred on by family, friends and her by now very raucous home crowd, she pushed herself hard and won the race by an enormous margin. Bill Howcroft had trotted up and down alongside shouting encouragement in his inimitable style. Such were his comments as he leant over the ends of the pool at the turns that the crowd began to realise they were there to see yet another record fall. At the final turn he nearly burst as yelled "Go on, you'll do it!" at the top of his high pitched voice, apparently even drowning out the ever raucous Garston faithful as it echoed back down at them from the rafters.

After the stopwatches were carefully cross-checked, Howcroft was even offered the honour of announcing the time because the result was nothing less than spectacular. Maybe she had been back on the bananas, because after her defeat at the weekend Hilda had managed to pull her finger out, demolishing her own 220 yards Ladies English Record time by a massive 5.40 seconds. Not only had that record gone, but at the 100 yards turn she had been timed another 0.20 seconds inside Connie's new mark. Because there wasn't a second team officially timekeeping Connie kept her record, but it was crystal clear that The English Comet was back to form. Once again she had announced her intention to the Nottingham star.

Following the big race, the carnival atmosphere finally broke out in full and overcame the proceedings. After being ceremonially thrown into the pool, Hilda was again presented with flowers and the usual basket of fruit. There is obviously no need to guess what that contained! There was a speech from Bill Howcroft, telling the packed crowd about some more of their experiences in America.

At the end of his address, he waited patiently for silence so that he could deliver an important public announcement for the benefit of the reporters present. On behalf of the Garston Club, Bill Howcroft issued sincere congratulations to Connie Jeans (in her absence) on her new 100 yards English Record. His comments were indeed reported in the press and taken to be a genuine gesture of friendship, a fact which apparently didn't go unnoticed in Nottingham. Afterwards, although they would never be friends, the two star swimmers did finally begin appearing regularly together again at meetings, to the enduring benefit of the sport as a whole.

The Bootle MP and Cunard Chairman Sir Thomas Royden was in attendance, and he also gave an address welcoming Miss James home. He officially thanked her and Bill Howcroft for all the impromptu coaching they had done aboard his ships. He added that he had already started receiving reports from his staff, plus several letters from passengers, about the hugely popular swimming displays Hilda had given during her two voyages. In fact, if they were half as good as her impression of Mr. Handley he really wished he had been there to enjoy the show.

Lastly the Lord Mayor made a speech praising the club and all Mr. Howcroft's swimmers. Hilda received a personal accolade, before accepting a small gift from him to show the City's appreciation. As a further surprise, His Honour was pleased to announce that local businesses in South Liverpool had come up with the unusual idea of starting a fund to commemorate Hilda's achievements in a way that would form a lasting legacy. Mr. and Mrs. James had been consulted, and with Hilda's brother Jack in mind it had jointly been decided with the fund secretary that Hilda was to have a children's cot named after her at the local hospital as a testimonial. More than all the other tributes, she was really touched by that.

Not wanting anyone to think that her new 220 yards record was just luck and clearly back to enjoying herself hugely, Hilda emphasised her return to form just two days later at a Cunard gala across the River Mersey at Seacombe. Garston was her home pool of course, but the Guinea Gap baths at Seacombe was definitely her preferred venue for record breaking because she liked the salt water.

Hilda turned in yet another startling performance. On this particular occasion, she smashed both the English and World Records for 150 yards. There was another huge celebration. It was a pity for Cunard that they had allowed Howcroft to hold onto Hilda until the end of the season because the 150 yards World Record performance at Seacombe was a Garston Club record. In fact it was the last occasion on which the name Hilda James would be noted in the record books as a Garston Club swimmer.

Hilda knew that Eppie would undoubtedly have looked her straight in the eye afterwards and said sternly "Always remember, good sportsmanship is greater than victory, Hilda". Of course technically she would have been right but sometimes though, just sometimes, Hilda James might have privately disagreed with her.

18/9/22
220 yards Freestyle - Won
Time 2:51.40
Garston, Liverpool
English Record

20/9/22
150 yards Freestyle - Won
Time 1:48.00
Seacombe, Wirral
English Record
World Record

21/9/22
NCASA 4x100 yards
Squadron Championship - Won
Retained by Garston 3rd year running
Burslem, Stoke

Following yet another Squadron Championship win by the seemingly unstoppable Garston girls at the end of September, Hilda James stood next to Bill Howcroft and faced the team at club night for an announcement. Hilda told her friends that she would be formally leaving Garston to join the Cunard Swimming Club at The Adelphi Hotel with effect from 1st October. There was a gasp of disbelief.

Howcroft explained to his team that it had been a condition of the travel for the summer tour, and under the circumstances he felt that Cunard had exacted a fair price. Anyway, it would largely just be a banner change as he would still be her coach, so she would swim regularly at club nights in Garston. Indeed, he added that the club had decided that regardless of whose colours she wore, she was to become a lifetime honorary member at Garston with effect from the same date. In spite of all this, Hilda's friends were genuinely saddened that she would no longer swim or record times under their banner. To them, it felt like the end of an era.

CHAPTER 10
PARKGATE BATHS

Unexpectedly, 1923 would herald the start of a new prosperity for John James and his family. The swimming business was about to impact on all their lives in ways that the Garston window cleaner and his wife could never have imagined. Early in the New Year and completely out of the blue, John was approached by a well to do gentleman by the name of Algernon George (AG) Grenfell, owner and Headmaster of the independent Mostyn House School at Parkgate in Cheshire.

Grenfell had an interesting and what would turn out to be very generous business proposition for John. He was near to completing a major project to build the country's largest open air salt water baths on the banks of the River Dee near the school. Adjacent to the pool there was also a rather grand detached house nearing completion, providing very spacious family accommodation in addition to a completely separate self contained apartment. The idea was to locate a resident pool caretaker and manager on the premises, with room for an extended family if needed.

Grenfell was wondering if John and his family might be interested in such an opportunity. The basic income would not be large, but as part of a working contract the new house would be rent free. There would also be opportunities for the new manager to increase their income by possibly opening a tea shop and ice-cream stall. There would be plenty of space available to offer bed and breakfast, or even holiday rentals. John asked the Headmaster if there might be room for an allotment and was told the house would be surrounded by a huge garden, from which he could requisition as much as he cared to work.

Facing North West into the Irish Sea, the Wirral peninsula is bounded by the River Dee and the River Mersey. Lying between the mountains of North Wales and the City of Liverpool, it is approximately rectangular and less than ten miles across by twenty long. Where it faced Liverpool on the banks of the Mersey, it was a land of docks and shipyards in the 1920s. It was every bit as industrial, ugly and built up as the Liverpool Docklands across the river. A very short way inland the conurbation gave way to gently rolling farmland and quiet countryside dotted with small hamlets.

Even today Parkgate is a small and peaceful village. There is a decidedly remote feel about the place, with no through traffic as the main road is located further inland. An attractive old promenade called The Parade sits atop a sandstone sea wall a dozen or so feet high, looking out over the Dee estuary. Sheep now dot the wide salt marshes, which are also an important haven for wildlife and birds. The once majestic River Dee has gradually retreated into a narrow channel nestling against the Welsh Hills some miles away to the south west.

The entire James family was invited on a day out to visit Mostyn House School, inspect the nearly finished pool complex and tour the new Bath House, as it would be known. In a straight line it is only a few from Garston, but after setting off by train to Liverpool they then had to cross the River Mersey to the landing stage at Seacombe on the famous ferry. Back on a train, they travelled through the Birkenhead and Wallasey dock complex, before finding themselves out in the countryside on the way to the town of Neston. From the station there it was still a walk of about a mile to reach Mostyn House at Parkgate. All things considered, it was quite a trek.

In the early part of the 20th Century the river was still properly tidal as far as Parkgate. At high tide the water lapped against the old sea wall and local fish could be landed. They walked along The Parade enjoying the sense of tranquillity and space in the small village. To John and Gertie James coming from South Liverpool's land of docks and industry, they may only have travelled a few miles, but it might as well have been at the other end of the World.

After being treated to hospitality at the school, the family walked to the far end of The Parade with AG Grenfell, continuing along a seaside lane from the corner of the promenade to reach the new swimming pool. The facilities were indeed excellent and Grenfell proved to be a genial and interesting host. Hilda could hardly believe her eyes when she saw the actual pool, because it really was huge. It was actually just over 100 metres long, but she asked the Headmaster why it wasn't exactly 100 as the ASA would not allow any records to be broken there unless it was a regulation size. She told him that with a 100 metre salt water pool she could swim the 300 with only two turns, and that would definitely make her capable of taking a World Record time off the Americans. Mr. Grenfell said that it was a shame he hadn't considered that, as it was already far too late to do anything about the pool design.

The James family were shown around the new house, which seemed absolutely palatial, and John knew for sure that it would be one of the few times in their long marriage that he and Gertie would find no need to argue. With the prospect of proper paid work and a beautiful new house in the country thrown into the bargain, the answer to Grenfell's offer would be a resounding "Yes please".

Grenfell also wanted Hilda for the new baths if he could get her. If John James took up the offer he was already planning to trade heavily on the school's new link to her family, by using the name of Hilda James to promote all the benefits of his new pool and draw in the crowds. Ideally he wanted Hilda to become the resident swimming coach. At that suggestion her parents did turn him down.

Bill Howcroft soon became involved, explaining to the Headmaster that Hilda was planning to remain swimming under amateur status at least until after the Olympics in Paris the following year. He also warned Grenfell that her parents could be somewhat difficult on the subject of Hilda's swimming career. Her mother especially was best handled very carefully, or even better still left for John to deal with. Grenfell was smart enough to realise that he could still use the family name even without actually having Hilda on the payroll. He was content to wait for the meantime, and see if he could catch her when she finally decided to turn professional.

In the meantime, Grenfell's deal with John James went through. The Bath House was completed and the family moved to Parkgate to oversee the final touches to the swimming pool. The new Parkgate Baths opened in a blaze of publicity on 12th May 1923. It was advertised as being managed and run by "Mr and Mrs James, the parents of the Champion Swimmer Hilda James of Garston". Like the greengrocer's shop in Garston, the ASA couldn't stop Grenfell trading on Hilda's name as long as he was careful. Naturally Hilda was asked to officially open the pool, and there was the usual gala event.

At 335'6" long by 50' wide (102.26 x 15.24m), Parkgate's new open air baths could justifiably boast about having the largest pool in the country. There was innovation too, as it had shallow and deep sides rather than ends. It instantly became a roaring success, with thousands flocking in to swim and play. There were slides and diving boards, large terraces for sunbathing and excellent changing facilities.

Sea water was pumped from the estuary through filters via a 40 hp electric pump and was constantly being refreshed to keep it clean. The boys from Mostyn House School were allowed free admission in return for having helped foreman George Cannon with the building work. They were always happy to tell bathers that "They had built the pool."

Shortly after the new baths opened, an anonymous letter appeared in the local press complaining bitterly about "A threat to the moral tone of the neighbourhood caused by the sight of partially clad females sunbathing at the new Parkgate baths". When a friend of Grenfell's remarked to him that it was a pointless and silly letter, he replied by saying "Not at all. After all my dear fellow, who do you think wrote it? The young men have been visiting in droves ever since!"

IN 1923 THE NEW PARKGATE BATHS BOASTED BRITAIN'S LARGEST OPEN AIR POOL AT 335'6" (102.26m) – THE BATH HOUSE IS VISIBLE ON THE LEFT (© THE FRANCIS FRITH COLLECTION)

CHAPTER 11
FRANCONIA

Cunard were also more actively courting Hilda by the time Parkgate baths opened in May 1923. They had already reaped the benefits of her high visibility trip across the Atlantic by having her picture splashed all over the papers alongside their name, both in Europe and America.

Their new mid-size liner, RMS Franconia was being completed for service entry in a few weeks. They were planning to use her for some cruising as well as the regular passenger work, and she was going to feature a modified interior for the purpose. Instead of a rear cargo hold there would be a spectacular vaulted indoor swimming pool situated between a racquet court and a gymnasium. If she was a success in the cruising role the next new ship would feature a completely new kind of accommodation in all classes, as designed specifically for the purpose by their dynamic and visionary Deputy Chairman Sir Percy Bates.

While at the Adelphi Hotel one afternoon following a swimming session, Hilda was approached by some senior Cunard people and asked to take tea with them. She was beginning to realise that these occasions were significant over and above the tea itself, and this time it would be no different.

The Company was planning to send Franconia on a three day shakedown cruise through the Irish Sea to Western Scotland and back. The idea of a shakedown was to give the engines and all the systems a thorough workout, with the crew having an opportunity to get to know their new ship and each other. Would Hilda like to go along for the ride, inspect the new pool and sports facilities and maybe give a swimming demonstration or two for the assorted guests and dignitaries involved? Cunard would mark the occasion by holding a ceremony so that she could officially open the pool.

As a Cunard Club swimmer that would fit neatly within her amateur status. After all, apart from swimming and a bit of coaching at the Adelphi it was just the sort of thing she had offered to make herself available for after her Cunard sponsored visit to New York the previous year. The subject of having celebrity crew members involved in the new World Cruises was raised once again, and the point was made that in the Company's view Hilda was very probably just what Cunard was looking for.

Hilda wasn't sure if any more cruising would go down too well at home and said so. She was surprised to hear that Cunard had remembered her having some problems in that department and had planned accordingly. Keen to avoid any further family difficulty, Hilda was actually told that Mrs. James would be welcome to join her on the cruise, and she was asked to pass on the invitation with their compliments. And so, accompanied by her Ma who finally felt she was going to get something out of it all, Hilda once again sailed from Liverpool in June 1923.

As usual Cunard had an ulterior motive. They wanted to encourage Mrs. James to feel that she could let her daughter travel safely with them. During the cruise Mother and daughter were invited to tour the ship, with careful emphasis being given on the subject of the crew's quarters. Their hosts were at pains to point out that the ladies were all accommodated in one part of the ship, which was a strictly male-free zone. As the ship wasn't nearly full and with it being a shakedown cruise, Hilda and her Ma were also made to feel utterly spoiled and were naturally given a first class stateroom to try out.

As usual, Hilda's swimming demonstrations were a big success, and she was definitely found to be in approval of the facilities. In fact she was very impressed with the new layout as the pool was actually bigger than the one aboard Aquitania, but in a liner with less than half the tonnage. Chairman Sir Thomas Royden was on hand to watch as she actually dared to make fun of his deputy Sir Percy Bates on the subject of cruise ship design. After the Garston homecoming gala he was already familiar with Miss James' comedy lines and trick swimming, and he was particularly delighted to witness Percy getting ribbed by her. He whole-heartedly agreed with Percy; one way or another the Company had to get her on board.

At the evening dance Hilda was pleasantly surprised to see the same young officer to whom she had taken a liking on Aquitania the previous year. She was thrilled to be asked to dance by him again. Hugh McAllister - of course, that was the name she couldn't remember! He then surprised her by turning up the following afternoon to watch one of her swimming demonstrations, but they didn't get to talk because she was kept busy by the Cunard senior management.

Hilda did meet Mr. McAllister for a long conversation later in the day before they finally parted, wishing each other the best of luck for their futures. Hilda found that she had actually taken quite a liking to the young officer. She had remembered correctly that he had the most incredible, piercing pale grey eyes. When they looked at her, she somehow felt like she had stayed looked at. Fortunately, he hadn't had the same effect on her respiratory system that Johnny Weissmuller seemed to! Hilda was glad that her Ma had been busy elsewhere, as she would not have been the slightest bit enamoured.

Back on dry land, Bill Howcroft had found himself in a state of complete exasperation with Hilda. With very little notice, the Franconia cruise had clashed with two important dates on the swimming calendar, namely the annual Olympic Tests and the opening of a new open air baths at Blackpool. Hilda had previously been booked to appear at both of these events. In fact he had actually asked her not to go on the cruise, because after all hadn't she had already done some pretty spectacular cruising the previous year?

Hilda told him that during her recent meeting with Cunard she had been reminded of the loose publicity contract she had with them. As yet they had not asked much of her, but they did want her approval and comments on the Franconia as a potential cruise ship. She had felt duty bound to accept the offer and didn't want to jeopardise her chances of securing a career with them later on, a possible development the Company seemed to keep on alluding to whenever she met them. For the second time in less than a year, his protégé disagreed with him and went off to do things her way.

Apart from her tricky family situation, which between them they so far managed to circumvent, Howcroft felt that Hilda was now beginning to cause him some difficulties in her own right. As her coach he had a fair point, because on this occasion he had actually been put in a pretty bad position. He dared not let on that Hilda was missing previous engagements by casually sailing away on a last minute free cruise. In the end he was forced to make excuses for her, a situation which he didn't like one bit.

It didn't actually come to another row, but the Franconia cruise certainly marked the beginning of a cooler period in the relationship between the coach and his star pupil. Deep down, he knew that she was getting ready to spread her wings and he just hoped she would manage to avoid her parents' wrath when she did. Unfortunately he was to be proved wrong. In fact sooner than he might have imagined, the coach would find himself helping to pick up the pieces.

At the new swimming pool, 15 year old Jack was managing to help out a little, and was already benefiting from being away from the smoky city in the clean coastal air. Elsie and Walter were both available for work during the holidays when the baths were at their busiest. Gertie had quickly taken to offering refreshments from her own kitchen, and was rapidly building up a reputation for serving a first class cream tea.

As the Manager, John ran the whole operation well. Uneducated but ever resourceful, by now he had been kicking around swimming baths and clubs long enough to know how they worked. He was also enough of an odd jobber to look after most of the equipment by himself, which ultimately saved Grenfell a lot of money in annual maintenance charges. He did indeed have plenty of space available and eagerly started work on a large new kitchen garden to replace his allotments in Garston.

John even managed to find time to put in some other work for Grenfell at the school on weekdays when the baths were not so busy. During the first winter closed season Grenfell had him engaged in upgrading the facilities at the baths. During the summer, he and his pool manage had been working on plans to make the pool even more of an attraction. John was kept busy realising some of their joint ideas to enhance the bathing experience when the baths reopened at Easter. One of the winter projects Grenfell paid for was to have John build his wife a proper tea shop adjacent to the pool.

Hilda was still very busy with swimming fixtures of course, but Grenfell offered her a proper job working for the school's Matron. On moving to the Wirral she had finally had to quit her greengrocery job in Garston. Although the shop had only ever managed to employ her in a part time capacity because of the swimming commitments, they were sorry to lose their helpful assistant and favourite champion.

Grenfell was still keen for Hilda to come to the school in a proper swimming capacity, but was mindful that she could not be paid for anything to do with that until she decided to turn professional. Much as her former employers had done, he arranged to allow her the time off she required for all her swimming activities. Like Cunard, he was positioning himself to try and secure her services after the Olympic Games, when it was generally reckoned that she would turn professional.

It seems probable that Hilda was also beginning to think further ahead by this time. With the new Parkgate deal, her family was becoming involved in the actual swimming business. She realised that there was a supreme irony in their having been encouraged to turn professional while she couldn't, at least until after the Paris Olympics. Maybe the time was coming for her to find ways to use her talents to bring in some proper money while she was at peak form. After all, some serious offers seemed to have started coming in recently. Time would tell.

Failing that, there seemed to be no reason why she shouldn't have some fun. Ocean cruising could definitely be filed under the heading of fun. If she ended up throwing in her lot with Cunard there seemed to be the distinct possibility of being given the chance to combine two important aspirations, fun and money.

Hilda was officially a Cunard swimmer, but she still trained with Bill Howcroft and the Garston team. When she was heavily committed at Garston, she had begun to stay with her father's younger sister Margery and her husband Jim Brooks. They had a house at Hunts Cross, not far away from her old club where of course she now held an honorary life membership. Her aunt and uncle ran a much more modern and relaxed household than her parents and she was always made very welcome. The Brooks' had long been of the opinion that Hilda's family were too hard on her, and they delighted in spoiling their niece a bit whenever she came to stay. They had a four year old daughter, also called Margery, who Hilda adored. Little Margery loved her big cousin and always looked forward to having her come and stay.

There was still a full swimming calendar. Following the ocean races off New York the previous year and with approval from Howcroft, Hilda had decided to try a couple of the longer distance river events. In typical style she won both of them by huge margins. During the summer she was again beaten by the ever improving Connie Jeans in both the ASA 100 and 220 yards championships. Once again Hilda quickly exacted revenge for one of those defeats on 10th October by breaking the 220 yards World Record in her favourite pool at Seacombe during yet another six week, nine record purple patch. The two stars were forging a solid rivalry in the pool which was once again good for the sport and would remain a popular crowd pleaser.

6/6/23
Scottish ASA
200 yards - Won
Dundee
Scottish Record

17/7/23
NCASA Championships
100 yards Freestyle - Won
Burslem, Stoke

30/7/23 ASA Cert. 306
Thames Long Distance Championship
Kew to Putney - Won
5 miles 60 yards in 1.09:46.40

26/8/23
Seine Long Distance Championship
Pont Nationale to Passarelle Debilly - Won
8km in 2.32:00.00

Hilda won the River Seine race by well over 300m. Two other English ladies featured prominently, Elsie Annison of Croydon Ladies taking 4th place and A.

McHattie, swimming in for the Lyons club to claim 5th. The three were jointly presented a very large trophy which immediately "had to be donated to" (i.e. was appropriated by) the English ASA because of the amateur status problem. It is still in annual use as a prize for the British Swimming Women's 400m championship.

In a newspaper interview following the River Seine race the usually magnanimous Hilda made a rare complaint, describing the race as a swimmers' nightmare. She reported that all manner of vessels including steamboats, pleasure cruisers and rowing boats had been tearing about on the river, greatly endangering those in the water and making it unnecessarily choppy. What she didn't tell the press was that the Seine was absolutely filthy and the competitors had been swimming through raw sewage for much of the race. Had the boats not been creating such waves she would probably have contrived to swallow less of it. Privately she said that it was so awful she would have actually preferred the canal in Antwerp. Win or no, Paris would be a one-time only event. It was the one race she would definitely not be accepting an invitation for in the future.

20/9/23
Liverpool & District Championships
100 yards Freestyle - Won
Time 1:07.20
Southport, Lancashire

10/10/23 ASA Cert. 427
220 yards Freestyle - Won
Time 2:46.60
Seacombe, Wirral
English Record
World Record

15/10/23 ASA Cert. 422
300 yards Freestyle - Won
Time 4:06.40
Garston, Liverpool
English Record

30/10/23 ASA Cert. 424
150 yards Freestyle - Won
Time 1:46.80
Southport, Lancashire
English Record

31/10/23 ASA Cert. 425
440 yards Freestyle - Won
Time 6:01.60
Seacombe, Wirral
Own English Record **lowered**
by an unprecedented 15.00 seconds

2/11/23
300m Freestyle - Won
Time 4:21.00
Seacombe, Wirral
English Record
World Record

5/11/23 ASA Cert. 426
500 yards Freestyle - Won
Time 6:57.60
Seacombe, Wirral
English Record

28/11/23 ASA Cert. 429
300 yards Freestyle - Won
Time 3:58.40
Seacombe, Wirral
Own English Record **lowered**
by another 8.00 seconds

CHAPTER 12
SHIPS IN THE NIGHT

After having had some time to familiarise himself with the 20,000 ton ships, Hugh McAllister was detailed to lend a hand with the wireless office aboard the next new one being completed. He arrived aboard Franconia during the final fitting out process. Although built in a different shipyard, she was from the same drawing board as two of the ships he had been working on. She had been designed with similar equipment to Samaria and Laconia so he knew what to expect in the way of hardware to assemble. He had learned a lot during his winter on the Atlantic as well as aboard Aquitania, and he already had a few ideas to try out.

After taking a quick look at the plans for Franconia's wireless system he promptly set about suggesting some major alterations to the equipment before it could be installed. He asked to be given enough time to make some modifications within the radio shack itself. Relocating several key pieces of equipment would make life a lot easier for the Wireless Officers, therefore improving the overall efficiency of the task. To add to the internal changes, he also needed to adjust some aspects of the external aerial setup.

Cunard had engaged his services with the aim of gaining a proactive and confident Wireless Officer who would hopefully show some real initiative. They got exactly what they paid for with Hugh. Time was tight, but they duly provided him with the manpower he needed, along with carte blanche to improve the facilities as he saw fit. Sea trials followed, culminating in a short shakedown cruise out of Liverpool during June 1923 with a party of invited guests and dignitaries aboard. They were treated to a leisurely few days of the legendary Cunard hospitality as they sailed to Western Scotland and around the Island of Mull.

Hugh was surprised and pleased to spot the champion swimmer Miss Hilda James at the ball, this time travelling with her mother. On her transatlantic voyage aboard Aquitania the previous year she had been accompanied by her coach and his wife. Feeling lucky and frankly a little bit star struck, he didn't wait patiently in line as he had on the previous occasion. As he was now a regular Cunard Officer, protocol definitely permitted him to ask her for an early dance.

Miss James told Mr. McAllister that she was really pleased to meet him again. She had half hoped that their paths would cross on the voyage back from New York, but she had forgotten there was a choice of three ships and had ended up sailing home aboard Mauretania.

She told the young wireless officer that she was aboard at the invitation of Cunard to declare the swimming pool fit for purpose and officially open it. In return Hugh told the young swimming star that he was a regular Cunard Officer now, and he was aboard to declare the wireless office fit for purpose and officially open that. They both laughed. He added that actually he had jolly well better declare it fit because he had insisted on delaying its completion so that he could re-design the whole thing. If he didn't approve the final layout, his Cunard career might end up being shorter than he hoped.

Hugh took himself along to watch Miss James' swimming demonstration the following day. Captain Milsom was there, hosting the Cunard Chairman Sir Thomas with Lady Royden and Deputy Chairman Sir Percy with Lady Bates. Before diving into the spectacular new pool Miss James announced that although very luxurious, it was naturally just a bit smaller than she was used to performing in. Having already calculated how many turns she would need to complete she would like to offer her apologies in advance, as there was no chance of her breaking a record for the assembled guests. After all, with a proper racing dive she could only manage a few real strokes in each length.

She cheekily added that she couldn't see why Sir Thomas and Sir Percy couldn't design ships twice the size of even the vast Berengaria, so that at least they could have a full-size competition pool for the poor swimming instructors. The assembled dignitaries laughed, Sir Percy burying his face in his hands and pretending to cry. He was actually laughing hard at the joke, delighted that Miss James appeared to be so at ease with these important folk. Nevertheless Hugh was more impressed by her swimming, especially when she showed off some of her now famous trick routine. The demonstration went down very well, and as Hugh left he noted that Miss James was engaged in conversation with the Company Chairman and his Deputy.

Feeling very forward, Hugh managed to arrange a meeting Miss James later in the day, and they found some time to chat in one of the lounges. He asked after her coach who he had been introduced to aboard Aquitania, and she told him that she didn't think Mr. Howcroft was actually speaking to her at the moment. She was supposed to have been swimming in the Olympic Tests event and then opening the new Lido at Blackpool, but Cunard had invited her on the cruise instead. She went on to explain that in return for the Atlantic crossing when they had met the previous year, she had a loose contract with Cunard to be available for publicity work when they asked her. Anyway, you couldn't possibly deny that cruising was much better fun than opening new swimming baths. She had lost count of the ones she had already opened.

Miss James confided in Hugh that her mother was only along on the cruise because she didn't like her daughter travelling. Cunard had felt obliged to invite Mrs. James in the knowledge that otherwise the star would not have been allowed to come, even though she had recently turned nineteen. Telling Hugh that she had met some women with much more modern attitudes than her mother on her tour of America, she added that she might even consider living there in the future. She said that she would definitely be turning professional in 1925 as soon as she turned 21. She had already received a tentative job offer as an on-board Swimming Instructress for Cunard, and she thought that inviting her on the current cruise was partly intended to keep her interested. They finally parted cheerfully wishing each other good luck in the future. Ships in the night and all that.

After completing the work on Franconia and seeing her safely off into service Hugh found himself back on board Laconia for a while, once again plying the Atlantic. Soon afterwards, he received a pleasant surprise in the form of a plum posting aboard the Company's flagship, RMS Berengaria. The 52,000 ton Berengaria was Cunard's largest liner of the 1920s and actually the third largest ship of the entire age. Launched in Germany for the Hamburg American Line in 1912 as the SS Imperator, she had been seized after the war along with all the other German liners. Following some trooping duties, she was finally allocated to Cunard as part of a reparation deal for the loss of several of their ships including the ill-fated RMS Lusitania. After an extensive refit at Liverpool, she had finally entered service with the Company in 1920.

Hugh immediately liked the mighty Berengaria even better than Aquitania. Sporting three very large oval funnels which had actually been reduced in height during the refit, she looked decidedly more modern and rakish than the other two big Cunard ships. Although they were both smaller than the flagship, they were four-stackers with the taller, slimmer funnels which gave them a somewhat more old fashioned look in his eyes. The wireless office aboard Berengaria was particularly well equipped, and even more spacious than the one aboard Aquitania. He even had his own personal cabin located nearby.

Once again he was able to settle quickly into a comfortable routine of watch keeping. During the posting he made over a dozen more round trips across the Atlantic on the Cunard express service from Southampton. The interior of the liner was luxurious in a vast kind of way that even Aquitania couldn't match. The public areas were designed on a heroic scale, and dances in her enormous ballroom were said to be one of the great features of 1920s transatlantic travel.

At 23, Hugh was a striking looking young officer. He was still skinny, with a somewhat bony face and those piercing pale grey eyes that had so attracted Miss James. He had a grand time working on the Atlantic liners. Wireless officers came into contact with the passengers as they delivered and received messages, and there was enough off duty time available to be able to engage in some serious socialising. He was easy company and certainly managed to attract the special attention of more than one wealthy travelling lady. He would remain lifelong friends with one or two of the people he met aboard the Cunard express liners.

There was definitely a regular girlfriend from New York City during that period, and he would always visit her while docked there. She eventually married a millionaire, but she and her husband would remain close friends with Hugh throughout their lives, occasionally visiting England until they were all very old.

A NEW CUNARDER

THE FRANCONIA'S FIRST TRIP

The Cunard Steamship Company recently added a new ship to its fleet of Atlantic liners. The new vessel, the Franconia, arrived at Liverpool yesterday afternoon from a three day cruise among the Western Isles of Scotland. The trip was designed to test the qualities of the vessel and give an opportunity to the directors of the Cunard Company and a considerable number of the Company's guests to make acquaintance with a type of ship which in certain respects excels its predecessors. The Franconia is not nearly as large as the Aquitania and many others of the Cunard Line – it is only a 20,000 ton ship – but it has special features which commend themselves to travellers on the sea. By feeding the boilers with oil fuel instead of coal there is a much larger space for cargo and passengers' accommodation. The new boat has been designed not only to meet the needs of all classes travelling between Europe and America, but for special cruises and occasionally a sail around the world. In a ship of this kind, therefore, you find as you would expect to do, exceptional facilities for physical exercise and recreation. Besides extensive promenades, reading and writing rooms, lounges and smoking rooms, there is a well equipped sports arena, in which the traveller can have a swim or indulge in a variety of other athletic exercise.

The provision for the comfort of passengers in other respects is excellent. The old system of berths has disappeared. In their stead you have bedrooms fitted with one or two beds and a constant supply of hot and cold water. Many of these rooms have their own bathroom attached. The accommodation for second and third class passengers, and also for the crew, bears evidence of a desire to give them a good deal more than they used to have, and a fairer share of life's enjoyments. One need only add that the decoration and furnishing of the vessel, and the arrangements for cooking, laundry work, ventilation, lighting and heating are as perfect as may be. The new Franconia will for a time be engaged with her sister ships Caronia and Carmania in maintaining the Liverpool, Queenstown and New York services. She begins her first Atlantic voyage, under the command of Captain Milsom, on the 23rd inst. Towards the end of the year she is to begin a cruise round the world.

AN INTERESTING ARTICLE WHICH APPEARED IN THE MANCHESTER GUARDIAN ON 12th JUNE 1923 DETAILING SOME OF THE FEATURES OF THE BRAND NEW CRUISE LINER FRANCONIA

97

CHAPTER 13
BREAKDOWN

It was inevitable. Matters with Hilda's parents would eventually come to a head one way or another. She had long known that she would eventually be forced to confront them, but she had always banked on having time to plan ahead and formulate a proper strategy. In the event it suddenly all came apart without any warning. The final drama of 1923 was a desperately sad episode, and it was also a defining moment which would damage the James family for ever.

In November a furious and prolonged row erupted in Parkgate when Gertie finally decided to put her foot down once and for all against Hilda travelling abroad. Whether her Ma had actually calculated it or not, and privately Hilda thought that she probably had, the timing could not have been worse.

Everybody in the country who read a sports page already knew that The English Comet's selection to the British team for the 1924 Olympic Games would surely be just a formality. Hilda would celebrate her 20th birthday just before the Games, and even with her considerable talents she was very obviously at the very pinnacle of her form. The VIIIth Olympiad, to be held between 4th May and 27th July in Paris, was widely anticipated to be her finest hour. The country was expecting Hilda James to bring back medals, with talk of possibly as many as three Golds. Bill Howcroft quietly concurred with that prediction.

Hilda's mother had other ideas. She had decided that if the Olympic Committee wanted Hilda to be on the team so badly then they would have to be happy to accept her as part of the package. Gertie insisted that she would be travelling to the games as chaperone to her daughter. Unfortunately, the Olympic Committee didn't consider her influence in the same way as Cunard had.

As with the games in 1920 and in line with policy, Mrs. James was told that perfectly acceptable chaperonage was already in place, and there simply wasn't any money available to pay for her to accompany her daughter. She was of course most welcome to travel with the British team at her own cost if that was what she wished. Unfortunately it wasn't. Gertie had been introduced to free travel, and the short Cunard cruise had inadvertently spoiled her forever. If she was not going to gain anything else out of it all, then Hilda would simply not be competing.

So far, albeit occasionally with considerable difficulty, John had always managed to prevail over Gertie's objections during Hilda's amateur career. His wife had eventually been made to see sense on each of the previous occasions she had tried to dig her heels in, but this time it would be different. Argue though he might, for the first time in his life he was unable to change her mind. The couple fought bitterly about it on and off for several days.

Hilda's far less controversial sister Elsie even got in on the act finally, and in a very rare event the elder James daughter had an almighty row with her mother. In absolute frustration Hilda cried and pleaded with both her parents. Pa told her that he was trying to change Ma's mind, but after all was said and done the answer from Ma still remained a flat no.

Grenfell soon got wind of the difficulties and came over from the school to try and pour oil on troubled waters, but to no avail. Hugely distressed and irritated, Bill Howcroft eventually took it upon himself to travel all the way over from Garston for a face to face meeting with Mrs. James. She was adamant on her stance and absolutely furious with the coach for trying to interfere. Eventually she became downright rude. If she wasn't going to the Olympics for free, then Hilda was simply not going at all and that was final. She couldn't see why he was being so nosy anyway, as it was family business and nothing whatsoever to do with him.

Under this onslaught, even though he had expected it, the coach's usually calm and correct demeanour wavered. Suddenly he lost his usually even temper and found himself roaring at the stupid woman as loudly as he could manage. And that was seriously loud considering all his years training swimmers in noisy pools; on this occasion his team probably heard him in Garston! After all the time he had personally given up for Hilda, the years he had spent training her for these Olympics, what was the matter with her? Why didn't she want Hilda to be the success she should be? Could she not see that she was ruining everything for Hilda just to satisfy her own petty jealousy? At that the distraught coach had finally gone too far. Following his outburst, he was immediately shown the door by John and told that he was finished as Hilda's coach. John James told Bill Howcroft never to speak to them again.

As had happened so many times before, for some unknown reason John would simply not stand up and overrule his battleaxe of a wife. Deep down he knew that the coach was right, but there had to be agreement in the James' household. Unlike Gertie, who had always contrived to reward Hilda's successes with extra chores, John was actually very proud of his daughter's achievements. He also fully understood that it was solely as a by-product of Hilda's success that the family now found themselves in such a fortunate position. In fact he was just as upset as Hilda about the situation, but by choosing his wife's unreasonable demands over his daughter's moment of glory he missed his last chance to do the right thing for all concerned.

After he had seen Howcroft off his premises John staged an ignominious back down, telling Hilda that although he didn't agree with Ma he was sorry, but she was not going to compete in Paris and that was to be the end of the matter. Even though he consistently failed to control his wife, once John finally issued their joint decree in his own house it became His final word and was The Law.

Shattered by the sudden turn of events and completely overwrought, Hilda then made a serious and what would rapidly turn out to be a near fatal mistake. Like her coach, she completely lost her temper and began screaming at her father after his Law had been laid down. It was not fair and Ma was stupid and mean and in the end it was his own stupid fault anyway because he should be more of a man and just tell Ma to let her go and he was a coward.

That was enough!

John would not stand up to his wife, but suddenly here he was faced with his headstrong daughter standing up to him and yelling like a fishwife. Hilda's Pa did not simply shout back at her like she might have expected her Ma to do. Somebody had taken it into her head to get ideas above their station. While he might be challenged by his wife and back down he was never, ever going to take it from his younger daughter. With all the frustration and resentment that must have been boiling in him something finally snapped and he saw red. Hilda's father had used force sparingly over the years, but on this occasion and for the only time in his life he shamefully vented real anger on one of his children.

John James sternly ordered his 19 year old daughter straight to her bedroom and, following her up the stairs he menacingly removed his leather belt. After making her take off her skirt and lie face down on her bed, he raised the belt and began to give her a cruel and sustained thrashing. Viciously he hit her, again and again, not stopping until his arm was so tired that he could no longer swing the belt. His daughter lay as still as she could with her face buried in the pillow and tried not to make a sound. Hilda thought that her father had lost his mind and she was actually going to die. Finally, mercifully, she passed out completely.

As soon as John left, Elsie arrived and helped Hilda during the long night, but Ma never came to the room. Elsie was worried because her poor sister was badly injured and she wanted to send for the doctor, but Hilda would not let her for fear of starting another row. Elsie quietly bathed and bandaged as best she could, moving silently about the house in tears as she fetched supplies and warm water. Like Hilda, Elsie would never forgive either of her parents.

The following morning Hilda could not sit down and was almost unable to stand either. She was badly injured, but there was no way they were going to break her spirit. She was leaving home, whatever that took. Overnight, she and Elsie had decided that was the answer, but in the morning Hilda had finally managed to persuade Elsie to go to college. Elsie had reluctantly left home at the normal time, expecting Hilda to be there when she got back so they could start to plan ahead. Hilda had been carefully considering her situation and doing her planning during the long, painful and sleepless night. She had made up her mind to take immediate action, difficult though it was going to be.

Nothing was going to stop her getting off the bed and she somehow managed to dress in the loosest clothes she could find. Any movement made her dizzy and sick, so it took her ages. True to form, once she had decided on a course of action she would complete it, painful or not. Gasping with pain, she got herself downstairs and clung to the kitchen doorway, breaking down as she told her mother exactly what she thought of her. There was no sympathy from Ma, who simply glazed over and started lecturing her daughter about her behaviour and the many Sins she would still need to be saved from. Hilda crept away, leaving Ma in the kitchen ranting to nobody else but herself.

While her father was out of the house Hilda packed a few things and quietly left home for the first time. She gritted her teeth and managed a few steps at a time, painfully struggling to carry a small case. She had to stop several times as she felt faint, but eventually reached Parkgate station which was closer than Neston. Somehow she managed to get herself all the way to Margery and Jim Brooks' house at Hunts Cross without collapsing. On the journey she felt dizzy and desperately ill, having to try and stand all the way in the trains and on the ferry.

Hilda knocked on the door and Margery answered. She was horrified at the sight that greeted her. Hilda's skin was grey and she was actually fainting as she reached sanctuary and her body finally gave in. Margery's favourite niece actually had to be bathed to soak her clothes off as everything was stuck fast to her wounds. Even though she had been beaten through her underclothes, her back and thighs had literally been flayed raw. Her aunt and uncle were completely sickened at the state she had arrived in.

They Brooks' found it almost impossible to believe that Hilda had managed the journey at all. Hilda was given no choice this time about seeing a doctor and was soon properly salved and bandaged. More than once over the next couple of days Margery actually had to stop Jim from going over to Parkgate and dealing with John in a way he would understand. Their niece eventually stayed with them for several weeks.

For three days Hilda lay on her front and refused to even let Margery and Jim tell her family where she was. She knew Elsie would have guessed. When Margery finally got the chance to speak to her brother, she told him that she fully agreed with his daughter and added that she considered him a coward too. She then tried her hardest to frighten him by saying that Hilda had needed to be treated in hospital and was so badly beaten that the police had been informed. She asked him why he would not stand up for himself just for once and do what was right, instead of pandering to his wife's obscene jealousy. Why could he not see that it was obvious he should overrule Gertie and allow Hilda her chance at Olympic Gold? For goodness sake, England herself was depending on it. She failed to change his mind. In Margery Brooks' opinion, John had beaten the wrong woman. For the rest of her life she would never forgive her brother for what he did to her favourite niece.

It was more than two weeks before Hilda's injuries healed such that she could very carefully put on a specially modified loose swimming costume. That would actually be the longest period in her entire amateur swimming career that she didn't get into a pool. To her eternal credit, as soon as her tender new skin healed enough and she could manage the costume Hilda headed straight for the baths at Garston. She was still covered in welts and bruises, so she was forced to begin very gently as she worked up a few simple exercises with her coach. Several of the team were moved to tears, such was their feeling towards her and the clear evidence of her father's temper. Over several sessions during the following weeks, one or more team members would always be in the water with her, staying close as Hilda carefully exercised her battered body in the pool.

Jim Brooks had escorted Hilda to the baths and ended up having a long talk with her coach. Bill Howcroft apologised profusely to Jim for not rescuing Hilda from her family the day he had been at Parkgate. If he had maybe insisted that she leave with him, or even sent for help from Grenfell things might have turned out very differently.

When Jim told him what had actually happened immediately following his retreat, the thought that as he walked back to the station Hilda was being half beaten to death had made the coach feel physically sick and he had needed to sit down suddenly. He told Jim that if he had indeed gone across to Parkgate to deal with John James, he would have been proud to accompany the younger man and hold Jim's jacket. The two men reached an understanding that they would never allow Hilda into any danger with her parents again. They would be keeping a very close eye on matters across the Mersey in future.

The coach was shaken to the core and deeply saddened by the change in Hilda's fortune. He also apologised to her, saying that he blamed himself in part. He explained that he had known full well who he was dealing with, and wished that things could have turned out differently. He told his protégé that Cunard might be her club now but Garston Baths was her real home, and somewhere she would always be able to find her true family. He and Agnes even invited her to visit their house when she was a bit stronger and in an emotional moment for all three of them, they actually offered her a permanent home. Once again, she was genuinely touched by the unsolicited kindness.

Of course there is no knowing for certain what Hilda would have achieved had she been allowed to attend the Olympic Games, but as a minor she had finally been denied any say in the matter. Bill Howcroft had his own opinion, and that was that three British Olympic Gold Medals had been recklessly squandered by an unpleasant and weak man to satisfy the whim of an equally unpleasant and jealous woman.

Austin Rawlinson had an equally powerful opinion on the same subject. He said that in all his long life, he would never meet a braver soul than his friend Hilda James on the evening she turned up at Garston baths to swim with her team, still covered in half healed scars and bruises and struggling to even get into the pool. That took real guts.

In December 1923, The Garston coach and his star pupil were therefore left with no other choice but to write a joint letter to the British Olympic Committee to inform them that, with the deepest regret, Hilda James would not be available for selection to the 1924 British Olympic Team. Privately Hilda had also finally made up her mind on another matter. She resolutely told her coach that whatever happened in the next eighteen months, the day she came of age on 27th April 1925, she would be leaving her broken family behind for good and finding a job as Hilda James, Professional Swimmer.

CHAPTER 14
THE LOST OLYMPICS

Without doubt 1924 was the lowest point in Hilda James' short but spectacular amateur swimming career. She and Bill Howcroft had finally lost their long struggle against her parents, just in time to miss the Olympic Games in Paris. After recovering sufficiently from the physical and emotional effects of her beating, she eventually moved quietly back to the Bath House at Parkgate in the New Year, having spent Christmas with the Brooks' at Hunts Cross. At best there would be an uneasy truce at home, but Hilda knew that given time there would undoubtedly be more trouble ahead. Neither of her parents deigned to mention the events leading up to her departure.

In fact it would be many years before Hilda's relationship with her parents would improve significantly, but even then the recovery would never really be complete. Between them her mother and father had completely destroyed their credibility as parents and she would never dare to trust them again. In their mean and narrow way they would always see her as an uncontrollable rebel, lost to Sins and Damnation.

In the meantime she spoke to them as little as possible and then only at mealtimes or when addressed directly, willing herself to say what they wanted to hear and to survive the next eighteen months without incident. She began to spend more and more time swimming, often returning to stay with her aunt and uncle at Hunts Cross. That way she could be with what she now knew for certain was her true family in the pool at Garston as much as possible.

Once again, Hilda received an unexpected invitation to an afternoon meeting tea at Cunard Headquarters. Cunard were aware that Hilda's Olympic dream had been shattered. In fact the whole country knew about it because the papers had made much of the lost opportunity without properly delving into the underlying reasons. The ASA had carefully made no comment but the press seemed to have assumed that either she was inexplicably off form, or had spoiled her chances of selection when she had recklessly missed the Olympic Tests. There was also some press speculation that Hilda might even be planning to turn professional before the Olympics, capitalising on her recent success by taking the money and running. Of course nothing could be further from the truth.

In spite of Bill Howcroft's best efforts, the fact that she had swanned off aboard Franconia had in fact appeared in the press when Cunard published some details about the new ship. That had led to further embarrassment for the coach as he had obviously been caught giving out false information about her non-appearance at the Tests and the Blackpool Lido opening event. He had been horrified initially, but he no longer cared what the press thought of him because he now knew for sure just what swimming had cost her, and he felt at least partly to blame.

Fearing that she may have other offers to consider and fully aware that if she was to miss the Olympics there would be no bar to her turning professional, Cunard had decided to make their move. Over the usual excellent tea she was formally offered the chance to take up an immediate full time position as the resident professional with their swimming club at the Adelphi Hotel. The role would be an extension of the work she was already undertaking for them as an unpaid casual instructor.

There would be an added twist. Apart from her regular duties at the Adelphi, Cunard actually wanted Hilda to engage in extensive travelling and demonstration tours, both across the UK and worldwide. She would be tasked with finding new places and ways to use her headline-grabbing shows and crowd pleasing swimming antics to publicise the Company, laying special emphasis on their new World Cruises. After watching the star entertain his invited guests aboard Franconia, Sir Thomas Royden had thrown his full weight behind Sir Percy Bates' assertion that Cunard actually needed Hilda James for publicity, whatever they had to do to get her. She cast her mind back to the travelling swimming show she had daydreamed about over the years, and realised with some amusement that it was probably the exact thing they were asking for.

Of course the idea would be a complete non-starter with her parents, and she knew it. On tentatively raising the subject at home the kitchen suddenly fell silent. Pa turned his head very slowly and looked straight at her. For a second Hilda felt herself turning cold. She suddenly thought that she had inadvertently just made the dreaded serious mistake and was about to suffer badly for it. In the event, Pa sternly warned her that even in mentioning it she had already gone too far. Amateur club swimmer would be the height of her aspirations, and after the way she had behaved already she should consider herself very lucky that she was even allowed that. Hilda suspected that if they didn't actually live at and run a prominent swimming baths, she might not actually be allowed near a pool.

It had been made crystal clear to her that as far as her parents were concerned, there would be no further discussion on the subject of turning professional at any time in the future. Once again Pa had laid down his Law, and on this occasion his daughter was not yet ready to challenge him again.

There was no doubt that the very next mention of her turning professional would provoke another encounter with his belt, but at least she now knew where they stood on her future in the longer term. By now, Hilda didn't really care anyway. She was already working on a long term plan, and when the time was right she was going to be fully prepared to exact her revenge.

Hilda wrote to her Cunard contact to inform them that as expected, her parents had refused her permission to accept their offer. She added that while she would not be available until she turned 21 the following April, she personally liked the idea and hoped that the Company might still be in a position to offer her employment after that date.

She received a surprise hand written letter back by return of post from none other than the Deputy Chairman, Sir Percy Bates. The letter said that on no account was she to worry herself about Cunard dropping their interest. She could rest assured that the Company had already waited for some time, and were willing to wait patiently for just a little longer if necessary. It went on to invite Hilda to visit Sir Percy and his wife for tea at Hinderton Hall, his home on the Wirral and just a mile or so from Parkgate. They would like to have a more informal chat with her about the future. She was dumbfounded.

As it was such a short distance, Hilda was able to walk to Hinderton Hall for her appointment. Sir Percy and Lady Bates made her feel very welcome and immediately put her at ease. Over tea they told her how much they had enjoyed her highly entertaining performance aboard Franconia the previous year. Sir Percy was impressed by how well at ease she had seemed to be with an audience of what he irreverently described as stuffed shirts.

They then discussed at some length Cunard's continuing interest in Hilda. Sir Percy was adamant that ever since the successful American tour had been arranged in 1922 he had been keen to have her work for the Company. In fact, several prominent passengers had asked if she might be available to travel and give lessons on the Atlantic crossings again in the future. His idea of inviting celebrity crew members aboard was beginning to take shape, and following the Franconia cruise Sir Thomas Royden fully agreed with him.

As a ship designer by training Sir Percy said that was busy working on a series of new liners especially for the speciality ocean cruising market, and he was keen to stress that there would always be a place reserved for her aboard one of them as soon as she cared to take it. He also joked about the Bates' and the James' being close neighbours, and remarked that their ten year old son Edward loved to visit the Parkgate baths when he was home from school. Hilda immediately offered to teach young Edward some trick swimming strokes in the summer, which Lady Bates said was a lovely idea.

Something odd happened during the afternoon. While his wife was out of the room Sir Percy quickly wrote down the Hinderton Hall telephone number for Hilda, with strict instructions to call immediately, "if there was any more family trouble at home". She suddenly realised with some horror that he might be talking about the beating she had suffered. She was rattled at the thought that he might know about it. After all, Sir Percy was the High Sherriff of Cheshire and a JP. Hilda worried for a long time about what a High Sherriff might be able to do to her Pa if he chose to. Sir Percy certainly knew AG Grenfell, but she didn't think that even the Headmaster had known about that particular episode. She was left feeling uneasy; something was bothering her but she just couldn't put her finger on it.

Finally, Hilda was given a rare treat and offered a ride home in Sir Percy's new motor car. She asked if she could be dropped off at the corner of Parkgate Parade, in case her father saw her and started asking awkward questions. Once again Sir Percy was reassuring and told her not to worry. If she did eventually choose to take up employment with Cunard, he would personally see to it that she was properly looked after for a change.

Hilda instinctively liked Sir Percy and Lady Bates. In spite of their being decidedly upper class and extremely well off she didn't find them at all stuffy; in fact quite the reverse. They were very pleasant, and she had been genuinely surprised to be treated like an equal. Sir Percy was entertaining and funny. He liked to share a joke with her, but underneath he seemed to be genuinely concerned for her welfare.

The fact was that by the mid-1920s the English Comet Hilda James was one of Great Britain's first true sports celebrities. Modestly she never really learned to appreciate that whether she was comfortable with the idea and whether her parents liked it or not, that was how people saw her. By that time, it was often the people that she came into contact with who were surprised when she treated them with deference and respect, rather than the other way round.

At Mostyn House School, Grenfell had also caught wind of Hilda's possible move to professional status. He thought that it might be better if he made her a formal offer through the official channels; i.e. by asking John James rather than the still underage Hilda. He still fancied he might persuade John to allow her to be a swimming professional at Parkgate, but once again he would be disappointed. His pool manager was not the slightest bit receptive to the idea. Even for his generous and likeable employer, John's answer was still a flat and heavily emphasized no.

Fearing that it might eventually lead to more trouble, Hilda walked along to the school and met Grenfell privately. As she had managed to do with Cunard, she persuaded him that she might still be in a position to consider his offer once she turned 21. Grenfell was actually pleased that she was developing an independent streak, and told her that if that was the case he would be content to wait. They agreed that it would definitely be best if he didn't approach her father about it again. He was actually worried about her safety, and told her to come straight to the school and find him, or even send a runner if there was ever serious trouble at home. Privately he considered that she would be better off away from Parkgate, but time would tell.

At least there were people offering to look out for her. In fact as Hilda walked back to the Bath House she realised that she was surrounded with kindness. In their different ways, AG Grenfell, Sir Percy Bates, Margery and Jim Brooks, and of course Bill and Agnes Howcroft had all offered her sanctuary in one form or another since her father's temper finally got the better of him.

Hilda had left Mostyn House in the knowledge that Grenfell did in fact know about the episode with her father, and reckoned that must have been how Sir Percy found out. In fact she was unaware that after agonising with the problem and his feelings of guilt, Bill Howcroft had actually taken it upon himself to warn Grenfell. He had also managed to contact Sir Percy Bates via Ernie Jones at the Cunard Swimming Club. Now that they were aware of just how precarious her home situation was, both men had willingly taken to keeping an ear to the ground for trouble. There was even a certified spy in the James household, because Grenfell had actually charged Hilda's sister Elsie with the task of keeping him abreast of any developments. Elsie was happy to help.

In March, Hilda was invited to appear at the Olympic Gala at Pollockshields in Glasgow. In spite of not being available for selection to the Olympic Team, she was still the star of the day and in constant demand. Hilda liked events in Scotland, where she always received an especially warm welcome. She left Parkgate to meet the Garston swimmers and Bill Howcroft at Liverpool's Lime Street Station, not knowing that she was inadvertently about to use the gala as a final release for much of the tension she was feeling. Deep down she was still really hurt about the Olympic fiasco and she had already decided to try and give one of her all out performances at the gala just to show the whole country what they were missing.

During the train journey up she sat with Bill Howcroft. Coach and pupil had plenty of time to reflect at length on the long and exciting road they had travelled together and to mull over the current sad situation. Hilda had felt unusually emotional all day and worried that her frustration and anger might get the better of her. Howcroft could feel it too, and he knew his protégé well enough to be able to play the psychology game a little. He carefully alluded to the way her parents had treated her, trying to tease all her emotions out into the open but she remained stoic.

Finally, just as they arrived at the baths Howcroft made the unusual decision to openly goad Hilda by letting on that he had recently been speaking to Sir Percy Bates about certain matters relating to the Cunard club. Suddenly it all fell into place. At last she knew how Sir Percy had found out about her being beaten; bloody Howcroft had told him. How dare he! Suddenly she found she was absolutely livid with her coach, but somehow she managed to keep the emotion bottled up just long enough. She could sometimes use strong emotion effectively like a prize fighter, but this time she was nearly bursting with anger. This was the limit. This time she was going to show the whole bloody lot of them once and for all.

Once in the pool and still fired up by real anger, she duly delivered a classic Hilda James performance. It was fortunate for The Olympic Committee that when asked, they had not tried to use poor form as a possible excuse for her non-selection. Following her usual solo routine Hilda took her place on the starting blocks to race. She had performed her tricks without feeling any emotion; usually she would enjoy herself hugely but on this occasion she had just done it by the numbers.

Now, balancing on the block she had finally let her hold over the emotions go loose, and she could feel herself physically shaking from the adrenaline rush of her pent-up frustration. At the gun she shot off the block like a torpedo being launched and thrashed mercilessly up and down the pool, soundly beating the entire Olympic team over the 300 yards and lowering her own Scottish Record by a significant margin.

Hilda was treated to a long standing ovation from the appreciative crowd, but having worked off all the anger she was left totally drained and almost too exhausted to struggle up the steps out of the water. For once she didn't know what to do with herself and as she stood meekly by the pool she was suddenly overcome with tears. Also completely choked, Bill Howcroft rushed along the poolside to her. His plan had worked and Hilda had shown them all what they would miss in the summer. Good for her.

In a rare demonstration of real affection the rather staid Lancashire man actually folded his champion into a towel and held her close, trying to apologise to her for the things he had so cruelly said earlier in the day. Hilda countered by batting weakly at him, no longer knowing whether she was crying or laughing, or even if he was for that matter. What a pair she and her gruff coach were, blubbing in public. But golly, she thought, what a team. What an amazing team!

25/3/24
Olympic Gala Event
300 yards Freestyle - Won
Time 4:04.20
Pollockshields, Glasgow
<u>Scottish Record</u>

The press were as stunned as the selectors by Hilda's cracking performance in Glasgow, but they were confused by the out of character emotional breakdown which had followed. Awkward questions soon started to appear in the swimming columns. If their English Comet's current form was that good, why on Earth wasn't she going to Paris? If she was being punished for not appearing at the Olympic Tests by not getting selected for the team there was going to be trouble. Something wasn't right. It didn't add up, and they were going to get to the bottom of it.

They apparently did some digging on the situation and came up with a few surprising answers. It would seem that they might well have been intelligent enough to talk to some swimmers in Garston and enquire about what was really going on. A few days later Hilda's parents were subjected to what Austin Rawlinson would later describe as a vicious, unpleasant and in his opinion a fully justified attack in the papers. Of course he had been one of the Garston club swimmers keeping watch over their friend as she gently exercised her battered body in the pool on club nights the previous winter. If a reporter did happen to have quizzed Austin on the matter they might have discovered that, like the other Garston Club members, he didn't feel at all charitable towards Mr. and Mrs. James.

Following such a severe press savaging, the home situation at Parkgate once again became particularly fragile, and Hilda rapidly escaped to stay at Hunts Cross until the dust settled. In the summer of 1924, the British Olympic Team for the Paris Games was once again coached by Bill Howcroft. Sadly, without the in-form Hilda James and probably feeling less like a complete team because of it, the British Ladies would again come back from the Olympics beaten to Gold Medals by those Americans.

Charlotte Epstein met the British team and there was a long talk about Hilda. She sent her best wishes home with Bill Howcroft and asked him to invite Hilda to visit her in New York again whenever she could manage it. She reiterated her assertion that there was always a warm welcome and plenty of work if Hilda did ever decided to emigrate. Eppie was pleased to finally meet Austin Rawlinson after seeing Hilda take on his back crawl stroke in a day and beat her swimmers to an American title. She told Austin that she hoped he could win a Backstroke Gold Medal for England because she thought so much of them as a team. In private she knew her superstar Johnny Weissmuller was on top form so there was really no chance of that.

Things did calm down for a while during the spring. It was all hands on deck to ready the Parkgate baths for their second season. After another of Grenfell's off-beat publicity campaigns, the baths finally reopened and immediately it was even busier than the previous year. As Grenfell had hoped, Hilda James often appeared in the water to host impromptu coaching sessions, and the chance of meeting the star or just seeing her larking about in the pool was an added draw. Grenfell had a major success on his hands. Gertie no longer had to run refreshments from her own kitchen because she was now the proprietor of a proper tea shop. Hard work it might have been, but for all their many faults nobody in the James family was ever afraid of that.

CHAPTER 15
TREADING WATER

For Hilda's parents at least, life at the Parkgate baths was really good. They were doing very well out of the move, which of course had been offered to them as a direct result of Hilda's fame. It was her success that had brought their prosperity, but they just accepted it without showing her any gratitude or allowing her any development. Hilda couldn't understand why they always wanted to stifle her ambitions. In any case, she had absolutely no idea what they expected her to do with her life if they ever managed to stop her from swimming professionally. Somehow they were missing the point, just like they had during the winter of 1917 when Jack had nearly died. Times were difficult then but it was her employers who had helped them manage, out of respect for her and how hard she worked.

It seemed to Hilda that everyone around her respected her except her own parents. About this time and to her utter disgust, she discovered that her mother had casually been giving away her hard won trophies and souvenirs, not only to relatives and friends which was fair enough, but to various clubs and swimming organisations. With the current climate at home Hilda knew better than to argue about it, but she carefully started to hide her remaining treasures. Margery and Jim Brooks gradually became the first keepers of the Hilda James collection. She felt like she was drifting about without a proper goal, treading water until she could come of age and swim away, free of her family.

The University of Liverpool had asked Cunard Swimming Club if Hilda James would be prepared to accept an Honorary Degree. After some consultation between Bill Howcroft and the ASA she was forced to decline the offer, as it would definitely be seen as an infringement of her amateurism. Howcroft wrote to the University suggesting that Hilda would be happy to accept the usual work around in the form of "a small token of their esteem" if they still wished to make a gesture. The gift had to be technically worthless, although the acceptance of various small souvenir trophies and cups etc. was the norm at the time and usually overlooked by the authorities.

Already a BSc, having gained the degree the previous year, Elsie was still at Liverpool and would be receiving a Diploma of Education in the summer. Hilda was duly invited to attend the ceremony along with her sister. She was presented with a magnificent tooled leather folder measuring 20 x 15½ inches and bearing the inscription "HILDA M. JAMES SWIMMING CERTIFICATES". She accepted it with good grace, but still feeling somehow distant from all the fuss she couldn't really see the point any more. It was

112

many years later that she finally began to treasure it.

Their youngest brother Walter was at Grammar school by this time, having followed in Elsie's footsteps and won a scholarship. After Elsie received her qualifications, she promptly decided to stay at home in Parkgate for a while and take up a teaching job locally. She knew how hard the family had worked to help her achieve the dream of getting a good education, so she wanted to cover the entire cost for her brother to try and repay them all. Nor was she going anywhere until she had seen Hilda safely out of danger and away from the family. Elsie had promised Grenfell that she would monitor the situation, and she was sticking around.

Elsie was also a creditable club swimmer in her own right. Because they obviously lived next to the baths she had started to join Hilda in training, and for a while they pushed the boundaries of the demonstration swim and trick routines as something of a double act. Since the baths had opened the previous year she had been inviting groups of her University friends to Parkgate at the weekends, including a rather exotic architectural student from Hong Kong called George Hall, who was half Chinese (George would laughingly describe himself as technically being two quarters Chinese, as his parents were both half).

George was already a diving champion in his native Hong Kong and he immediately hit it off with Hilda, so for the first time in her life she unexpectedly found herself with a boyfriend. Elsie was readily sworn to secrecy and they managed to keep the fact really quiet at home. George also had a car which he called Mabelle, and as Hilda was always able to get away on the pretext of visiting the Adelphi she could arrange to meet him. They would take a picnic and head for the open road, visiting various places on the Wirral and further afield. Sitting on a picnic blanket up by the sandstone outcrops at Thurstaston Hill she might only be about four miles from home, but just when she really needed changes Hilda began to feel a sense of freedom for a while.

Several years later Elsie would be hospitalised with peritonitis, which sadly left her unable to have children of her own. She would finally marry at the age of 46, causing the usual series of blazing rows with her parents by choosing to marry a wealthy divorcee. In lieu of having her own, Elsie spent the whole of her long life giving generously to children across several generations of her extended family. She may never have become a mother, but to her everlasting delight she gained special status with many as a much loved favourite aunt.

Aside from the ongoing dramas involving the family, as an accredited superstar Hilda was still in demand as much as she had ever been. She continued to sustain good form as a distance competitor, winning the Kew to Putney River Thames race by a huge margin for the second year running. With a shudder at the thought of the River Seine, she politely declined the invitation to once again compete in Paris. Although she didn't break many records during 1924, she was still enjoying herself, and still opening galas and new pools with her trademark trick swimming act;

7/24 ASA Cert. 499
Thames Long Distance Championship
From Kew to Putney - Won
5 miles 60 yards in 1.11:24.40

28/8/24
ASA Championships
220 yards Freestyle - Won
Time 2:58.60
Hull

/24
ASA Championships
440 yards Freestyle - Won
Garston

This was the first time that the ASA had staged the 440 yards as an annual event for women. Hilda made much of the fact that this in particular was a prize she really wanted to win. As usual, sheer determination drove her to turn in one of her classic performances and she duly received the trophy to hold for a year. And the reason she had wanted this one so badly? It was an old friend of hers, none other than the same large silver cup that she had jointly accepted in Paris after winning the race in the River Seine, and that the ASA had immediately appropriated. If only for a year, she had been absolutely determined to be its holder and see it standing in the Cunard Building's trophy cabinet.

There was only one record event to note in 1924, but by any standards it was a significant event. At a meeting in Hartlepool Hilda swam an absolute corker. There must have been an expectation of record breaking, because the race was officially timed for three distances. As previously discussed this was a tricky task that in this case required no less than nine official timekeepers. She competed in a one mile event, winning it by over a length of the pool and smashing three English Records in a single race. The previous times for both the 880 and 1000 yards had stood for well over ten years. Frustratingly there was another unofficial World Record, and once again it was by an enormous margin. As usual FINA denied her an official World Record because of their beastly timekeeping rules. Hilda would therefore once again be left holding an English Record with a time significantly below the official World Record;

27/9/24 ASA Cert. 546
880 yards Freestyle
Time 13:57.20
English Record

Also ASA Cert. 547
1000 yards Freestyle
Time 15:57.60
English Record

Also ASA Cert. 548
1760 yards (1 mile) Freestyle - Won
Time 28:49.00
Hartlepool
English Record
Unofficial World Record
Due to timekeeping discipline

1924 – SHOWING OFF SOME SILVERWARE
APPROACHING THE END OF AN AMATEUR CAREER

CHAPTER 16
HULL NO. 586

Back at home in Cullercoats on England's north east coast, young Douglas McAllister idolised his half brother Hughie who was 19 years older than him. He didn't see as much of his Hughie as he would have liked. When on leave Hugh tended to stay with his aunt rather than his step-mother, but he would always find time to visit his family home. Douglas usually had a lot of fun when his half brother visited, as Hugh had never really lost his sense of mischief. On one occasion Hughie brought Douglas his very own soldering iron and they built radio receivers and speakers. For the rest of his life Douglas would always have a wired-in radio and later a stereo system with speakers through his house, together with a workshop full of tools and spare parts just like Hughie.

On another visit they famously tinkered with a large chemistry set supplied by Hughie, experimenting with explosives until they managed to blow up the curtains in Douglas' bedroom. That got the pair of them into trouble all right. Hughie might have been grown up and working, but their father sternly escorted the pair of them to the sea front like a pair of naughty children. They were made to very carefully dispose of the rest of their mixture in the water. Hugh had told his father that he was sure they had managed to produce nitro-glycerine. His boys!

As soon as he was old enough Douglas would follow Hugh into the engineering industry, eventually far surpassing his half brother's technical knowledge. In fact he would spend most of his working life as a design and technology specialist. Starting out in January 1936 with an apprenticeship at CA Parsons of Newcastle, he would actually spend an entire 47 year career with the same company. He became a recognised expert in a vast range of turbine and fluid technologies, extending his design and testing expertise to all manner of industries from Shipbuilding to Nuclear power. He was always adamant that Hughie was the inspiration for him to become an engineer.

In fact, Douglas ended up owning an interesting and very unusual Cunard souvenir. Sadly, the mighty Berengaria had a spectacular but relatively short 25 year career. Having suffered a couple of serious fires aboard she was finally deemed unfit for service in 1938. She had already been replaced by RMS Queen Mary anyway, but was initially expected to stay in service until the introduction of RMS Queen Elizabeth. Cunard tried their hardest to get the unfit order lifted, but yet another fire broke out while she was stored at Southampton and her fate was finally sealed. Scrapping her was to prove a long and painful process, lasting through the entire duration of the 2nd World

War and not being finally completed until 1946.

There was a long tradition of auctioning absolutely everything from the ships that could possibly be carried away. There is even a pub in Bristol called "The Mauretania" whose interior walls are furnished with panelling from that ship. While Berengaria was waiting to be broken up at Jarrow on the River Tyne, Hugh asked Douglas to attend the auction of fittings and see if he could secure the ship's bell. Predictably that article sold for far too much, but Douglas wanted his own souvenir and went away having secured a rare complete wash stand from one of the first class staterooms. Douglas' souvenir would serve for the rest of his life as his tool store and workbench, and he would forever keep a close connection to his half-brother's favourite ship.

Hugh thought he had hit the big time with Berengaria. He hoped he might work his way up towards a more senior position, so the next posting he was offered came as a real surprise. In January 1925 while on leave in Cullercoats, he received a letter asking him to travel to Liverpool for an important meeting at Cunard Headquarters. Hugh arrived in uniform not really knowing what to expect. He was most surprised to find Sir Percy Bates himself hosting what appeared to be an afternoon tea party rather than a formal meeting. Of course he already knew something of the Deputy Chairman; they had met and spoken on a couple of occasions, notably aboard Franconia during the 1923 invitation shakedown cruise. There were several other young officers at the meeting, some of whom Hugh already knew. He sensed that they were all equally as mystified. Sir Percy introduced each of them to one of his most senior Captains, EG Diggle. The Deputy Chairman had a unique way of doing business, and it wasn't at all what Hugh might have imagined. Once tea had been served, the assembled company were treated to an informal address.

Sir Percy started by refreshing his audience on some facts they already knew. The Company had hosted a few highly successful World Cruises, thus far experimenting with their new fleet of post-war mid-sized liners, the 20,000 tonners that Hugh liked so much. In fact Laconia had been the trailblazer, and the brand new Franconia had been modified to improve the interior by introducing some changes to the public areas.

In general, the ships were already proving very popular as a class, but the luxurious Franconia was causing quite a stir amongst the travelling rich and there was a clamour for more of the same. The rear cargo hold of the original design had been sacrificed, allowing Franconia ample space for an extra-large pool and gymnasium complex. The immediate reaction and feedback from passengers aboard Franconia had been so positive that during late 1923 he had finally made the decision to forge ahead with the complete interior redesign that he had been working on for several years.

Vickers Ltd. was just completing the last of the current series of five 20,000 ton ships for Cunard at Barrow-in Furness. Ordered as Hull no. 586, she was originally due to be launched as RMS Servia and destined for use on regular transatlantic passenger duties. As interior work had not been started when his decision was made, she was the lucky ship chosen to have the revolutionary new interior fitted. A bit of a favourite of Sir Percy's, she now boasted such modern luxuries as hot and cold running water in all the staterooms and cabins, together with the widest mattresses of any ship afloat. There were better designed wardrobes and storage spaces in newly created cabin layouts. Even in third class the dining room was equipped with individual tables for families.

The public areas aboard were designed to be as spacious as possible, with themed rooms and lounges carefully outfitted to echo the space and grandeur of the much larger flagship liners. In fact, by having the ship fuelled by oil from the outset rather than coal, much more space instantly became available to incorporate all kinds of innovations not possible on any previous generation of ships. No. 586 would become the first of a new breed of ocean liners specifically dedicated to the lucrative and rapidly expanding luxury and leisure cruising market.

In the opinion of the Company, the name "Servia" sounded far too hard working for such a vessel, so a change of image had also become a priority. 586 was due to be launched just a couple of weeks hence on 24th February 1925, and in a long established Cunard tradition she would be reviving the name of a much earlier ship of the line. It was still a secret, so would they all please keep it to themselves just for now, but in the personal view of Sir Percy Bates the dawn of the Golden Age of Cruising would be heralded in by Cunard with their all new Luxury Ocean Cruise Liner RMS Carinthia.

Carinthia had to be fitted out and completed by the late summer if at all possible, and huge resources were being made available to achieve that. In lieu of a shakedown trip she was already due to be scheduled for a regular crossing to New York before embarking on her first World Cruise. The plans for his new liner started with a leisurely World Cruise each winter. There would be shorter summer cruises as demand required. She was capable of carrying a large number of third class passengers, as she would have to be available to slot in on some transatlantic crossings to keep the regular schedules up when other ships were in dock. In spite of this, Carinthia was to be an ocean cruise liner first and foremost.

Sir Percy went on to explain that along with a new kind of ship he was busy putting together a crack team for a completely new kind of assignment. Normally crews came and went, transferring between ships in the fleet as single individuals and often losing track of friends and colleagues, but he had come up with an altogether more radical idea. All those present already either had some ocean cruising experience, or more practical technical experience relative to the 20,000 ton fleet. Would any of them be interested in becoming part of his new Senior Officer team aboard Carinthia? Each would be given carte blanche to hand-pick their own people from across the fleet, with the aim of keeping the new crew together as a complete unit as much as possible. The only real problem to consider might be long periods away from home, as the World Cruise itinerary would typically last over four months.

By now, all the officers present were becoming equally enthused. Sir Percy went on to describe some more of the facilities they would have aboard. The liner would have passenger accommodation for 240 in first class, 460 in second and 950 in third, although even third class cabins would be more comfortable then ever before. It was planned that on most cruises and especially the full World Cruises, a limit of about 500 tickets would be sold. The American travel agents Raymond-Whitcomb were selling the cruises, and they intended to market only first and second class staterooms.

He already had someone special in mind to take charge of the swimming pool and activities department, but she was out of the country and couldn't be present. Hugh felt a sudden thrill as he realised who that was going to be. Hugh McAllister smiled to himself, as the new appointment he was being offered immediately took on a completely different kind of significance.

Finally the officers were all issued written orders for their consideration, and they left the meeting having been given a few days to think it all over. Apart from Sir Percy and Captain Diggle, the group reconvened at a local pub. Having rapidly decided that the opportunity was just too good to miss, Carinthia's new officers elect proceeded to indulge in a spot of team building, celebrating their luck together in the traditional manner.

CHAPTER 17
SOUTH AFRICA

Towards the end of 1924, Hilda was still pondering the major changes to her life that she had been anticipating for so long. She was excited by the prospects, but also apprehensive as she knew that whatever she decided to do, there would once again be serious trouble with her parents. There was really no way to avoid it, but she was absolutely determined that whatever their reaction the final choice would be hers, and hers alone.

The options available at the time seemed to be either to stay at Parkgate baths, throwing in her lot with AG Grenfell and her parents as a resident swimming professional (if they would let her, of course), or taking the much bigger gamble with Cunard. Deep down she worried about staying at Parkgate, knowing that she needed to break away from her difficult and increasingly domineering family. The more she thought about it, the better she liked the idea of working for Cunard, even with this vague and unspecified role that they kept vaguely talking about.

At a training session in Garston one evening, she received an extraordinary invitation via Bill Howcroft. He gave her a letter from the South African Amateur Swimming Union (SAASU), which had arrived at the club asking if Hilda James would consider participating in a tour of the country, extending all the way into Rhodesia "(Zimbabwe)". Unlike the American tour two years previously, their all expenses offer even included first class passage for two people. It would mean being away from home for nearly three months. They discussed the options, but the outlook looked pretty bleak.

He told her that this would be a fantastic opportunity, and in his opinion it looked even more exciting than the American tour. Unfortunately the dates fell before her 21st birthday, so she would still have to be chaperoned. After his furious shouting match with Gertie James, Bill Howcroft had been dismissed from the Bath House by John with orders never to cross their paths again. As he was still persona non grata, this time there would no opportunity for him to help her grease the wheels. If she wanted to accept the invitation, it looked like Hilda would have to deal with her parents on her own. Her coach was adamant that she should go at all costs; adding that the expression "at all costs" probably meant that she would have to consider taking her mother. In fact he had been trying to come up with an alternative plan for several days, but without success.

At first Hilda didn't believe what she was hearing, and scolded him for making the situation worse by joking about it. They batted the options back and forth for a while, but in the end she had to agree with him that it was probably the only possible solution. It galled them both to give in to the threat that Gertie had made to the Olympic Committee just over a year before, that to get Hilda they had to have her too. As they had done more than once in the past, the two old hands put their heads together and contrived a cunning plan on how to best put the question to her parents. This time they both knew that their aim was to do it very carefully, without compromising Hilda's safety in any way.

There was a gala coming up at Garston. Out of courtesy Bill Howcroft still normally wrote to Hilda's parents asking them to attend, but they had not chosen to respond to an invitation from him in over a year. On this occasion, he arranged for the club secretary to invite them instead, without mentioning his name. As Hilda had predicted they duly turned up.

Hilda competed with her team as usual, but the club coach kept a lower profile than normal and didn't appear poolside during the racing. It was a classic team effort, with everybody at the pool having parts to play. Between them the whole team had decided to lull her parents into a false sense of security, before springing their trap. At the end of the evening Hilda and Howcroft waited nervously in the lobby, to literally block the James' exit from the building.

Their victims were the last of the audience to leave the pool, having been surprised to find themselves engaged in conversation by some of the team for a few extra minutes. After all, some of them knew the James' very well and hadn't seen them for ages. John and Gertie were pleasantly surprised that a few of Hilda's old friends wanted to share a few words. However, when they finally reached the lobby there seemed to be an unusually large number of Garston team members hanging about outside the changing rooms. Bill Howcroft and Hilda were standing there too. The trap was sprung.

In a carefully rehearsed set piece Bill Howcroft braved John and Gertie James, calmly staring them both down as he silently offered John the envelope. Usually a genial and forgiving soul, he had to work hard to keep his temper in check as he reflected on the injuries this detestable man had inflicted on his own daughter. Bill Howcroft just wanted to punch James as hard as he could, and that emotion was very close to the surface as he patiently stood there. John looked at the letter, but didn't take it from the coach.

Hilda broke the growing silence and told her parents what the envelope contained. She must have had her fingers crossed, because in a barefaced lie she immediately said that if they would allow her to accept it she really wanted her Ma to go with her to South Africa. She quickly pointed out that the dates conveniently fell during the closed season at Parkgate. Between them all, they had carefully contrived to corner John and Gertie in a position with plenty of witnesses, and where they could not start a fight.

There was apparently another awkward and prolonged silence as the whole Garston team and their coach held their collective breath. In an unrehearsed addition to the original plan several team members, including her great supporter and close friend Austin Rawlinson, quietly moved in from the background to stand with crossed arms alongside and around the coach and his star.

The implications were not lost on John. He knew in that moment that he was facing the people Hilda considered her real family and they were not going to stand for any trouble. He apparently turned white, before suddenly snatching the letter from Howcroft's hand. John James then gripped his wife's arm roughly and brushed past the team without a word. As the door slammed behind them, you could probably have heard the collective sigh of relief across the Mersey. Hilda wisely went to Hunts Cross and stayed with Margery and Jim.

Hilda never really found out if it was the exchange at Garston baths that had the effect, but something certainly did. In the end she wasn't really surprised that her Mother suddenly changed her tune and decided to accept the invitation. There was something in it for her. The pair duly left from Southampton on 9th January 1925, travelling in a first class cabin aboard RMS Saxon, a 12,500 ton mixed traffic passenger and cargo ship built in 1899 and operated by the Union-Castle Mail Steam Ship Company. There would be one stop at Madeira on the 16 day voyage to Cape Town.

Saxon was just over half the size of Franconia, the liner they had cruised on so comfortably the previous year. However, unlike the luxurious Franconia she was a working ship hauling mails and mixed cargo as well as some passengers. They were comfortable enough, although Hilda decided that what Union-Castle was passing off as first class travel was frankly a bit over rated. Worse still, there was no swimming pool on board. No, it definitely wasn't Cunard.

Even aboard the Saxon they didn't get along well with each other, although Hilda refused to let it spoil the experience. She loved the sea and any excuse to be on it was acceptable. During the voyage she finally came to the realisation that she was definitely going to talk to Cunard about that job when she got home. Having at last taken that major decision she felt hugely relieved. She discovered that the uncertainty had been bothering her more than she had acknowledged. She put it behind her and resolved to enjoy herself on the tour. To do that she would simply have to ignore her miserable Mother, but that was easy to achieve.

Hilda decided that when they arrived back in England she would probably hide out with the Brooks' at Hunts Cross until her birthday and then formally leave home and do as she pleased. With a wicked kind of excitement she started to look forward to telling her father just that. At the stop in Madeira she managed to get a good workout, swimming vigorously in the ocean for a while and loving the warmer water.

On arrival in Cape Town, they were met and hosted by Gilbert Reynolds, President of the SAASU. Gertie had sunk to a new low, arbitrarily deciding to award herself the joint roles of coach plus gracious and deserving Mother and positively simpering at everybody she was introduced to. Previously she had never appeared to take any interest, but now she was instantly the big expert on swimming strokes, racing and records. Talk about not being allowed to have airs and graces, Hilda simply couldn't believe the naked hypocrisy. Used to travelling with her pragmatic and forthright coach, poor Hilda was immediately disgusted and highly embarrassed by her mother's antics.

In fact, during the entire visit they didn't speak to each other much. Hilda cheerfully started accepting invitations out with groups of young swimmers in several of the places they visited, effectively dumping her Ma by simply pushing off out of various hotels without telling her, thus avoiding having her tagging along as the oh-so-precious chaperone. Good riddance too; Hilda James really was through with her Ma.

Hilda even contrived to enjoy a bit of fun at her mother's expense. From day one Mrs. James had spectacularly failed to impress their hosts, by making a series of bitter protests to the swimming authorities about finding that events had been scheduled for immediately after their arrival. She was reported in one newspaper article as having said that Hilda should have at least two weeks of training time allocated before being booked to compete anywhere. She was also quoted as saying that South Africa would never see the best of her daughter without proper training. They weren't sure what to make of this rather scary and outspoken woman. Hilda quietly put them right.

Explaining to Mr. Reynolds, she said he should be made aware that her mother was not actually her coach and was in fact just being difficult. She assured the SAASU President that their visitor was in fact happy to make her own decisions, and fully ready to start swimming any time they liked. She also indicated that her mother had actually insisted on travelling with her instead of her coach Mr. Howcroft. Anyway, she was not even acquainted with her Hilda's training regime, having never taken the slightest interest in her swimming career. After that the word was quietly passed around and from then on, however she fawned and simpered, the South Africans just ignored Mrs. James.

Much of the travel was by long distance train, but even that had its problems. On one journey they had to wait most of the day while the rails were repaired after a washout. Travelling by road was apparently an altogether more pioneering experience. In the 1920s, the idea of a "road" in South Africa was nothing more than a vague concept across much of the nation; often it meant simply following dirt tracks made by tribesmen or animals. As there had been a lot of rain the travelling party had to contend with some serious flooding, which held them up for another whole day in one place.

They did manage to make one serious transport mistake however, electing when offered a choice to travel by boat from Durban to Port Elizabeth. What kind of boat it was is not recorded, but whereas they had been fine aboard Saxon, both ladies were terribly seasick. In agreement for once they vowed to stick to overland travel for the duration, difficult though that was.

There were galas and invitation races at every town they managed to visit. At each, she was given a rousing welcome as huge crowds chanted a traditional greeting "Yea Hilda! Yea Hilda! Yea Hilda! Forrum! Forrum! Forrum!" As usual Hilda managed to delight children with trick swimming and lessons during the day, often hosting several successive groups for an hour each. She also had to give the famous trick act and demonstrations most evenings, and cheerfully raced all comers at every gala. In most provinces they were entertained by local Governors and dignitaries, finding themselves put up in the best hotels available and usually invited to some form of gala evening.

In spite of the practical difficulties, and casually disregarding her Mother's antics, Hilda's tour progressed throughout South Africa and Rhodesia in much the same way as across America in 1922. The country was obviously much less developed than anywhere she had been before, and she was fascinated by it. Fortunately there was enough time built in for delays, and when they could her hosts made the most of it, taking her to see all kinds of wonders. Without a doubt the highlight was a specially scheduled visit to Victoria Falls. It was breathtaking, although in hindsight she liked Niagara Falls better because she had nearly got right underneath that one in a boat. There were ancient rock artworks to see and of course the ever present wildlife.

As usual, everywhere they visited Hilda was showered with gifts. Without Howcroft alongside her to protect the oh-so-precious amateur status and already planning to turn professional the moment she arrived home in England, she was happy enough to accept them for once. In South Africa the English ASA was not present to check every trophy for value; it was the only thing Hilda could find that was good about not having Bill Howcroft in tow.

There was an absolutely enormous mounted springbok head which she somehow managed to bring home from Bloemfontein. She eventually left that at The Bath House to keep a glass eye on her parents, and it carefully watched over them for the rest of their lives! There was a tiny gold ingot from Johannesburg, and gold badges and brooches which were presented to her at the various mining cities. At Port Elizabeth, she was given a fantastic set of ostrich feathers which she carefully brought home for her favourite cousin, Little Margery.

As she had been in America, Hilda was offered the chance to do some unusual things and to visit some extraordinary places that were usually off limits to the general public. She found herself suited up in an outfit about six sizes too big, standing in a mine elevator between two huge burly foremen for the long drop underground to see the workings of the Nourse Diamond Mine at Kimberley. Ma James had to sign the indemnity forms to allow her still underage daughter to visit the mine, but to Hilda's delight she flatly refused to go underground. At a reception the same evening, Hilda was presented with a gift from the town, a large and beautiful uncut Kimberley diamond mounted on a silver stick pin.

MISS JAMES'S TOUR

ENTHUSIASTIC RECEPTION IN BLOEMFONTEIN

Miss Hilda James, the English champion lady swimmer, fulfilled the second engagement of her tour of the Union on Saturday night when, before close on a thousand spectators she gave a wonderful exhibition of fancy swimming strokes and diving. Her reception was most enthusiastic and there is no doubt that interest in natatory sport will be quickened as a result of her visit. At the conclusion of the gala given in her honour by the local Swimming Association, the Administrator of the Free State, the Hon, E.R. Grobler, presented her with a handsomely mounted springbok's head as a gift from the people of Bloemfontein.

A STRIKING DISPLAY

After that she gave a stimulating display of the various crawl strokes, of which she is so famous an exponent, and concluded with a striking exhibition of "stunt" swimming. Her graceful movements were a pleasure to behold, and she secured a great ovation.

On Saturday morning Miss James held the attention of several hundred school children, to whom she lectured and demonstrated, and on Sunday she was taken out for a drive and a picnic, She left in the evening for Durban. During her stay her modest and charming personality won her a host of friends.

**35/1/25
BLOEMFONTEIN**

**20/3/25
NOURSE MINE
KIMBERLEY**

On completing the tour, there was another surprise in the form of a new invitation from the SAASU. The demand had been so great and adulation about their visit so intense, that the visitor and her mother were asked if they might consider staying in the country for an extra six weeks. The SAASU were being inundated with requests from people and clubs that had missed out on the spectacle, and had decided to ask Hilda to reprise the tour and go round the entire route again. In their own ways, both Hilda and Gertie realised that this was really their last chance and so graciously accepted.

Gertie sent a letter home to John explaining the situation and it left aboard the very ship that they had been expecting to be sailing on themselves.

There was actually a mild protest in some sections of the South African press that it was all too much to ask of the visitors and the Union was being greedy, but it was soon drowned out in the excitement. In every town plans were hastily being made to host an even larger event than the first time around and make an even bigger fuss of the champion. As usual, even after taking her surly chaperone into account The English Comet was in big demand.

It continued to rain. There was an English invitation XI cricket team playing in South Africa at the same time as Hilda's swimming tour. One match against the Transvaal at the old Wanderers Stadium in Johannesburg was completely rained off. One of the South African papers carried a large cartoon, which showed the two captains standing together in heavy rain, up to their ankles in water on a flooded wicket. The English captain, The Hon. Lionel Hallam Tennyson is wearing a rain jacket and hat. The Transvaal captain and former rugby star VH Neser looks much more optimistic in cricket whites and a team cap. In the background stands a grinning Hilda James, standing in typical pose. She is wearing her signature dark blue one piece silk racing costume and hat. She is holding a cricket ball with a spinner's grip and obviously very much in her element.

As they had stayed so long beyond the original planned duration, Hilda passed her milestone by finally celebrating her long-awaited 21st birthday in South Africa. April 27th 1925 was a scheduled gala day at Stellenbosch in the Western Cape, just a few days before leaving for home. The whole town had been in raptures since finding out that they would be hosting the visitor for a gala on her special birthday, and a surprise had been organised.

Hilda and her mother had discovered months before that the South Africans liked a party, and on this occasion the entire town turned out to host a Hilda James Birthday Gala to commemorate her coming of age. Before the swimming pool extravaganza there was even a carnival parade, with a float made up to look like a pool for her to ride on as she accepted the whole town's greetings. She delighted the organisers by turning out dressed for the pool.

1924 CARTOON – SOUTH AFRICA
BOWLED JAMES!
NESER; "IF WE HAD PLAYED I THINK WE MIGHT HAVE BEATEN YOU". TENNYSON; "MY DEAR MAN, YOU HADN'T AN EARTHLY. I WAS GOING TO INSPAN* MISS HILDA HERE AND PUT HER ON AT THE RAILWAY END!"

*The Afrikaans word "inspan" translates as "to draft in".

Hilda was mindful of an episode from earlier in the tour, when two police officers on duty had to call for reinforcements when a crowd of more than 300 had forcibly gate crashed a sold out event. Although it was her 21st birthday, she insisted on reorganising the entire evening so that she could perform two complete shows because demand was so high. She addressed both of the audiences, thanking them for their hospitality and adding that she had never had quite so much fun as on the tour. She said that she had personally asked to swim twice in one evening because South Africa in general and the Stellenbosch crowd in particular deserved it. The other swimmers gave her the bumps at both performances, and both times they ended up by throwing her in the pool to the obvious delight of the audiences. She was given a card signed by all the swimmers and dignitaries present "To a great little sportsman – Happy Birthday Hilda James".

While in South Africa, Hilda had naturally broken most of the local records, but there is scant evidence to demonstrate the actual races and times. She did comment that she had enjoyed the warmer water to be found in the nation's swimming pools, usually at least ten degrees better than she was used to at competitions in England. The only practical drawback that she could identify was due to the high altitude in some places. She found that she had to modify her breathing schedule during races longer than 100 yards to get enough oxygen through her system and avoid suffering from leg cramps.

At the close of the reprise tour there was a much more formal event than the birthday party. The English visitors were invited to a gala dinner hosted by the Prime Minister, Barry Herzog. SAASU President Gilbert Reynolds made a long speech thanking their visitors for giving up more time than they had planned, so that thousands of South African people who couldn't get tickets originally could enjoy her performances. He presented Hilda with an engraved gold watch, and a magnificent citation mounted in a gilt frame which read;

South African Amateur Swimming Union
HQ Durban. Natal
Season 1924-1925
Certificate of Appreciation and Thanks Presented to Miss Hilda James in recognition of the valuable services rendered during her tour of South Africa
Jan 26 – May 1 1925
The Union on behalf of all swimmers throughout South Africa and Rhodesia records its grateful appreciation of the very sporting spirit in which Miss James carried out her most strenuous tour which included special coaching to thousands of school children and demonstrations at more than twenty swimming galas in all the leading towns
Gilbert Reynolds, Pres.

Hilda and her mother finally left for home from Cape Town after being in South Africa for over three months. The tour had undoubtedly been another raging success for amateur swimming. Standing at the rail watching Table Mountain recede, Hilda allowed herself to bask in her past glories just for a change. She mused over what she now considered a fitting end to a pretty spectacular amateur career.

On reaching home she would definitely be retiring, having variously broken and lowered the English Records at almost every yards distance available (100, 150, 200, 220, 300, 440, 500, 880, 1000 and 1760). Many of these she still held. There was a string of six FINA ratified World Records, two of which were still current. In addition to those were the many unconfirmed times, mostly recorded as fastest swims over distance with many hailed universally as unofficial World Records. She would also retire as the undefeated champion of the River Thames Long Distance Swim and as an Olympic Silver Medal holder. She was quitting at the top, which she definitely saw as a positive thing. Yes she would miss the racing, but she would still train with the Garston team when she could. In spite of the difficulties it had all been a great deal of fun. In spite of all this, it was definitely time to move on.

CHAPTER 18
CASTING OFF

Hilda and her Ma arrived back in Parkgate at the end of May 1925. Hilda did wonder if her Pa would be told tales about her being disrespectful to her mother, chaperone dumping, or even simply that they had not got along at all well whilst away. As far as she could tell nothing was said, even if it had been she certainly didn't hear about it. She reckoned that to be a sign that either one or both parents actually knew just who had been surly with whom.

Apart from a delayed birthday party, there was a huge pile of mail waiting at the Bath House. There were 21st birthday greetings from relatives, swimmers, friends and many cards from various swimming clubs and societies. There was also the usual series of swimming invitations. Elsie had cleverly singled out a particular envelope from Cunard and had it carefully hidden in case it might fall into the wrong hands. She had correctly guessed what it contained, a request that Hilda contact the Company as soon as possible on her arrival back in England. Aha!

Over the usual sumptuous tea at Cunard headquarters, which on this occasion was hosted by Sir Percy Bates himself, Hilda was made a new offer. He started by offering her belated birthday greetings and congratulating her on yet another hugely successful foreign tour. Sir Percy then told her that Franconia was turning out to be a roaring success as a cruise ship, and the American travel agents were already clamouring for more of the same. The brand new liner RMS Carinthia was therefore having his new interior design fitted out, and she would be the very first Cunard ship specifically configured for a World Cruise. The layout of the recreational facilities would be the same as Hilda had seen aboard Franconia, with the gymnasium and racquet courts located each side of a magnificent swimming pool and sauna.

By now he knew that she felt relaxed enough around him for a bit of joshing. The Deputy Chairman went on to apologise in advance that unfortunately Carinthia's pool was to be the same size as that on Franconia. In mock severity he growled at her about how embarrassed he had been at her swimming display during the Hebrides cruise, when she had commented that the pool was not the regulation size for competitions. He then relented, chuckling as he recalled how Royden had been completely beastly, merciless even, when making fun of him about it afterwards. Remembering Sir Percy's display of comedy horror at the time, she enjoyed a good laugh with him about it. Sir Percy was pleased that the young star no longer seemed to feel overawed by such occasions.

Anyway, he continued on to the serious business. Carinthia would be sailing on her maiden voyage from Liverpool to New York and back via Queenstown (Cobh) on 21st August, a little over three months hence. There was no invitation cruise planned on this occasion as time was tight, so the first transatlantic trip would have to serve as shakedown time. After that Carinthia would head straight back to New York for the start of her first World Cruise. The plan was to complete a World Cruise each winter, usually interspersed with summer Mediterranean and North Cape cruises, and occasional transatlantic work when not otherwise required.

Sir Percy told Hilda that actually, Carinthia was a bit of a favourite of his and the culmination of a long process to reinvent the Cunard liners as speciality ocean cruising ships. He added that in case Miss James had not realised it for herself by now, she was also a bit of a favourite of his. He had been busy asking some of his other favourite, mostly younger crew members to serve aboard Carinthia. Along with the ship herself, he was breaking down other barriers. For this mission he wanted a dynamic and, dare he say it, a modern and lively crew.

Sir Percy then asked her the question she had been waiting to hear. With her recent coming of age he now considered the timing to be right with respect to Miss James' possible availability. Would she like to formally join Cunard, officially in the position of Swimming Instructress aboard the new liner? Although the concept of celebrity crew was something she knew Cunard had been working on since the beginning of their association in 1922, if she was to accept Hilda would actually be the very first person to take on that kind of role.

He explained that apart from the regular pool and swimming duties, he planned on her becoming much more visible in the public areas of the ship than a lot of the other crew, basically playing the role of entertainment hostess to the paying guests. He told her that it was little use him trying to tell her what to do as he wouldn't be there; he was hoping that she would be comfortable with being expected to show some initiative. The Company would provide some basic guidance and rules, but in conjunction with the gymnasium staff Hilda would be expected to pioneer and develop the new role herself. She would have to find a balance which she could then define before reporting back in person to him.

At long last here was the moment. It was the very thing Hilda had been waiting so long for, a definite offer that she could finally accept without hesitation. By now, she knew Sir Percy well enough to ask him for a small favour. She asked if it could be arranged so that it came as a complete surprise at Parkgate, as she didn't want any further trouble with her family.

He was in hearty agreement with that sentiment and as usual he told her not to worry. In spite of the fact that it would slightly hinder his pre-event publicity he told her that would be more than happy to make it so. He told her that in their different ways she absolutely deserved it and so did her family. He pledged to make sure that apart from Carinthia's Captain who had been working with him on the crew postings, nobody else would find out about her new career until it actually happened.

He didn't really think it might happen, but Sir Percy was mindful that she could still technically be poached. If she accepted the post, he also offered to put her on the payroll from 1st July 1925 and immediately grant her an extended shore leave until she sailed. The only minor problem was that after that date she would no longer be able to swim in amateur competition, but she told him that she was happy enough to manage that. Late in the afternoon Hilda finally left the Cunard Building having signed up without involving her parents. She walked out of what was now her new headquarters and went down to the Pier Head to catch the ferry as Hilda James, Cunard Swimming Instructress. She was walking on air and felt at once rebellious, sneaky, justified and absolutely triumphant at the new found sense of emancipation.

For the meantime Hilda somehow managed to drag herself back to normal duties, training at Garston and at home. On 27th June 1925 Newcastle was unknowingly treated to the final performance of Hilda James' amateur career. A spectacular new salt water pool had been blasted out of the bedrock at Tynemouth Long Sands Beach. As usual, Hilda was invited to officially open the pool and star in the gala.

She duly treated the crowd to the full trick routine before unusually giving a short solo speed swimming demonstration rather than appearing in any of the races. She had already signed away the right to compete, and although she would not actually start getting paid officially for four more days, for once she was worried about what the press might say if they caught wind of it. Her parents were there too, and feeling utterly indifferent to their possible reaction she told them that they had made the trip in vain. There would be no records broken and she wasn't even going to race because she was tired and feeling under the weather.

There was a six week gap until Carinthia was due to set sail on her maiden voyage. Hilda had to miss one gala she had been expected to attend, also telling Bill Howcroft that she was under the weather. If the coach knew something was afoot, he didn't let on. Mostly, she kept herself busy at the Adelphi pool and at Parkgate, where she was often to be found helping out and giving free instruction. By now it was well known that a visit to the baths might mean free coaching from the champion and that in itself had become a major draw for visitors. Lady Bates would often bring young Edward to the baths, and as promised he started to learn some tricks from Hilda.

Margery and Jim Brooks brought little Margery for a day out at Parkgate baths, but they stayed in the outdoor pool area and pointedly refused Gertie's usual offer of tea in the Bath House. Neither of them was prepared to even speak to John, and for his part he wisely kept well out of Jim's way. They also quietly accepted another bag of Hilda's remaining souvenirs to be stored safely with them at Hunts Cross.

George Hall and a friend of his stopped in at the baths, staying overnight as bed and breakfast customers. They were off on a summer driving tour of Europe in his car, Mabelle. As they prepared to leave the next day, Hilda told him that she was also leaving soon. She told George that they probably wouldn't see each other for, well at least a long while. She confided in him about the new job and how she would by away for months at a time. They were both bright enough to know that it marked the end of a gentle romance. George was really excited to hear that she would be visiting Hong Kong on the World Cruise, and told her to make sure to take a ride on the electric tram which carried visitors to the very top of The Victoria Peak. They parted as friends, and would remain so for many years.

Her parents may have been left completely ignorant of the developments, but there were several people to whom Hilda felt she did owe an explanation before she left. She was reluctant to tell anybody about her next move for as long as possible in case word got back to the Bath House.

Eventually she had to own up to Grenfell that she would not be returning to her job at the School in the autumn term, having finally accepted a generous offer from Cunard to sail on the new Carinthia. The Headmaster was philosophical about it, having already decided in his own heart that she would have to leave and knowing how badly she needed to escape from the family. Hilda told him that if there was trouble she was ready to deal with it this time, but that if her parents ever calmed down enough she would probably visit Parkgate between cruises. She also said that as the Parkgate baths were already closely associated with her name, she was happy if he continued to use her for publicity as he saw fit. Even though she could now charge for her services, she at least owed him that for free.

As with Bill Howcroft, she and AG Grenfell had both grown to respect and trust each other. For his part, he said that he was more than happy not to tell her parents. Thankfully the girl was 21 now and to his thinking the pool manager and his wife would find nobody but themselves to blame once she was gone and the dust had settled. They had stubbornly put themselves in the position where what their daughter did was no longer any of their business, and they were about to find themselves soundly punished for it. Whilst there was no doubting that they were hard working and trustworthy employees, thankfully he didn't actually have to like them. His respect for the couple as people had waned significantly. He didn't think that they had ever learned to appreciate their daughter. They didn't deserve her, but in his view they were definitely about to get exactly what they did deserve.

Hilda visited Hunts Cross and brought the last of her treasured belongings to be stored there. She broke her big news to Margery and Jim, adding that there was bound to be serious trouble when her parents finally found out. If things broke badly she might even need to stay with them before the ship sailed. They were delighted that she was finally leaving Parkgate, and in some style too. They discussed the fact that it was indeed her big opportunity, and how delighted they were that she was ready to grasp it and move forwards. They were proud of her achievements and were happy to share those feelings in a way that her parents seemed incapable of. Like the Howcrofts had done before them and after having discussed it between themselves for years, they finally offered her a permanent home if she was not welcome at Parkgate at any time in the future.

Hilda took the Brooks' into Liverpool for afternoon tea at the Adelphi Hotel. Any time she arrived there with guests there would always be quite a stir, as the hotel treated anyone in her party like proper celebrities. Before tea Little Margery enjoyed a swimming lesson with her big cousin in the gorgeous pool. She loved having Hilda teaching her to swim there, and the excitement she felt when the hotel staff made such a fuss of them.

On one such visit Margery innocently told the hotel manager how much she loved the swimming pool's huge fluffy towels, and later as they were leaving the child found herself being solemnly presented with one of them tied up with ribbon as a gift. Whenever she was in Liverpool, Hilda would either invite the Brooks' to meet her at the Adelphi, or visit Hunts Cross and spend some time with them if she could manage. They too would remain close all their lives.

The Cunard Management were delighted with themselves for finally securing the services of Hilda James. The week before Carinthia's maiden voyage Sir Percy Bates once again invited her to headquarters for tea with himself and the Company Chairman Sir Thomas Royden. Unusually she was asked to bring her swimming gear. As there was no pool at the Cunard Building, she was left mystified. Although by now they already knew each other well, it was an occasion for Sir Percy to formally welcome the Swimming Star Hilda

James into the Company.

Before tea Sir Percy introduced her to Captain EG Diggle, who would be in command of Carinthia. For her benefit, he fixed his captain with a stern eye and personally charged him with looking after Miss James, who he once again described as a bit of a favourite of his. Sir Thomas left after tea, and the Deputy Chairman and Captain invited Hilda to join them for a guided tour of "her" brand new liner. The pair escorted her to a waiting car as if she were some sort of royalty and they were driven north along Liverpool's famous Dock Road to reach the vast Huskisson Dock complex, where Carinthia was in final preparation. On the way, Sir Percy asked Hilda if she was coping at Parkgate and for a change she spotted an opportunity to tell him not to worry. He laughed and told her to remember how close she was to Hinderton Hall if she needed to bolt.Hilda was given an extensive tour of the new ship, including the small cabin she would be sharing in the ladies crew area. Sir Percy then revealed the reason for the swimming costume. He politely asked Hilda if she would mind getting changed for a commemorative photograph to be taken in the beautiful marble pool, and joked that it was definitely a much nicer office than his. Hilda really liked him by now, and already felt comfortable enough to joke back. She told her new boss that although still somewhat smaller and entirely unsuitable for racing, it was definitely a much nicer swimming pool than her father's!

She posed happily for the pictures, and then took a ceremonial first dive into the new pool. Carinthia's Swimming Instructress was delighted to pronounce the facilities fit for purpose to her new Captain and a beaming Sir Percy. That photograph of Hilda poised for the dive would appear in the papers on the morning of Carinthia's maiden voyage, alongside one taken the same afternoon up on the deck with Sir Percy himself formally handing over his fabulous new liner to Captain Diggle.

On the Tuesday prior to the maiden voyage, Hilda finally decided to break some more of her links. As she travelled between Parkgate and Liverpool it felt like being in a dream, as if she was watching herself from a distance. She was carrying a small case as she had gradually started to move the things she would need to the Adelphi Hotel, from where Cunard had made arrangements to have them taken on board the ship with the passengers' luggage. All she needed to do on Saturday was leave Parkgate as if she was going swimming. She was probably going to leave behind a letter for her father, thereby avoiding another scene.

Passing through Wallasey docks on the train she absent-mindedly noticed a ship untying from the quayside, and suddenly the daydream came into sharp focus. It felt like she was looking at herself. She was just like that ship, starting to coil in the ropes one by one and waiting for the final line to be cast off so she could finally set sail. Her plans were sound, but she had a nasty inkling that in her case, that last line would not be unhitched from its bollard without a struggle.

Leaving the Adelphi later on after swimming, Hilda caught a train to Garston where it was club night at the baths. She wanted to say goodbye to Bill Howcroft and ask him to explain to the team why she couldn't tell them all individually before she went. Just occasionally, maybe once in a long career a teacher will have the good fortune to come across a pupil that they will always think of as "Their Special One". There can be no doubt that Hilda had been his, and for nearly ten years the pair had been a formidable team. Together they had carefully navigated the troubled waters of her home life, developing her talent to the point where she had finally outgrown a club swimming pool. They had shared extraordinary success and weathered several major storms together. There had been highs and lows, they had laughed and cried together, but most of the time it had been an awful lot of fun.

After telling him all about her new job and apologising for the secrecy, Hilda promised that she would definitely make it to the first possible club night when she got back from the initial crossing to New York. She added that if she was no longer welcome at home, she would be staying at Hunts Cross and would always train at Garston whatever happened. He was delighted to hear her news, and wished her every success.

Things then went slightly wrong when the newly confident young lady started to act like Eppie might, bravely abandoning the usual formality and calling him "Bill" for the first time. The tough coach was suddenly lost for words and had to fight back tears as he responded in an equally out of character manner by spontaneously hugging her. He had come to think of Hilda not only as that one special pupil, but a favourite niece, or maybe even another daughter. She was genuinely touched by his emotion, and promised to call in and see him and Agnes whenever she was home.

Two days before she was due to leave, Hilda cast the line off another quayside bollard, breaking the dreaded news to her big sister late in the evening. Naturally a lot less confrontational than Hilda, poor Elsie was horrified at the thought of the storm that would surely blow up once their parents got wind of it. They spent half the night tucked up in Elsie's bed, talking quietly and reminiscing. Elsie especially spent a lot of it in tears, because she genuinely believed that she might never see Hilda again. She thought that her little sister would probably just sail away out of their lives for good. Hilda tried to reassure her, but with Elsie it wasn't easy.

In fact, privately Hilda thought that Elsie might actually have a point. She wasn't even sure herself whether she would ever want to come back. Well, very possibly not back to Parkgate anyway. Every one of the lines she had cast off left her feeling as if she were drifting further away from the safety of the dock.

She had not planned to say anything at home, just quietly leave her parents their letter and go out as if she was on her way to Liverpool to swim at the Adelphi. Quite unexpectedly on the day before she was due to leave the plan suddenly fell apart. As usual, Ma snapped at her in the kitchen over something trivial, and Hilda reached breaking point.

With horrifying finality the storm broke over her and she couldn't stop herself in time, hearing her own voice announcing that she was 21 now and she had been snapped at quite enough, thank you. From now on she would damn well do as she pleased. She was sailing from Liverpool the next evening on the new RMS Carinthia as the resident Professional Swimming Instructress and they might as well get used to the idea. There was nothing left they could do to stop her.

Her mother tried to shout at her, but couldn't actually string any words together. She was so incoherent that Hilda briefly thought she was going to have a stroke. Then, with considerable force Ma suddenly threw the heavy pan she had been holding straight at her daughter and took to screaming. So loud was the noise that Hilda's father ran straight in from the pool thinking there had been an accident. Hilda had successfully dodged the pan and fearing that he would surely attack her, she made a run for it. She pushed straight past her Pa and just managing to escape.

From outside the open kitchen window she shouted at them that it was their own fault and she was never coming back, before finally abandoning ship. Hilda knew that Pa would be hot on her heels and would probably head straight for Neston station. She would manage without the already packed bag and there was nothing left in the house that she desperately needed. She briskly walked in the opposite direction to the next station at Heswall, keeping to the fields and lanes while avoiding the main road. Needless to say she stayed the night at Hunts Cross as per the provisional plan. She arrived to discover that they had been waiting for her.

On Saturday afternoon, 22nd August 1925, Hilda arrived at Liverpool's Pier Head to board the brand new liner. There was a carnival atmosphere and the usual Maiden Voyage send off, with a band playing and good luck speeches. Apart from passengers and luggage carts everywhere, there were press photographers and crowds of well wishers and relatives. When Carinthia finally sailed there would even be a water salute from the River Mersey fire boat.

Outwardly the smart new Carinthia was almost identical to her sisters Scythia, Samaria, Laconia and Franconia. Powered by four oil fired steam turbines driving twin propellers, she was designed to attain what was for the day, quite a respectable speed of 16.5 knots. She was a handsomely proportioned ship with a single tall funnel. At just over 600' long and weighing 20,000 tons she was small by today's cruise ship standards, and under half the weight of Cunard's big liners of the era, Berengaria, Aquitania and Mauretania.

The ocean cruising idea was only just beginning to catch on properly, and nobody could have imagined the 200,000 ton monster cruise liners that would ultimately follow. Unlike the first three ships in the series and the modified Franconia, at long last here was the first of Cunard's new generation of genuine ocean cruise ships. To Hilda she was more than the sum of all these things. She was a lifeboat, and the means to escape from the gradually sinking wreckage of her family life, fatally holed in the storm of November 1923 when she was beaten by her father.

A figure shouted to her, and came running from the large crowd. Elsie was in floods of tears and carrying the bag Hilda had been forced to leave behind after her hasty exit the day before. The sisters hugged fiercely. Elsie had long been dreading this moment, because even before Hilda had told her she knew that her sister would have to break away sooner or later. Elsie told her there had been the most dreadful scene after Hilda had left the previous afternoon. Ma had been beside herself, and had screamed and yelled incoherently until she had actually made herself sick, before finally collapsing motionless into a chair. She had then refused to speak or acknowledge anybody for most of the evening.

Pa had slammed out of the house in a blind rage and disappeared after Hilda, yelling as loud as he could for her and hoping to catch her at the station. He turned up again hours later, after Elsie had quietly fed the boys out in the tea shop and closed up at the baths for the evening. Ma had started up again as soon as he came in, her broken voice weakly wailing in a tirade about Hilda and Sin and Eternal Damnation in Hell, but Pa had shouted and screamed at her to pipe down, goading her into round two proper which had raged off and on well into the night. Elsie and her brothers were actually frightened for their lives and had quietly taken themselves off to hide.

Over breakfast Pa had fought with his emotions, crying as he announced that Hilda was gone forever and was hereafter expelled from his family. He wouldn't hear her spoken of again. Ma was still flaming, and started on yet another loud tirade about the ways of Sin. She nearly choked as Pa actually broke down and loudly cut her off again, before sobbing uncontrollably as he ordered Elsie to clear Hilda's room immediately and get rid of all her belongings. He finally shouted at Ma as loudly as he could that he would rather she had left than Hilda, then once again slammed out of the house.

Elsie showed Hilda the Liverpool Daily Post, which featured the pictures of her in the new pool aboard the ship, and Sir Percy with Captain Diggle. They laughed wryly about it, but Elsie was sure that it would have caused yet another row at Parkgate during the day, and she was glad she had crept away from the Bath House as soon as breakfast was over.

Finally Elsie produced a thick envelope and told her sister that it was something for later on after the ship had sailed. She had been waiting there for hours, not really expecting to spot Hilda, and was planning to hand it to the ship's crew to be delivered with Hilda's bag. She wished Hilda luck and asked her to write care of Grenfell at the school if she found time, because she wasn't sure anything from Hilda would get to her at the Bath House. They finally parted with another long hug, and Hilda went tearfully aboard the beautiful liner to start her new life.

The New Cunarder.

On right, Sir Percy Bates, deputy chairman of the Cunard Line, wishing bon voyage to Captain E. G. Diggle, of the Carinthia, before the departure of the vessel on her maiden trip on Saturday; on left, Miss Hilda James, who is swimming instructress on the new liner, taking her first plunge into the swimming bath on board.

22/8/25 – LIVERPOOL DAILY POST
SWIMMING INSTRUCTRESS HILDA JAMES IN HER NEW OFFICE
AND SIR PERCY BATES FORMALLY HANDING CAPTAIN EG DIGGLE
HIS NEW LINER

CHAPTER 19
SETTING SAIL

When Hilda James left her sister and walked up the gangway to board the brand new Carinthia she was still crying, but trying hard to put on as brave a face as possible. The last 24 hours had been a disaster and frankly she wasn't making too good a job of it. She was welcomed aboard by a kindly man by the name of Archibald MacDonald, known deferentially but fondly as "Sergeant Mac" on the ship.

Originally from North Uist in the Western Isles of Scotland, the softly spoken crofter's son had joined the Lancashire Police Force as a teenager after applying for jobs in both England and Scotland. Following a successful 30 year career, retirement from the Liverpool Police as a sergeant at the age of 50 hadn't suited the still youthful MacDonald. He had quickly found himself a job with Cunard at the Pier Head. His quiet but firm demeanour was ideal for the Company and he progressed smartly through a second career. Moving swiftly up from his initial position as an Inspector at the ship's gangways he became a Master at Arms, effectively a one-man ship's police force. He had two daughters in the same age group as Hilda, and seeing straight through her stoic act he realised how distressed she really was. Mac quickly put her in the care of one of the other female crew members who took her down to her cabin.

Hilda's cabin was in the strictly male-free crew quarters, located near the medical room. She learned that she would be sharing with one of the hairdressers. There was a corridor with rows of twin cabins for the female crew which included ladies engaged in all kinds of tasks, from cleaners and laundry staff to nurses, a physiotherapist and now of course a swimming instructress. Her luggage had already been delivered, so she set about trying to find places for her belongings. It was a good job she didn't have too many clothes, because with only half the already meagre storage space available for her things there certainly wasn't going to be much room.

At precisely 17:30 on Saturday 22nd August 1925, Captain Diggle gave the order for Carinthia to be untied. In a massive blaze of publicity, Cunard's first purpose built cruise liner sailed out of Liverpool to undertake a regular scheduled transatlantic voyage to Queenstown and New York. The passengers threw streamers and the brass band played as loudly as they could, completely drowned out by cheering both from on land and aboard the ship. At every window in Cunard Headquarters overlooking the Pier Head, employees waved papers and shouted greetings.

A few moments later Carinthia was finally under way. There was an age old Mersey tradition requiring a noisy send off for new ships, so from up and down the river and from the vast dock complexes on both the Liverpool and Birkenhead sides there was an enormous bellow of whistles and hooters from every ship on the water. A new ship had joined the fleet.

Elsie still stood in the crowd worrying about what might have happened at home in Parkgate. She hoped that her father hadn't seen Hilda's picture on the front of the Daily Post, but she knew he would have done. She tried to spot her sister among the lines of people waving from the ship, but didn't see her. Finally, with no more possible excuses left she headed for the Mersey ferry and wearily started off home to Parkgate to see if she could start to pick up the pieces.

In fact Hilda had missed the entire show and was sitting on her bunk feeling completely lost. All the lines had finally been untied, but far from being underway she had only been cast adrift. She had managed a quick hello when her roommate had arrived to drop her bags, but the other girl had rushed outside to watch the departure before they had a chance to chat properly. About half an hour out, once they were past the Mersey Bar Lightship and into the Irish Sea, Hilda found herself being dragged to the crew dining room by some of the other women to get something to eat. Following dinner, and realising she hadn't even visited her swimming pool, she went to see if anybody was there but it was locked. She really didn't have a clue what was expected of her yet. Unless you could count Sir Percy and his "You develop the role" talk with her, nobody had really given her a proper job description.

Later on in the evening Hilda sat alone again in the tiny cabin. Suddenly she remembered the envelope Elsie had given her and brought it out to open. It contained the long letter her sister had been planning to hand to the ship's crew in case they hadn't managed to meet. Elsie told her not to worry about the boys; she would make sure they stayed out of trouble with Pa. She also told Hilda that Mr. Grenfell had spoken to her, and asked her to make sure that Hilda knew he was going to keep an eye on the family. She also owned up that she already had a track record in that field, as she had already been watching over Hilda on instructions from Grenfell for over a year. The wily pair!

Hilda could just picture him giving out his instructions too because she had become very fond of the Headmaster and considered him as a kind of extra uncle. Deep down she knew that in his own mind he had let the idea of employing her at the baths go months before, and she was grateful for his understanding. There was a separate envelope inside Elsie's package which contained a large sum of money carefully folded inside, along with a label that simply said "some savings to keep you going, x". It was so typical of Elsie. Throughout her long life she saved hard and always cheerfully gave her money away.

Hilda was well used to ships and travelling, and she had always tried hard to meet new experiences and challenges with relish. She had expected to be able to sail away and not even think about her family for a while. Coming to see her off had been a wonderful gesture for Elsie to make, but her sister had unwittingly shaken Hilda's resolve and she suddenly felt utterly heartbroken. She should be rejoicing at the prospects before her, but instead she was sitting alone and already feeling a very long way from home. Hilda couldn't believe she felt so depressed.

A tidal wave of emotions had been rushing toward her over the turbulent waters of her life during the past weeks. Hilda finally curled up in the small bunk and felt the pressure from the huge wave build up until it finally crested and broke over her. Exhausted from swimming her best stroke against the tide for so long, she cried herself to sleep.

The rest helped, and things did look a bit better in the morning. She lay awake feeling calmer and beginning to look forward to the challenge at last. In fact over breakfast there was a great deal of excitement when the other girls finally found out just who they had in their midst. "Hilda James? But you shouldn't be down here with us – You're a Star!"

She explained how she was going to be part of the working crew in a new role, but so far didn't really have a clue what was actually expected of her. Hilda was quickly taken to heart and drawn in to the extended family that makes up any ship's company. Being a new crew, they were the usual mixture of old hands posted in from other ships and new starters like Hilda, so at least she wasn't the only new girl.

The day's programme gave her the times she was expected to be available for coaching at her new pool, so at least there was something for her to work with. When she arrived there just before the published opening time, one of the Pursers was waiting to see her. He had been detailed by Captain Diggle to take Miss James under his wing, so she would have a contact point and some proper guidance. The pool was situated between the gymnasium and the racquet court, so Hilda was taken to be introduced to the gym instructor with whom she would be organising activities. Sergeant Mac had apparently given him the pool keys the previous day and kindly arranged for him to cover for Hilda by closing the pool in the evening while she pulled herself together.

Even having seen it before, Hilda had to admit that the facilities were pretty spectacular. Apart from the pool there was a proper sauna bath, and more changing rooms than Hilda could ever imagine she might need. The pool itself was designed in the Roman style, with attractive marble columns and built in seating around it. It had a vaulted ceiling and was reached down a dramatic set of curved staircases from the deck above, giving the impression of even greater space. She was given a key to one of the larger corner changing rooms which had been set aside for her to use as an office, containing a small desk and a chair. At least that added to her available storage space.

One or two passengers drifted in to visit the pool, but her first morning was quiet. After a brief lunch time stop at Queenstown near Cork, Carinthia steamed out into the Atlantic Ocean for the eight day maiden voyage to New York. A few people took a dip during the afternoon pool session but Hilda still wasn't particularly busy. Passengers stopped in from time to time to have a look while touring the ship, and one or two were surprised when they recognised Hilda James in charge.

The situation finally changed the following morning, and Hilda found herself properly busy for the first time. The word must have been passed around over dinner the previous evening, because suddenly she found her hands full with requests for coaching. Somebody had seen her perform before and asked if she would mind demonstrating a particular exhibition dive from her routine. Back in her element at last, over the next few days she gradually began to relax. When she was off duty she still had a lot of emotions to deal with, and would find herself crying in her bunk some evenings. What on earth had she gotten herself into?

About half way to New York, Hilda arrived back in her cabin one afternoon to get ready for dinner and found an invitation waiting. Captain Diggle requested the pleasure of Hilda James' company at dinner in the Adams Room. That meant First Class dining. There was a pencilled note added underneath saying that he might have a small surprise arranged for her. She was intrigued. The idea of a surprise immediately brought back to memory the occasion when she had been presented with a cup for swimming aboard Aquitania, but now she was being paid for her services. Surely they didn't expect her to accept another trophy.

Hilda was instantly faced with a new dilemma. She had carefully packed the beautiful and monstrously expensive American gala dress she had been given in New York at the end of the 1922 tour. It was the only garment she actually owned that had any real value. It had never been worn since, as she hadn't ever dared to let her Ma see her in it. She wasn't certain if it would be the correct style, or out of date, or even too grand for a Captain's Dinner. She had one or two other dresses with her, but they were all pretty old, and if the truth be told she hadn't really given much thought to her wardrobe. In spite of Sir Percy's comment about her being part of the more visible crew, she had imagined that she would be largely slopping around the bilges below decks with the other invisibles when she wasn't in her swimming gear.

Seeking advice, she took the gala dress to show it to the on board seamstress. It was quickly pressed for her and she was made to try it on. The advice was simple. It was a stunning and beautiful dress and completely wasted sitting on a hangar. And what was she thinking? Nothing could be too expensive or chic for the first class dining room. So what was the problem? Just wear it and knock them all out! She was paraded before some of the other girls and they immediately wanted to hear the story behind the dress. Predictably it turned into quite a hen party.

Her parents' strict indoctrination did come in useful sometimes. The girls in the crew had quickly realised that Hilda James might be an accredited superstar, but actually their new Swimming Instructress had turned out to be a humble and ordinary young working class woman who fitted in easily with them. Once they heard why the dress had been pressed, they delighted in making a fuss of her. One of the hairdressers immediately whisked her off to the salon for a bit of a tidy up. She was also lent a make-up kit, but to the girls' amazement she had to be shown how to use it.

Hilda explained that apart from the gala dinner at Madison Square Garden for which the dress had originally been bought, she had never actually worn any make up. She laughed about it, and said that as she had spent well over half her life so far variously diving into, thrashing about in, or getting out of a swimming pool, there had never seemed to be any point. The others also had real difficulty in believing that make up had never even been allowed at home.

When she went on to mention that she had never had an alcoholic drink, they simply refused to believe her. The good news was that all these things could be remedied, so Hilda started on a whole new education. Ma would have had another fit! She laughed as she told them about that. There, now that felt better. At last, her home port was beginning to feel a long way back for all the right reasons.

Entering the Adams Room, Hilda was escorted to the Captain's table. Captain Diggle was facing her as she approached and rose to introduce his new swimming instructress to a group of passengers. He had planned his surprise very carefully. Another officer was sitting at the table with his back to her. As he also stood up and turned round, Hilda caught her breath - Unbelieveable! Carinthia's new Senior Wireless Officer Hugh McAllister fixed her with those piercing grey eyes and an absolutely enormous grin. A small surprise indeed, eh? They could have presented her with the biggest swimming cup ever made and she would not have been more surprised.

She was instantly pleased that she had worn the American dress, and glad of the make up because she could feel herself blushing underneath it. As she took her seat next to Mr. McAllister, Captain Diggle asked Miss James if she liked his surprise, but he could see that the question was unnecessary. Over dinner, Mr. McAllister told her that he had known for months that she was joining the ship and had been waiting for the opportunity to meet her again. He had casually mentioned to the Captain that he and the famous Miss James were already certifiable "ships in the night", as their paths had crossed briefly aboard two different Cunard liners. Hilda enjoyed an evening of luxury dining and dancing. It felt very odd slipping back out of sight behind the scenes to the tiny twin berth cabin afterwards.

Within a day or two Hilda was busy paying back some favours below decks by teaching several of her new colleagues to swim when they were not all on duty. She had been well trained by her Ma and was good with a needle and thread, so readily helped with sewing and dressmaking. She became very friendly with the hairdressers and soon began to take lessons from them at the salon. Hilda also realised that the job came with perks; there were opportunities for what Sir Percy Bates had described as "Her Office" to be used outside the published hours. Hilda quickly developed a reputation for hosting a girl's swimming pool party, especially when they were in port for a few days and there were no guests about.

The Maiden voyage ended on the last day of August when Carinthia arrived at Manhattan's Chelsea Piers, where the Company had its terminal. There was a five day break before she was due to leave for the return trip, so apart from a photo call for the American Cunard people to take some publicity pictures Hilda had time to renew some old acquaintances. She was permitted to bring Charlotte Epstein and a few of the other American swimmers on board the ship for lunch, and proudly showed off her shiny new pool and the corner changing room office. In return she was invited over to the Women's Swimming Association pool, known as "The Tank" for a swim with them. Hilda packed her racing gear.

The WSA Captain Charlotte Epstein was delighted to see Hilda again, but felt that on pure form she had been forced to quit too early. She and Hilda had exchanged the odd letter and Bill Howcroft was still writing to the American coach Louis Handley, so Eppie knew all about the personal disaster Hilda had suffered over the Olympics. She could sympathise with Hilda's need to break away and earn a living. Always direct and honest, she told Hilda that if she had been involved, the situation with Hilda's mother would most certainly have been concluded differently. Hilda knew that Eppie could be really tough, but said that she didn't think any force on the planet could have helped her with that.

The Americans had been watching Hilda's record and trophy list growing, and had been certain that the British team would take Gold Medals at the Paris Olympics the previous year. In the event, Eppie's girls had once again wiped the floor with the competition, but Eppie actually thought it had been too easy for them without Hilda competing. Eppie told her that it was a damn shame, and if Hilda could only have been there she would gladly have seen her own team beaten to some Olympic Gold Medals. Well, maybe just one or two.

Hilda told Eppie about wearing the 1922 gala dress, and they laughed about betting odds on meeting the same Wireless Officer three times in a row. Eppie simply told her it was "Third time lucky" and obviously meant to be. The conversation turned to dressmaking in general. Hilda said she was planning to make some new clothes for cruising as she had discovered that she was a bit under-equipped. Eppie boasted plenty of connections in the fabric business, and after a trip to Manhattan's famous Garment District Hilda arrived back on the ship with yards of material to work with.

By the time Carinthia arrived back in Liverpool, Cunard's new swimming instructress was busy writing her new job description to pass on to Sir Percy. He had placed a lot of trust in her, and she was determined to justify his investment. Given the circumstances leading up to her joining the Company it was understandable that it had taken her a few days to come to terms with shipboard crew living, but when Hilda arrived back at Liverpool, she had finished pulling herself together and was in full control of the situation.

While Carinthia headed across to Huskisson Dock for a rest and a spot of attention, she had nearly two weeks ashore to work on the task of defining her new role. Hilda accepted Margery and Jim Brooks' offer to stay with them at Hunts Cross. Her aunt and uncle had definitely made life a lot easier for her, because she would have had to find another alternative as there was no way on Earth she was appearing in Parkgate. With her new found confidence growing all the time, she had decided that her parents would have to get on their knees and beg her for that. And so they would, but not yet.

The following day was Tuesday and a club night at Garston baths. Although it was less than a month since she had bid Bill Howcroft farewell Hilda purposely turned up a few minutes late, getting changed when the team were already in the water. She walked out of the changing room and quietly stood by the wall waiting to see if anyone noticed. It took less than ten seconds before the first squeal of delight erupted from the pool, and she rushed to dive back in to enjoy a familiar evening's fun with her . . . family.

While on her first shore leave, Hilda got busy revising the swimming pool availability on board Carinthia. She wanted to modify the opening and attended times to better fit the general flow of entertainment around the ship. She had also begun to take on the role of deck games mistress, and had already hosted all sorts of impromptu competitions to the delight of many passengers. One thing she wanted to discuss with Sir Percy was how he saw her role developing with regard to visibility. Did he think she should just pop out into view from below decks at pool opening time, or was he serious about her being more visible around the ship as part of her defined duties?

In keeping with the publicity part of her original informal contract which stretched back to 1922, Hilda brazenly invited Sir Percy to meet her for tea at the Adelphi for a change. With Little Margery in school she was able to take Margery and Jim Brooks to meet him. He was pleased to meet them too, and amused all three of them as he made a point of thanking the Brooks' for helping to look after his investment properly.

He was also delighted to hear that Hilda was getting to grips with the swimming pool and games. The new ship would need organising properly, especially on the forthcoming World Cruise. Sir Percy told the Brooks' that he considered finally persuading Hilda into Cunard just at the same time as his specially designed cruise ship was finally available as a personal triumph. He twinkled at Hilda from behind his glasses and joked that it was simply no use owning the right tools, unless you were prepared to employ a master crafts-er-lady to wield them.

On the subject of his part in her planned role he was surprisingly firm. It was the start of the Cruising Age and he had done his part. It was now up to the younger people to redefine the leisure possibilities aboard the entire ship. Captain Diggle had reported back to him that Miss James had fitted easily into his crew, so she was now considered ready to accept the full challenge. As far as Swimming Instructress Hilda James was concerned, she was henceforth instructed to re-style herself as The Cruise Hostess. The document she had brought to their meeting was a good start, but by the end of her first World Cruise he would be itching to see what ideas she had come up with.

Cunard might own the ship, he might have designed it for them and the American travel agents Raymond-Whitcomb may arrange the World Cruise, but it was up to people like Carinthia's new Cruise Hostess to actually make it popular. Naturally the new post attracted a lot more responsibility than a swimming instructress, and he would obviously have to pay her more money with effect from the 9th October, the date of the World Cruise sailing and her promotion. Hilda was once again amazed at his confidence in her and the generosity that went with it. With Sir Percy, she never quite knew what he would do or say next.

He also wanted to know if she needed anything. She asked if something could possibly be done about her storage problem as she would need a lot more clothes if she was to take on the new role. She also asked if her changing room at the pool could be equipped with a cupboard. Bearing in mind the humid atmosphere at the pool, she would be better off with a wicker type chair than the upholstered dining room one which had been provided. Sir Percy laughed again as he said that none of it sounded too demanding, or desperately expensive for that matter. He made a few notes, telling her that he would see what could be done.

Hilda arrived back aboard Carinthia during the afternoon of Saturday 26th September 1925 for an early sailing to Queenstown and New York at 7 AM the following morning. The World Cruise would depart from New York on the 9th of October. Sergeant MacDonald was there to welcome her aboard, and asked her to visit the Purser's Office who had some accommodation changes organised. There was yet another surprise in store as she was handed the keys to a vacant 2nd class stateroom. This had apparently been allocated to her for the crossing to New York, plus the entire four month duration of the World Cruise.

The World Cruises were sold with a lot of exclusivity by the American travel agents Raymond-Whitcomb, with the liners being chartered from Cunard. Normally, only first and a few second class staterooms were advertised, with the total numbers rarely exceeding about 400 guests, who were referred to as Club Members by the travel agent. This further enhanced the sense of space in a medium sized liner that could actually hold upwards of 700 in those two classes alone, plus another 950 in third class which was left empty during the cruises. Therefore the ship had plenty of spare cabins available for certain crew members to use, and Sir Percy had obviously solved her storage problem by securing one for his new Cruise Hostess plus all the clothes she needed.

There was another, more personal surprise waiting too. Unlocking the swimming pool, she found that as requested she had been provided with a large cupboard. Her old upholstered chair had been substituted for one better suited to the atmosphere, and she had also been given a spare. Not only that, but in the corner there stood a fabulous and obviously very old cabin trunk covered in old travel stickers. The address label on it said "PE Bates". The trunk was empty, but lying at the bottom there was a single sheet of paper which simply read "HMJ from PEB – Bon Voyage!"

1925 – PUBLICITY PHOTO
CARINTHIA'S NEW CRUISE HOSTESS HILDA JAMES ABOARD THE NEW CUNARD LINER RMS CARINTHIA AT CHELSEA PIERS, MANHATTAN

CHAPTER 20
WORLD CRUISE

The crossing back to New York was fairly uneventful. Hilda was busy with the pool but made sure that she joined in off-duty activities below decks whenever she had the time. She may have found herself with a stateroom, but she was determined not to immediately burn her bridges with her new friends in the ship's company. She explained to them about the new role she had been asked to develop, and how she was under orders to be on view in the public areas more. Hilda had already been adopted into their team so the girls were fine; there would be no problems with them.

She started on some new dresses she wanted to make and having her own stateroom meant she had space to work on dressmaking, although she did get some extra work done by the seamstress. While visiting the sewing room, she had been measured up and told that there were already orders to provide her with a set of formal uniforms similar to the officer's whites. She accepted an invitation to dine at the Officers' Mess one evening, and was taken to visit the Bridge by Mr. McAllister, following a tour of his impressive and very technical looking wireless office.

When Carinthia arrived at Manhattan's Chelsea Piers on Monday 5th October, Hilda had four days to kill until the World Cruise was due to sail at midnight on Friday 9th. She had to check at the Cunard Building each morning in case they needed her for anything, but after that she would have the rest of the day to herself. She arrived there on the first day to find one of the Company's employees waiting to take her shopping. The girl was about Hilda's age and told her that she would need a completely different sort of clothes for the tropics, so she had been allocated an expenses allowance to help her prepare. She was also given a month's wages in US dollars in case she needed any other supplies.

Hilda was worried that they might be headed back to Bloomingdales where her 1922 gala dress had cost so much. The girl laughed, saying that they could do much better than that, and they made for the garment district where she had previously shopped with Eppie for material. Sitting over lunch at a local diner later on, Hilda said that she couldn't believe her luck. She was told that in case she didn't already know it, she was held in high regard at New York Headquarters, and the Company had high hopes for her on the cruise.

After arriving back at the ship and unloading all her shopping bags, Hilda decided to head back into Manhattan and make for The Tank. She managed to play the same trick as she had in Garston, quietly slipping out of the changing room and waiting to be noticed. There was soon quite a party, although the feel was different in New York. Like all the Americans she had met, the members of her swimming club there were somehow more relaxed than at home. A pleasant evening of pool fun was followed by an unexpected night's stay at Eppie's apartment. Eppie told Hilda that she was always welcome at the apartment whenever she was in town and issued a standing invitation for Hilda to base herself there between cruises. Yet again she had received an unsolicited offer of a home when she needed one. Eppie said sternly that it was high time she stopped sneaking up on them, so she was to let them know in advance when she would be in New York. If Hilda wanted to race they needed time to plan a proper WSA homecoming party and a meeting for when she got back from the World Cruise. Eppie said she would be sure and check the schedules with Cunard to make certain of the dates.

The days passed rapidly, and by Friday Hilda was ready to begin the serious work of keeping 400 or so paying guests entertained for five months. And there was no way these would be ordinary paying guests; the new World Cruise customers tended to be the wealthiest and most influential people. They were mostly Americans, from industrialists and financiers to theatre stars and the idle rich. Some of them would turn out to be charming and graceful, rich indeed but human for all that. She would come across others who she would find utterly spoiled and demanding. In fact, in spite of their backgrounds being so very different there would actually be very few people that she would come into contact with whom she failed to connect with on one level or another, with just the odd one or two she ever really disliked.

The long awaited 1925 Raymond-Whitcomb Winter World Cruise commenced with a leisurely four nights at sea, reaching Havana at breakfast time on Tuesday 13th October. As it was right at the height of the prohibition era in the USA, the first day out from New York dawned very peacefully aboard. Alcohol was not (officially) available at home, so as soon as Carinthia had left U.S. territorial waters and the bars were allowed to open, many of the Americans on board had enjoyed a serious all-nighter before retiring to sleep it off around dawn.

Nobody moved around much until a lot later in the day, and then many of the guests elected to have a quiet afternoon. In any case, having so few guests aboard meant that the lounges and public areas on the liner would never feel crowded, and there was an air of relaxation throughout the ship right from the word go. Hilda really had very little experience of it, but some of the more experienced crew found the emptiness of the ship quite odd to start with.

154

Even with the amount of ocean they would need to cover, the available time meant that many ports of call were used as an overnight stop, effectively giving a stay of up to two days in some cities. Some places would have longer stops to allow for several days of side trips. At every port possible, Raymond-Whitcomb had shore excursions organised for those who wanted to get involved, but there would be room for crew members to join a lot of the tours if they wished. Hilda immediately made the decision to take in as much visiting ashore as she could manage, because she viewed the whole experience as something between an education and a holiday. It wasn't really like work; well at least it certainly wasn't in the parts of the ship where she was usually working. On arrival back after that cruise, one of her recommendations to Sir Percy would be for Cunard to initiate the policy that endures to this day, of having a member of the ship's company leave the ship with every tour.

Cuba was followed by three days at sea cruising across the Caribbean in the hot sun, culminating in a night transit of the Panama Canal. Although Carinthia entered the canal at Cristobal at 9 PM, Hilda stayed up with the majority of the guests and crew to enjoy the unique experience. Most of the Americans would have used any excuse to keep the bars open anyway, but this was definitely something not to be missed. Predictably it turned into another unplanned deck party which lasted until the sun came up to find Carinthia slipping into the Pacific Ocean for the first time.

Once again, Sunday found a very quiet liner tied up at Balboa on the Pacific coast as few people were up and about. Sailing on in the evening, the next seven days were spent cruising north up the Pacific coast before arriving at San Pedro in Long Beach, the port of Los Angeles. Hilda accompanied many of the passengers there as they went ashore to tour Hollywood.

During the first couple of weeks Hilda worked hard to try and recognise all the guests by name, and to draw everybody into as much of the available fun and games as they wished. Of course, there were all the regularly scheduled dances and entertainments, but that was considered quite "Old School" by some of Sir Percy's more dynamic young crew. Hilda had the gym staff and several other crew members roped in for some more lively pastimes.

For a gentle start there was a badminton tournament at the gym plus tennis on deck, with most of the passengers becoming involved. The gym people already had all sorts of organised nonsense outside on the decks, including the usual handicap races, quoits and what could be described as a sort of manic version of croquet which was played with rope balls.

Indoors there was plenty of hilarity over board games too. Years before Hilda had devised her own game for the James family called "A Journey Home", which was a distant cousin of ludo. She quickly became something of a card sharp, introducing all manner of games she knew from the long evenings at home before the television age. A cruise usually included organised card events in the form of a staid whist drive or the altogether more cerebral game of bridge, but Hilda had other ideas for the more willing and progressive to try.

Alcohol may have been prohibited in the James family but by all accounts, apart from Ma who of course thought it was Sinful, everybody betted heavily on cards, playing for matchsticks with a fiercely competitive streak as there was no money. Hilda knew some great games to teach, some of which instantly became huge fads aboard. Below decks in the crew quarters where cards were apparently seen as a much more serious business and a lot of money did change hands, she was busy learning a series of casino moves to entertain the guests. Somebody eventually gave her a proper peak to wear so she could look the part. Fifty years later she could still handle a pack of cards like a seasoned professional and would perform all manner of spectacular trick shuffles and so on, throwing the cards around like the most flamboyant Las Vegas dealer.

Hilda had quickly taken to the latest craze sweeping New York, namely crossword puzzles. In fact while out shopping she had bought a book of the things in case she had to ward off any dull moments. She rapidly discovered that in her position any dull moment was actually to be cherished as a rare treat. She was soon spotted doing a crossword by a couple of the American guests, who begged her for a copy. It turned out that there were no crosswords aboard, so Hilda duly copied one out of the book and had it printed at the ship's newspaper office to distribute. She was immediately elevated to the new height of Official Crossword Mistress and received impassioned pleas from all over the ship until she did it again.

While in San Francisco she had to find a book shop and stock up on more puzzles. There was a set of encyclopaedias in the ship's library, so eventually she set her bright but uneducated mind about constructing her own crosswords, including such vagaries as clues to passengers' names for added entertainment. In those days each stateroom and cabin was furnished with a full passenger list at the start of every voyage, and these became invaluable tools for Hilda's quest to bamboozle her growing, but ever more frustrated crossword gang. She also initiated a sort of treasure hunt, forcing the increasingly desperate guests to solve clues so they could find a missing volume of the encyclopaedia which contained the final answer, so completing the grid. Devious she was, and equipped with a poker face too, but entertain them she certainly did.

The great crossword encyclopaedia mystery naturally led her on to devising a series of proper detective treasure hunts. For instance, one morning at breakfast a cryptic clue might be announced in the form of a supposed ransom note found by the crew. Worryingly it pointed to a kidnap victim possibly bound and hidden somewhere in the ship. Singles and teams would participate in a game which might develop over several days, especially on the longer ocean crossings. Riddles and clues would have to be solved, and often there would be various other crew members in possession of spoken messages, which had to be asked for in the right way once their identities were discovered.

Eventually it might all end deep below the waterline in parts of the ship not often frequented by the super rich, with the Purser being asked to open a certain third class cabin by a team of very excited Club Members. A "body" made of pillows would be discovered apparently tied up and waiting for rescue, the prize being a nice bottle or two of something standing near by. The clues would also add up to a resolution such as "The Wireless Officer Did It!"

Apart from her regular coaching and the obvious leisure swimming that went on in her pool, Hilda was delighted to organise games and entertainment. As the pool was not big enough for full size sports, she had to adapt the rules to suit. She had some goals made for mini water polo matches, or she would string up a line and have a water volleyball court. She couldn't really organise proper racing in the space available, but after doing some coaching she did get a diving competition running.

She delighted in giving her famous display, following on by teaching some of the guests a range of novelty strokes to take home. And what a conversation piece; "Look, I learned this one from Hilda James. You remember her, now, "The English Comet". Beat Helen Wainwright that time". Racing was really limited to those who would learn trick strokes because they could then be in, for instance, a feet-first race. There was no shortage of volunteers for such hilarity, and the pool became a centre of a whole new social circle.

Leaving Los Angeles, Carinthia steamed north for a day, arriving in San Francisco for another overnight stop. Hilda was on deck to enjoy the arrival, sailing into San Francisco Bay past the fortress of the Alcatraz Military Prison before docking at the city's famous Embarcadero. At that time, San Francisco was still only dreaming about the mighty bridges that would follow in years to come, and Hilda was amazed at the amount of ferry traffic and the massive crowds at the port as people thronged to and from the Bay's many ferry services. There were dozens more ferries than in her home port of Liverpool, with sailings seemingly around the clock to many communities across the huge bay.

Carinthia sailed at midnight the following evening, setting off across the Pacific to the Hawaiian Islands, another voyage of five days. She had picked up more guests at both the ports in California, and on leaving for Hawaii the Raymond-Whitcomb 1925 World Cruise had its full Club Membership.

Hilda James and Hugh McAllister were already getting on good terms. She liked the young wireless officer, and he thought the swimming star was quite wonderful. They had been on a couple of the tours together in various ports, although that could hardly be classed as proper dating. She had begun to find herself invited to the Officers' Mess more often in the evenings, something that was almost unheard of for a lady.

In return Hilda tried hosting one of her out of hours pool parties for them, which seemed to go down really well. She did notice from early on that Hugh never actually swam, although he would bounce around in the pool happily enough with the others. Naturally Hilda saw that as a challenge, and she tried to teach him properly on several occasions but without any visible success. She had often boasted that she could teach anybody to swim in just five lessons, but with very limited coordination Hugh McAllister seemed to have been put on Earth just to prove her wrong. In that respect he was probably her only failure.

The first stop in the Hawaiian Islands was on the Big Island itself, where Hilda went with many of the guests to visit the Kilauea Volcano. The liner then moved north to visit the island of Oahu and its major port of Honolulu. There Hilda swam at the beautiful and as yet largely unspoiled Waikiki Beach to the south of the city proper. It was the original home of her friend Duke Kahanamoku, and she thought it was almost perfect. Sadly there was none of the new sport of board surfing to be seen as the weather was too calm.

On leaving Hawaii, there was yet another long ocean crossing to reach Japan, a voyage of eight days which involved crossing the International Dateline. Carinthia left Honolulu at Midnight on Tuesday 3rd of November, but the ship awoke to Thursday morning on the 5th. It all seemed very "Jules Verne". In Japan there were two scheduled stops, with four days spent at the port of Yokohama in Tokyo followed by a day stop at Kobe, the port of Osaka. Two more cruising days brought the ship to China, with four days at Peking's Chin Wang Tao port (Qinhuangdao). After yet another four days at sea Carinthia arrived in Hong Kong for a two day stop.

158

Hilda told Hugh about the recommendation she had been given by her friend, Hong Kong Diving Champion George Hall, so the pair set off from the ship to catch the crowded Star Ferry from Kowloon to Hong Kong Island. Victoria Harbour apparently surpassed even San Francisco for shipping, with every conceivable shape of waterborne transport rushing in every direction at once. As a ship's officer Hugh was professionally horrified at the chaos in the bustling waters, but as a tourist he had to admit that he found it quite a sight.

From the ferry terminal there was an electric tram to take them to the foot of the Peak Tramway funicular. They were surprised at the steep gradient on the 1,200' climb to the top. At the summit they spent a couple of pleasant hours walking to several of the best vantage points and enjoying the spectacular panoramas, looking back across to Kowloon where Carinthia was docked in the port. They were both reluctant to get back on the tramway and descend into the hot and sticky city, because it was tranquil and much cooler on The Peak.

The Philippines were next on the tour, with day stops at both Manila in the north, and the exotically named southern city of Zamboanga. Following this there was a twelve day cruise to Auckland, with just a brief half day stop in Papua New Guinea. So far they had largely been following in the footsteps of Laconia and Franconia, but Carinthia was stepping out of the groove now and her pioneering cruise guests were about to break new ground. Raymond-Whitcomb had advertised this as the first World Cruise to visit Australia and New Zealand. Carinthia crossed the equator during the voyage to Port Moresby.

In a long anticipated afternoon of hilarity the Captain appeared on deck to oversee the traditional ceremony of Crossing the Line, echoing an ancient Navy tradition and a staple cruise ship favourite even today. He had been mysteriously reincarnated as Neptune in order to solemnly initiate all the Pollywogs (landlubbers) aboard into the Order of Neptune as Shellbacks (seafarers). This was basically achieved by crushing a carefully organised Pollywog fancy dress revolt against those aboard who were already Shellbacks, using those notoriously deadly weapons of buckets and brushes. For added effect, it also just happened to coincide with a supposedly pre-scheduled fire hose testing session.

Before battle commenced, Neptune waved his mighty trident at the Shellbacks present, sternly warning them that he might actually be forced to turn decidedly grumpy if any of the revolting Pollywogs were actually hosed overboard. After all, this particular sorry lot were rich enough to sue the barnacles right off Cunard! Shellbacks roared their disapproval, and the

159

assembled Pollywogs laughed nervously. The serious initiations began with each Pollywog being hunted down, duly resisting as they had been instructed, being subdued with brushes and then getting severely hosed!

In Navy style, having mercifully had all their souls saved from Neptune, the newly reinstated and rather benign Captain Diggle ordered up rum and sentenced all Shellbacks aboard to a measure. With the ceremony complete, this of course meant everybody (except those on duty). With it being a cruise liner rather than a warship and with his much more pleasant natural demeanour restored, he graciously commuted the sentence from rum to include any other kind of drink one cared to order. And obviously there was a party laid on afterwards. After all, what would be the point of entertaining such anarchy if it didn't result in a party? The very thought! Predictably, the following day was another of those oddly peaceful affairs, with few people moving about much.

Carinthia docked in Auckland for a two day visit on 20th December. As the ship would be at sea on Christmas Day, arrangements had been made to bring a Christmas tree aboard and decorate it. Many of the guests were off on various tours of New Zealand's volcanic offerings, or doing some shopping. As with many of the countries, some would travel ahead overland and meet the ship at a later port. From Auckland that meant a train journey to Rotorua, rejoining the cruise at Wellington on Christmas Eve. For those staying aboard, there was a spectacular cruise through the Cook Straight between the North and South Islands, before the Christmas Eve stop at Wellington.

Christmas Day dawned to find Carinthia steaming westwards across the Tasman Sea towards Sydney. There was a large heap of presents under the Christmas tree, one carefully chosen by various crew members for each of the guests and arranged during a frantic shopping trip in Auckland. Wrapping teams had worked overtime below decks for hours.

Captain Diggle led a carol service, after which there was a magnificent Christmas dinner, featuring the favourites of goose and turkey with all the trimmings. The kitchens had been busy, and there was plum pudding and Christmas cake. Even with the whole point of the World Cruise being to escape the northern winter, it seemed odd to many that Christmas could occur in the height of summer when they would traditionally be sitting around fires at home in Europe or North America trying to keep warm. Christmas dinner and sunbathing on deck – How utterly modern, how fabulously expensive, Oh how very World Cruise!

The cruise arrived in Sydney for a two day stop on 28th December. With many guests away on tours the crew organised their own day off with a picnic at the famous Bondi Beach, from where Hilda had once received an invitation to visit the Bondi Surf Bathers' Life Saving Club. A large number of crew members wanted to visit the beach, so they went by way of the city's huge electric tram system. The idea of a visiting celebrity had been fully embraced by Sydney, so Hilda was whisked off for a city tour of her own by the local ladies' swimming association, joining the party at Bondi Beach by lunch time. She persuaded her hosts to let her sneak up on the lifeguard station, opened the door and asked if the person who had sent her the old invitation might be available.

In short order a number of club members turned out to join the Cunard group down on the sand. The lifeguards produced all sorts of treats to add to the Cunard picnic, and predictably a proper party atmosphere broke out. Hilda was naturally invited to race all comers, and had a wonderful afternoon in the warm water. As expected they had some seriously good swimmers available, so she had to work hard to beat one or two of them but usually managed it. She did promise to let them know when she would be back for more, as they desperately wanted time to organise a proper pool event on her next visit.

As the sun started to go down and the visiting party was forced to drag themselves back to the port, Hilda left telling the lifeguards that for her it had been the best day of the cruise so far. She would have stayed longer, but although she had the whole day off work, she was expected at an invitation dinner in town later in the evening.

Leaving Sydney behind, Carinthia reached Tasmania on 31st December for a day stop at Hobart, before a Midnight departure amid New Year celebrations to cross the Bass Strait to Melbourne. Carinthia didn't usually hoot at Midnight, but on this occasion all the ships whistles were thoroughly tested. Following a couple of days in Melbourne there was a five day cruise along Australia's south coast, arriving in Fremantle for another day stop at Perth. There seemed to be an awful lot of Australia, and not enough time to really see any of it. From Perth to Batavia (Jakarta) was another five days cruise, followed by a planned two day stop in the Indonesian capital.

Another two day sailing brought the ship to Singapore for a couple more shore days, but the cruise through the Indonesian archipelago itself was truly spectacular. There was a mass of shipping both by day and night, and dozens of mysterious islands slipped by as Carinthia threaded her way slowly through. The early morning approach into Singapore itself was a highlight of the actual sea journey, and a sight to behold. Many of the passengers stood at the railings, marvelling as hordes of Chinese sailing junks seemed to form

161

an impenetrable barrier for the ship until the last possible minute. Although there was a lot of straight ahead steaming, Captain Diggle and his crew certainly earned their money on occasion.

Arriving in Singapore after so much sailing, Hilda was desperate to have a proper swim. It was blisteringly hot, and the water in the port was crystal clear and very inviting. Once alongside, a group of naked local kids swam around the huge liner, cheerfully calling up to the rails for the rich tourists to throw coins to them. They would watch the coins fall into the water and then dive to the bottom to retrieve them. In accordance with protocol, Hilda checked with Sergeant Mac that he had no objections, before taking herself off down the gangway dressed modestly in swimming gear and a bathrobe, with a towel over one shoulder.

Walking to the ship's bow, Hilda left the robe and towel on a bollard before diving into the beautiful water. It was warm and she was instantly at home. She swam right around to the outside of the ship, causing a great deal of excitement when the kids spotted her. Hugh remembered being out on deck having a cigarette and throwing pennies with some of the other officers, when one of them nudged him and said "Your girlfriend's crazy, HM". He looked along the ship and spotted Hilda swimming round from the bow. "Don't I know it", he replied.

Hugh stood and watched her for a while as she swam away from the kids doing one of her trick strokes, followed by a proper length of the ship to give herself a workout, having warmed up with the locals. She organised a race for the kids, letting them all beat her. They immediately wanted another race, but this time she showed them what she could really do. She spent much of the day diving off the quayside and playing among an admiring group of new little friends. And under the watchful eye of an admiring young Wireless Officer.

From Singapore, another three days at sea brought Carinthia to Colombo, the capital of Ceylon (Sri Lanka) where there was a three day stop. Sailing on to India, there was a long ten day stop planned in Bombay (Mumbai). Hilda wanted to visit Agra and see the Taj Mahal, but she had decided that she would only make one expensive tour during each cruise and on this occasion she just had to spend her money in Egypt to visit the Pyramids.

The Raymond-Whitcomb representatives on board usually allowed crew members to join the day tours included in the guests' original cruise price for free if there was any space available. On the longer trips, and especially those involving night stops, they were required to charge, albeit at a very generous discount. With fewer guests aboard the ship while tours were away it was always possible for crew members to cover for each other while side trips were undertaken, especially when they were in ports where the majority of the guests were ashore.

Hilda had a working agreement with the gym instructors, so there was no problem escaping for a day or two. Still, this time in Bombay she was content to find a decent swimming pool and get some serious training in while the ship was quiet. Having looked overboard at the local water, she decided a pool would be a much safer prospect than swimming around the ship. It actually looked worse than the Seine.

From Bombay to Suez there was another long nine day cruise. By this time he vast majority of the guests had joined in and become a great team themselves, with many forming lasting friendships through shared experiences. Hilda was of the opinion that the cruise actually became less like work and more like a holiday for a lot of the crew as the weeks wore on. Everybody was feeling relaxed and cheerful.

Reaching Egypt, Hilda missed out on the Suez Canal transit this time as she had departed by train for a five hour journey to Cairo. There she stayed in a top class hotel with the other guests and participated in a driving tour of the chaotic city. The following day she joined the tour to make her visit to The Pyramids before visiting the markets, the tour finally rounding off with another train journey to rejoin Carinthia at Alexandria.

Naples was next after another leisurely sail through the Mediterranean. This was another stop that Hilda enjoyed, joining a tour to visit the rediscovered city of Pompeii, where excavation of the ash-covered ruins had begun to reveal one of the World's most important historical sights. She found the experience at Pompeii fascinating and at the same time quite eerie with the Roman bodies preserved in plaster just as they had been covered by the volcanic ash on the day Vesuvius had erupted nearly 2000 years before.

The World Cruise was all but over by the time Carinthia reached Nice. Here, some passengers left to join various tours of Europe and would not be rejoining the ship. The same thing would happen at both Gibraltar and Cherbourg, but over half of them would stay with Carinthia until the final disembarkation at Southampton on the 2nd March. Carinthia sailed empty from Southampton for a final day and a half trip home to Liverpool, before having a 17 day layover and service.

Although some of the crew had left at Southampton, Hilda hosted a final evening crew party on the empty ship. The verdict from all was that their World Cruise had been a resounding success. Arriving in Liverpool at midnight, Hilda knew that if Sir Percy wanted her to go round again on next winter's World Cruise, she would definitely be able to afford the trip to visit the Taj Mahal in India. The Americans had turned out to be very generous tippers and the Cruise Hostess had a pocket stuffed full of US dollars. She was feeling decidedly flush and it was well after midnight when she stepped onto the Pier Head to set off for Hunts Cross. Professional Swimmer and Cunard Cruise Hostess Hilda James decided that for the first time in her life she could afford to take a taxi.

RMS CARINTHIA AT SEA
20,200 TONS, OVERALL LENGTH 624' (190.2m)

CHAPTER 21
MODERN TRANSPORTS

In the end Hilda stayed away from Parkgate for a year. Whenever she found herself in Liverpool she stayed at Hunts Cross with the Brooks'. Following the World Cruise, there was a crossing to New York for the start of a two month long Mediterranean trip which ended back at Liverpool. A round trip to New York followed. Next it was back across to New York to start a pair of back-to-back Iceland and North Cape Midnight Sun cruises with a change over at Southampton. After that there was another scheduled round trip from Liverpool to New York and back.

During one of the New York visits, Eppie proved she was true to her word by organising a major homecoming gala for Hilda. It was a mixed event and all her friends were there including Johnny Weissmuller. There was no need to avoid chaperonage on this occasion so there were a couple of raucous nights out, one to see a musical on Broadway and another for an evening visit to Coney Island, where the rides proved to be even more spectacular with all the lights on. Johnny and Hilda rode on one of the roller-coasters, and he daringly sat with his arm round her. The Americans never ceased to amaze Hilda with their forward attitude, but she wasn't about to complain. At the end of the evening, he somehow even managed to overcome his shyness and kiss her again. There was nothing official in her developing friendship with Hugh McAllister, so she enjoyed the moment.

Elsie, Jack and Walter had all been visiting their sister whenever they could manage if she was in Liverpool, either meeting her at the Adelphi Hotel or travelling out to their uncle and aunt's house in Hunts Cross. Her brother Jack was now 18 and fast becoming a bible study and scripture expert. In fact he was developing quite a style for preaching, borrowing much from his mother's tendency to wail and wring her hands as she predicted imminent doom for all.

Gertie managed to make it all a miserable affair, but Jack definitely had the kind of style that would have made him a powerful television preacher, had he been brought up in a later age. Although he had largely recovered from his dreadful accident as a child, he was still frail and clearly always would be, but also completely spoiled because his Ma absolutely doted on him. He wasn't expected to lift a finger at home and would never have to consider earning a living. In fact for the rest of his life one or other of the family would always support him financially, even after he had his own family.

In the end it was Jack who finally stepped up and made the decision that the time was right to try and heal the family rift. He enlisted the help of his eldest sister Elsie in persuading their parents that it should be they who made the first move to repair the damage. The family still kept strict observance to their faith by setting part of every Sunday aside for bible study, with Ma and Pa usually asking Jack to choose the week's topic. Elsie checked with Cunard when Hilda was due home for a reasonable stay, and the James children put their simple plan into action.

Over a couple of study sessions before Hilda's expected shore leave Jack chose the Parables of the Prodigal Son and the Lost Sheep for discussion. After the regular study time, he risked his parents' wrath by openly starting to talk about Hilda. Elsie bravely chipped in, questioning their part in her continuing absence and making sure they knew that their children all considered it unjust and against the teachings of Jesus. Once again John and Gertie James could not avoid the trap that had been laid for them, this time cunningly set by their own children and carefully baited with their outmoded beliefs. They were forced to accept that they had been bested, and finally capitulated.

On 17th August 1926, Carinthia arrived in Liverpool at the end of a North Cape cruise. There was a maintenance visit to Huskisson Dock scheduled, so Hilda could look forward to an extended shore leave of 11 days. She arrived at Hunts Cross to find a long letter from her parents waiting. They actually begged her to forgive them and asked if she might consider moving home to Parkgate, where she was sorely missed by all. There was even a very grudging acceptance of her decision to join Cunard.

For Hilda, even a return to Parkgate just for a visit was going to be a far from easy decision to make. The whole scenario brought back a lot of memories that she had gradually managed to deal with and lay to rest during the year away. She and Margery had to talk it over for a day or two, but eventually the two women decided between them that she should at least give her parents one more chance.

Hilda flatly refused to move straight home, but suggested a compromise by offering to make a trial visit to Parkgate for just a couple of nights. That would neatly demonstrate that she was willing to make some concessions, but was putting her parents on probation as they were not so easily forgiven. Margery and Jim would accompany her across, taking little Margery to visit the baths for the day. They all thought that having the Brooks' present might defuse the tension a little. Whatever happened at Parkgate, Hilda planned to spend the final night of her leave back with the Brooks' before Carinthia sailed once again.

Hilda sent a postcard to let her parents know what day she would be coming, and that she would be bringing visitors. She had done a lot of maturing during the year away, so Jack once again assumed the lead role in warning his Ma and Pa that they had to treat her as an independent adult. He made sure they fully understood that if they failed on this one chance, his sister had forged a new and successful life for herself and she could easily walk away without giving them a single thought.

It galled and offended John and Gertie that after all their efforts to rein in their daughter they had eventually been defied, but from a purely religious point of view Jack had them cornered. The headstrong girl was her own woman now. In reality they were just victims of the age because whether they liked it or not, by the mid-1920s a generation of girls everywhere was finally beginning to be very much their own women. Hilda didn't consciously realise that she was actually one of them, but she had certainly met a few. Charlotte Epstein was certainly on that list, her emancipation having greatly influenced the way Hilda now saw herself reflected against the backdrop of her parents' archaic attitudes and petty jealousies.

Nobody was certain how the visit would turn out, but thankfully in the event Hilda's Parkgate homecoming managed to be a fairly low key event. Ma James and Jack were at the station to meet the party, but of course Pa was busy at the baths. There was the expected round of hugging and tears, but Hilda had been feeling uncharacteristically nervous on the way across and was quite subdued. They arrived at the baths to be greeted by her Pa, who was very formal with his daughter, probably because he was feeling just as anxious.

Hilda promptly left her parents with the Brooks', and took her cousin into the pool. Before having a swimming lesson and her usual play on the big slides, Little Margery was content to watch for a while as Hilda treated herself to a really stern workout over a couple of laps before she could begin to relax a little. Her spectacular marble pool on Carinthia was just not big enough for serious swimming, so she always headed for a decent pool as soon as she landed anywhere with time available. In New York that meant a session at The Tank, but in Liverpool she was always able to find company among her old team mates at Garston baths as even the Adelphi pool was a bit tight for proper exercise. Over all these options, her preference for any serious swimming was always salt water, and the long 100m plus lengths at Parkgate gave her time to think.

On this occasion, Margery and Jim did accept Gertie's offer of tea, in fact they found a regular feast had been laid on for the whole family. Eventually the Brooks' were persuaded to stay for the night, returning to Hunts Cross the next day and leaving Hilda to get acclimatised to her family again. Although there was no real trouble on this occasion, her Ma and Pa were both pretty sullen with her and never asked her about her new life. In fact there was very little real conversation with them at all. Having been away getting a modern and practical education in the wider world, Hilda started to realise just how old fashioned her parents' views really were. She found the situation at home completely stifling, and she couldn't believe that her brothers and sister still put up with it.

Once Hilda had been introduced to alcohol aboard the ship, she had learned to enjoy a drink. In keeping with her image as a bit of a rebel she did prefer a glass of beer over wine or anything stronger, but never drank more than one or two. The Bath House at Parkgate was as dry as New York City. Well, as dry as New York City in the official sense of course. Strictly it was a poor comparison because she had actually been taken to some great speakeasies in the Tin Pan Alley district of Manhattan by her American friends for drinks and to experience some of the latest jazz music. She tried the drink, but they could keep their jazz. It was the one facet of modern life that she was not about to embrace. In fact she had thought most of it was absolutely dreadful.

She decided to walk along the Parade to Mostyn House School and visit Grenfell, who was delighted to see her and immediately wanted to hear the entire story of her first year away in one go. At least here she found an enthusiastic welcome. He told her how delighted he was that she had made the move away, and how he had always hoped and believed she would in the end. In fact, visiting Grenfell made the entire trip to Parkgate more worthwhile than just seeing her parents.

Walking back, Hilda was surprised to discover that she had actually missed the place itself more than her family home. As she approached the baths she realised that she really didn't want to arrive home just yet. She passed by and kept on walking along the shore for a while. The Dee Estuary is a beguiling and ethereal place, one of those peaceful out of the way spots which will enchant people and always draw them back to it. Enjoyable as her new life was, Hilda was always very busy, and a walk along that quiet coast with the seabirds for company was a great way to slacken the pace in her mind and find some valuable relaxation for a few hours.

Strolling quietly along the beach Hilda mulled over the major practical difficulty with Parkgate, namely access. It always took forever to get there from Garston or Hunts Cross, having to use two or three trains, plus the Mersey ferry. Nevertheless, she did make the decision to attempt splitting her shore time between the Brooks' and James' family homes in the future,

168

provided her parents continued to behave themselves. There were a lot of sour faces aimed at her at the moment, but she guessed that they would probably mellow eventually. With a sigh she supposed she would never know if she didn't come back. Frankly she was far enough removed from her past now to have conscious choices, but if they wanted her in their lives they already knew that it would be strictly on her terms henceforth.

In the end Hilda was glad that she had made the effort to visit, but relieved to be getting back to the far more serious business of enjoying her work aboard the ship. On the way back to Hunts Cross, she sat on the train mulling over a brilliant new plan which had come to her like a revelation. She just knew it would cause some real excitement. In her way of thinking it would also be the final test of her parents' ability to accept her lifestyle and independence, and she couldn't stop herself smiling. The show-stopping days were not quite behind her yet.

Hilda appeared at the annual Cunard Club swimming gala, which was held on the 23rd September at her favourite salt water pool, The Guinea Gap Baths at Seacombe. Cunard and its swimming club had actually planned the event months ahead so that their star performer could attend and give her crowd pleasing show. As a professional she was no longer allowed to compete in the racing, which was timed for records by the ASA, but there was something new up her sleeve.

Elsie had been a club member at Garston for years; she was a competent swimmer although never at a competitive level. Hilda had got Elsie roped in for some new tricks to add to the demonstration, and they had been putting in some time swimming together at Garston whenever Hilda was home. Following Hilda's own demonstration swim the sisters performed a short act together, the highlight of which was a couple of revolutionary dual dives. In one, Elsie would stand facing Hilda, who would be balanced on a handstand with her back to the pool. Elsie would hold Hilda's legs. Elsie would then dive as high and far as she could, Hilda pushing off sharply with her hands and entering the water feet first. As usual the new set piece was a success. They wore daring and very natty matching swimsuits, patterned in large hoops, which enhanced the whole effect.

A few weeks later Carinthia's Cruise Hostess arrived back from a round trip to New York and once again went to stay at home for a couple of days. Most of Parkgate knew exactly when she arrived this time because she didn't even have to walk down from Neston Station. Dressed in a long, heavy leather coat and sporting a very stylish beret, Hilda announced her presence by roaring along the quiet sea front Parade astride a large and extremely loud motorbike.

John and Gertie James were just dumbstruck. They thought that their tearaway daughter was just doing it for effect, to provoke a reaction out of them. They would probably have been right, but they also realised that it would be unwise to have a row with her again so soon. The timing was good on Hilda's part because her parents just had to grin and bear it, reluctantly choosing to ignore the infernal thing completely. She had her fun and enjoyed watching the pair of them biting their lips. She did have to take her brothers and sister out for some demonstration rides. That stopped Ma doing the ignoring act, she promptly started wringing her hands and wailing on about getting them all killed and taken straight to Hell.

More important than the sense of freedom Hilda felt was the knowledge that she now had two much more rapid routes available to get across the Mersey. If she wanted to get to Hunts Cross or Garston there was the mighty Runcorn Transporter Bridge, lifting vehicles to carry them over the southern end of the estuary where it narrowed sufficiently. To reach the Cunard Building or the Adelphi Hotel in central Liverpool she only had to ride the bike straight onto the luggage boat at Woodside Ferry in Birkenhead; on a good day that particular trip would take a lot less than an hour from door to door.

The adverse reaction to the motorbike that Hilda might have expected from her parents actually came from a completely different direction. Out of the blue she received a very strongly worded letter from the Tory MP, Nancy, Lady Astor. The Astors of Cliveden were close friends with the Grenfell family and Hilda had apparently offended them when she shot past with the bike giving out high volume while they were out on the promenade at Parkgate during a visit to Mostyn House. Lady Astor might have been seen as a progressive, but a supporter of such antics she certainly was not.

Asking if AG might know how to contact the young man with no manners, she discovered that it was actually a lady and worse still, a very well known one to boot. She immediately wrote to The Bath House sternly informing Miss James that to be seen tearing around the Cheshire lanes on a motorbike offended the peaceful nature of the countryside. She considered the riding of such a ghastly machine to be most unbecoming and unladylike, increasingly so when the so-called lady concerned was fondly held as a paragon of sport in the hearts of the nation; Miss James was henceforth instructed to cease all such impolite activity immediately.

The whole episode certainly appealed to AG Grenfell's wicked sense of humour. When Hilda told him about her letter, the Headmaster apparently laughed like a drain. She realised then that she didn't just like and respect the man. The fact was that she actually loved him.

1926 - HILDA AND HER FRIEND MARY DODD
ARISTOCRATS TERRIFIED A SPECIALITY!

There were still some interesting benefits to be had for an ex- amateur swimming star. Even though Hilda had not appeared in any amateur competitions for well over a year now, the invitations still flowed in. Because she was usually out of the country, her show had begun to acquire rarity status and she continued to receive some very generous offers. Cunard happily allowed her to appear whenever she wished and also to charge a personal fee, but she was always required to be billed as "The Cunard World Champion Swimmer Hilda James". That suited her fine as she had always enjoyed performing. It did usually limit her appearances to demonstrations and trick swims, although she would cheerfully compete in any staged invitation races that an event cared to schedule. Of course there were no longer any opportunities to break records as that was only for amateur competition, but if people still wanted to race her she would never object.

Hilda made one particular appearance at an evening gala on Tyneside, having ridden across the Pennines on the bike accompanied by a friend and Cunard colleague called Mary Dodd. When Hugh McAllister discovered that she was due to appear locally, he had contacted her to check what she had planned. On hearing that Hilda and Mary had booked to stay in a hotel overnight, he followed up with an invitation for them both to drop in and meet the McAllister family over lunch at Cullercoats in North Shields. He had spotted his opportunity, and was eager to introduce his father to the quite wonderful Hilda James.

After the gala, Hilda was passed a hand-written note that had been left with the baths management by one of the spectators. Inside was an invitation to visit the flying club at Cramlington Aerodrome the following afternoon. Following a very pleasant lunch with Hugh's family the two ladies roared up to the flying club astride the motorbike, which apparently impressed the flyers no end.

They were shown around the facilities by one of the flying instructors, a man by the name of PF Heppell. He had been so impressed at the previous evening's gala that he had been moved to extend an invitation to the star to try something new. He kindly asked if Miss James, and of course her friend Miss Dodd, would like to be taken aloft for a taste of flying. Had she been an amateur that would have been impossible of course, but if she was offered treats now, well that was fine.

As the brand new De Havilland Gipsy Moth was only a two-seater aeroplane, Mr. Heppell had to make a separate flight for each of the lucky ladies. Hilda's friend Mary went first and was given a choice of route, requesting a flight out over the beaches to the lighthouse and back.

When it came to Hilda, she had a plan. "Mr. Heppell, Would this aeroplane be able to perform a loop the loop?" she asked. He grinned at her, and she was duly treated to half an hour split between some proper aerobatics and actually having a go at the controls. It would prove to be the only time in her 78 years that she would ever take to the air. The picture shows Mary Dodd helping to secure a flying helmet on an excitedly grinning Hilda before her flight.

Inevitably the motorbike furore died down once Hilda departed back to New York aboard Carinthia, sailing on 25th September 1926 to be in position for the start of her second World Cruise. She would not be returning to terrorise the Cheshire lanes until the following March. AG Grenfell allowed himself a chuckle as he mused over her antics. Would she manage to create another shockwave on her next visit? After all, the girl seemed to have developed quite a talent for it since she finally spread her wings. With Hilda James on the scene, there was rarely a dull moment. What an amazing character she was turning out to be!

**INSCRIBED ON THE BACK OF THIS PICTURE
"MR. HEPPELL, MARY AND I.
CRAMLINGTON AERODROME, 1926"**

CHAPTER 22
A CUNARD ROMANCE

Once again Carinthia departed from Chelsea Piers on 14th October 1926 for her second Raymond-Whitcomb World Cruise. The tour started off in much the same way as the previous year, with the predicted lazy day at sea as all the Americans were nursing major hangovers following a heavy first night out. The same route as the 1925 cruise had been planned as it had been such a success. There would be two extra stops added at Chemulpo (Incheon) in Korea, and Athens, Greece. The crew team were looking forward to what could only be described as another working holiday for many.

Arriving in Havana at breakfast time on the 18th, the Captain met the Raymond-Whitcomb representatives and informed them that he had been forced to make an executive decision. For safety reasons he was going to shorten Carinthia's visit to Cuba. There was to be a day stop with an early evening sailing, instead of the planned overnight tie-up. A major tropical storm was heading towards the island from the south, and he didn't like the sound of it at all. If the ship was caught in harbour or too close to land, it could prove catastrophic. They were happy to let him take control. Raymond-Whitcomb chartered the ship, but where Carinthia's safety was concerned Captain Diggle had absolute authority.

In hindsight it proved to be a very wise decision, as the storm was already strengthening into a major category four hurricane with 115 mph winds and its path would subsequently cross directly over Havana. The island of Cuba was left with 600 people dead and $100 million worth of damage. Significantly for Carinthia, several ships were sunk at their moorings in the port of Havana. Christened 1926 Hurricane Season Storm no. 10 in the days before names were used, it continued in a north-easterly direction, heading straight towards Bermuda. Two ships were indeed caught too close to that island and sunk with great loss of life, before Bermuda itself also received severe damage.

By midnight, Carinthia had safely rounded the western tip of Cuba to find some sea room on the south-southeast run towards Panama. Storm forecasting in the 1920s was nowhere near the science it is today, so having worked so hard to avoid it they were probably just unlucky to get caught by the western edge of the storm late on the 19th.

The Captain was forced to turn and steam back to the north-west to try and avoid turning turtle, taking the wind and waves head on during the worst of it. Over a very long evening Carinthia battled slowly along with mountains of solid green water lifting up from the spray in front to crash over the foredeck and wash off the sides. Incredibly the ship herself fared really well with no real physical or mechanical damage being reported, but many of the passengers and crew were badly seasick by the end of it, poor Hugh McAllister being one of them.

Hilda immediately seconded herself to the nurse's team and helped out as best she could, but it was difficult even to get to people in their staterooms. In the end it was really just a case of helping to marshal the tidy up operation afterwards and starting on an emergency double-time laundry schedule. The major losses were suffered below decks where, in spite of the valiant efforts of the crew to tie things down, a lot of the crockery and glass on board plus some furniture were smashed. To add to the misery the bars didn't fare too well either, with a large amount of alcohol lost and carpets destroyed.

The following morning found Carinthia safely back on course towards Panama. Hugh McAllister had a specific mission during this cruise. Working with Cunard and the Radio Corporation of America (RCA), he was engaged in an experiment attempting to send and receive short-wave radio messages back from their Headquarters in New York City twice every single day throughout the World Cruise. It was a feat which had never been attempted before. The plan was to relay transmissions through a series of outstations situated on every continent.

It was interesting that RCA were involved, because the division of that company which Hugh was working with had formerly been a Marconi offshoot in the USA, so he knew some of the people involved from his early wireless days. Although he was not available in the wireless office during the storm, he had his office and staff well organised and they had managed to make regular reports in his absence. Once things calmed down a bit he recovered enough to pay them a visit.

Cunard Headquarters were very relieved to get the message that Carinthia had made it through the hurricane undamaged. The following day Hugh was able to rejoin the wireless effort, frantically sending messages ahead. They transmitted word of Captain Diggle's plan to make a technical stop, together with the anticipated new schedule. There were also extensive lists coming in from different departments throughout the ship for transmission to HQ, detailing their requirements for replacement items to meet them as soon as they reached port.

Instead of a quick night transit of the Panama Canal, Carinthia arrived at the nearby Panamanian port of Colon, eventually staying docked for 24 hours to take on supplies and give everybody a breather. With all the details from Hugh and the wireless office, Cunard had been busy with the arrangements, so most of the needed items would be available to get the ship restocked and the cruise restarted.

Literally hundreds of boxes of locally sourced new breakables were delivered to replace all the broken and damaged goods being taken ashore. Some badly soiled carpets and a certain amount of furniture were also ditched in Panama, although replacements were being despatched from New York by train to meet Carinthia the following week in San Francisco. Thankfully, the bars could be restocked fairly easily, so in the eyes of the many anti-prohibitionists aboard their major troubles were really over.

There was a great sense of shared experience aboard following the hurricane. Nobody ever thought cruising would be dull, but in hindsight the 1926 World Cruise had got off to an unexpectedly exciting start, if you were prepared to discount the sheer terror element of the excitement. Nevertheless it was definitely something to write home about, and once all their important work was complete the wireless office had been frantically busy sending cables home to rich American households ("HURRICANE SOUTH OF CUBA BAR DESTROYED STOP SHIP NOT DAMAGED STOP SEASICK BUT RECOVERING STOP ALL WELL").

Staying tied up in Colon overnight also had the effect of allowing a spectacular daytime transit of the Panama Canal. The passengers who had not opted to take the side trip of a land crossing and a visit to the canal's workings were able to enjoy a day of shipboard sightseeing, rare enough on a World Cruise with so many thousands of miles of open water to cross. Four days on from the horrors of meeting a full-blown hurricane, Hilda helped to organise a pleasant and relaxed daytime deck party and picnic to allow the most time to enjoy the views.

Once safely out into the Pacific, Hilda started her first detective game. She was looking forward to this one. The new game required passengers to spend a couple of days solving some particularly difficult clues found inside bits of damaged furniture and so on. There seemed to be no end to her conundrums. The prize was a corker too – a large stash of the last original booze left intact by Hurricane no. 10.

There was time built into the overall schedule to allow for delays, but even having left Havana early they had wasted some of it riding out the storm and then making the extra stop. Because of this, the stop at Long Beach was missed and shore excursions from there to Los Angeles cancelled. Carinthia had finally caught up with the schedule by the time she docked at San Francisco on 1st November, where guests booked to join the cruise at Long Beach also came aboard. Hilda and Hugh strolled through San Francisco and rode the streetcars together, enjoying the sights and sounds.

Hilda had the Officers' Mess right in on the card craze by now. There would be hilarious late evening parties with her dealing as they all played and, depending on the games involved, sometimes money would change hands. Their dealer would sip from a glass of beer and if they would let her she might join a game or two while one of the others dealt. Hugh finally pointed out that it was usually a mistake and regularly cost them all money.

Hilda had started to smoke the odd cigarette, and would find herself sharing one with Hugh late in the evening out on deck, chatting about this and that. They had the Raymond-Whitcomb guide book for the cruise and were beginning to plan ahead, studying which shore excursions they would like to take together. Hugh wanted to see the Hawaiian volcanoes, which he had missed the previous year, but Hilda still had her heart set on the Taj Mahal.

By this time they were starting to be seen as a definite item, usually going on trips together and spending a lot of time in each other's company aboard the ship. In Hawaii they joined the tour from Hilo to Kilauea by train and car. After a stop for lunch they were thrilled to see the lava lake, although the area was unpleasantly sulphurous and made everybody choke and cough. During the Tokyo visit they shopped in the Ginza district and toured the city's temples which they both loved. In China they managed to take in a guided tour which included a visit to the Forbidden City.

They had both been enchanted by Hong Kong and so reprised their visit to the Victoria Peak from the previous year, before enjoying the shopping delights of the bustling city. Spending the evening eating local Chinese food, they nearly came unstuck as they were the very last people to run up the gangway as the ship was already untying. The usually calm and benign Sergeant Mac was not pleased at all, and they were severely scolded like a pair of naughty school children. They escaped with a telling off though, just about managing to get away to safety before collapsing in fits of giggles.

Sydney would also be one of her highlights. Hilda had written ahead to the Surf Bathing Club with the cruise schedule, and she arrived to find that they had organised a proper afternoon event in the local pool. She participated in several races, managing to win some of them but having to work mighty hard in the process. She would never smoke heavily, but knew by now that shipboard living plus a cigarette or two had lowered her athletic ability to below competition standard.

There was also a large and hilarious evening party at the beach for the guests, who were expected to include everyone that had visited the previous year. In the end half the ship's crew got in on the act having heard about the last year's event, but there was plenty of food and drink to go round. The Australians had a revolutionary new idea for cooking meat, using a grill suspended over a pit dug in the sand and filled with burning charcoal. The steaks were smoky and delicious, but nobody reckoned it would catch on.

Of course Hilda had other, more impromptu appointments to keep. The local kids were still diving in the harbour when Carinthia docked at Singapore, so she was once again delighted to join them in the warm water for a hastily organised afternoon swimming gala. More and more of them turned up until she was surrounded by laughing, splashing children delighted to host the visitor some of them remembered from the great ship.

As usual, the very latest craze had been brought on the cruise from New York. The on-board dance orchestra had been busy adding to their normal repertoire by learning to play various numbers to which "The Charleston" could be danced. With plenty of evenings available for guests to practise they all had a whale of a time.

Hilda had acquired a wind up gramophone in New York to add to the fun. In fact Cunard had willingly supplied it, along with a large stack of 78 rpm jazz and dance recordings. It was all fine in a calm sea, but with any movement on the water the gramophone became somewhat unpredictable. She would never be a jazz baby, but there was a huge demand for the awful stuff so she had to grin and bear it. This meant that she could host dance competitions which even included the band themselves, as everybody was keen to participate.

There were plenty of dancing officers too, but Hugh McAllister simply couldn't learn to dance anything faster than a gentle waltz. Even that was fraught with danger as he struggled to co-ordinate any kind of complex action beyond a walk. It was odd, as he had definitely told her that as a child he had been something of a climber. Hilda finally realised why he couldn't swim either, he had permanently lapsed into being a Thinker; his agile mind was so damn busy being intelligent that the poor man's brain never had enough processing power left over for co-ordinated movement.

At last they reached Bombay for their long-anticipated tour to Agra and the visit to the Taj Mahal. They had both been saving up for it, as even the discounted price was hugely expensive. Hilda still suffered the odd pang of guilt about actually spending any money on herself but consciously hardened her attitude. It was her money, she had worked hard earning it and she was jolly well going to enjoy some of it!

The Raymond-Whitcomb "India By Train" experience was an incredibly exciting nine day tour, with all the nights spent in first class accommodation aboard sleeper services. They would be taking in day stops at Benares (Varanasi), Agra, Delhi, Jaipur and Ahmedabad. After two nights and a day on the first train the tour started in Benares with a carriage drive to visit the city's temples and shrines. A boat trip on the sacred River Ganges followed, and there were views of the Bathing and Burning Ghats.

The tourists were back on the train by dinner time in the evening for the overnight trip to Agra, where the day would be spent enjoying the sights including the fort and the Pearl Mosque before making a leisurely visit to the Taj Mahal.

The Taj Mahal was every bit as beautiful as the guide book had said, and in Hilda's opinion it had to be the World's most magnificent building. While Hilda and Hugh sat looking at the vista, he suddenly caught her hand and held it. She was surprised but very pleased that he had. After all, she hardly knew Johnny Weissmuller but he had dared to kiss her. She knew Hugh McAllister very well by now and he wanted to hold her hand, but she knew that he was making a much more significant gesture.

India's incredible Victorian railway system allowed for a very modern tour experience. The first class sleepers were comfortable, and all the meals were excellent. It all contributed to a feeling that they had actually both joined the rich set for a few days. On one train there was even a highly civilised piano bar where many of the guests on the tour gathered in the evening. While off the ship as paying guests themselves, the others were very inclusive, happy to treat Hilda and Hugh as Club Members rather than as crew.

After the Taj Mahal everything else seemed to pale into insignificance, but on one tour from Jaipur Hilda did remember the strange and rather alarming elephant ride. To reach the deserted city of Amber they had to sit in a huge howdah atop the enormous beast, and she was certain it would unbuckle and throw them all off. The ship definitely felt more stable. The Indian railways were organised on a military basis, but whenever the party stepped out of the comfort of the trains India was ready to assault them with heat, with noise, beggars, smells, traffic and the general disorganisation and chaos unique in its vibrant culture. She thought it was begging to be hated and loved all at once.

After completing the second World Cruise, Carinthia's schedule followed the pattern of the previous year. Following maintenance and shore leave, she

179

departed from Liverpool to pick up a two month Mediterranean Spring Cruise out of New York. For a brief change, it was Senior Wireless Officer Hugh McAllister's turn to be put squarely in the limelight. In New York he was invited to an official reception at Cunard Headquarters on Broadway. He naturally took Hilda as his guest. He was presented with a uniquely commissioned gold Waterman pen engraved with the legend:

W. H. McAllister
S. S. Carinthia
Commemorating consistent direct radio communication with New York during World's Cruise 1926 – 27
_R. C. A._

CHAPTER 23
THE CHANNEL?

Arriving in Southampton at the end of the Mediterranean Cruise in April 1927, Hilda surprised Sir Percy Bates when she unexpectedly asked him to accept her resignation. She had a new plan. In August 1926 her American friend Trudy Ederle had dramatically become the first woman to swim the English Channel, breaking the record by a huge margin. Hilda had been approached by a newspaper who wanted to sponsor a British woman to make the crossing. There was a lot of money in the deal.

As usual Sir Percy immediately made a joke of it. He would not accept her resignation for now, but instead wisely offered Hilda an unpaid leave of absence for as long as she needed, on the proviso that she would come straight back to him like a good girl if the attempt failed or she decided against it. He said that in the meantime he did have someone else in mind to try out aboard Carinthia for a while, although strictly on a temporary basis.

He told Hilda that for him, Carinthia would always be Her Ship and he constantly received praise for her administration and hosting. He would personally be very sad if she didn't come back as Cunard really couldn't afford to lose her. She asked about his cabin trunk and he said they might just move it to storage aboard for a while and see what happened. She had grown very fond of Sir Percy, not only because he always looked out for her but also because he made her laugh easily. He had insisted on leaving her options open, and she cheerfully accepted his terms.

Training for the channel began in earnest with miles of lengths in the long salt water pool at Parkgate. Hugh was away with Carinthia of course, so there was nothing for it but to train, and train, and train. Hilda found that she could easily swim ten miles, but it did seem to take forever. A few weeks later she participated in a publicity gala and demonstration swim at the baths which was attended by the Gaumont Film Company. They were making a newsreel piece about the Channel attempt for cinema audiences. The newspapers carried "Former World Champion Hilda James to Swim the Channel" banners on the front pages. Once again she appeared to be big news.

Shortly after the headlines appeared she started receiving letters. There was a long one from Charlotte Epstein in New York begging her not to attempt the Channel. After Trudy's channel swim, which had been sponsored by the WSA, Eppie had changed her mind on the subject altogether. She told Hilda that Trudy was still suffering from the effects of the feat nearly a year on.

She had been very ill afterwards and had taken a long time to recover. Even in the summer The Channel was so cold that Eppie thought it was foolish for skinny girls like Trudy or Hilda to even attempt it.

She lightened up a little, telling Hilda that the much sturdier Thelda Bleibtrey had laughed when she heard the skinny girls comment, joking that she had better go straight to England and show them all how to do it, but seriously she actually agreed with the WSA Team Captain. Eppie said that she was lying awake at night worrying about her English friend. Hilda loved Eppie and had huge respect for her, and she was horrified to learn of the problems Trudy had suffered. Thus far she had never known Eppie to be negative about anything. Eppie just wouldn't talk like she had unless she thought it really mattered. It was a worry and did indeed make Hilda think.

Completely out of the blue she received another letter about a week later, this time from Trudy Ederle's father. He backed up everything that Eppie had told her, adding that he knew Hilda would immediately think Eppie had put him up to it. He promised her that he had not known Eppie had written until he contacted her to ask for Hilda's address. He said that his daughter had been in such a state after the crossing that he had thought he might lose her for weeks afterwards. He told Hilda that not only was he prepared to meet her personally, but he would actually sail to England and plan on being there at the beach to physically prevent her from attempting to do the swim if he had to. It just wasn't worth dying for. In his opinion, brave as they were one of the girls was going to get killed sooner or later.

Faced with such credible opposition Hilda's heart just went out of it. She looked up to Eppie so much that whatever else happened, she would never be able to attempt the crossing without her stern American friend's blessing. Hilda had demonstrated over many years that whatever else she might be she was never a quitter, but she was just not prepared to risk dying for her art. Still, in the end she had to force herself to understand that the right decision had come from within. It upset her badly to back down from anything, but back down she eventually did.

One of the hardest things Hilda ever had to do was to call off the channel swim training and admit to herself that she had actually been scared right out of the venture. She contacted the sponsor and asked for a meeting where she told them that the deal was off. She carefully explained why and fortunately still retained enough kudos with the British press that she was allowed to make her own decision, without being destroyed in the papers. The story was simply allowed to melt away and no further reports appeared.

Hilda took a deep breath. Having got over the hardest task of dealing with the sponsors she had decided to be very forward for a change. She took out a scrap of paper that she still treasured and telephoned Hinderton Hall. Sir Percy was in and came straight to the telephone himself, immediately asking her if there was trouble. Was she all right? Once again she told him not to worry. She had just discovered that she missed that old cabin trunk and asked if he had moved it yet. She could visualise him grinning with delight as he asked her to meet him at Headquarters the following morning.

After a four month break from duty, Hilda James rejoined Carinthia on 27th August 1927 for two round trips to New York before the winter cruising season started. Hugh McAllister was delighted to have her back where he could see her every day and by now that just felt natural. He wasn't about to let her slip away again so easily.

She had written to Eppie with the news that her sponsors had let her off, and the Channel swim was not going ahead. On purpose she had neglected to mention that she was back in her old job. On reaching New York, Hilda once again managed to sneak up unannounced on the swimming team at The Tank but on this occasion she didn't get quite the reaction she had hoped for. There was the usual exclamation from one of the team in the pool as Hilda walked out of the changing rooms but tough as she was, Team Captain Charlotte Epstein just took one look at Hilda and burst into tears.

Carinthia was not scheduled to make a World Cruise in 1927. For a change there were three long duration cruises to the Mediterranean from New York, reaching as far as Constantinople (Istanbul), Beirut and Alexandria. The schedule then took the liner on her usual Midnight Sun and North Cape trips in the summer of 1928, also venturing deep into the Baltic Sea.

Hilda still enjoyed riding her motorbike when she was on leave. She would do all her local visiting and take in a Garston club night before heading over to Tyneside to visit Hugh and his family. Mary Dodd had acquired her own bike by this time, so the intrepid pair took off to do some exploring in Scotland during one shore leave.

On one visit home in the summer of 1928 Hilda traded in the old motorbike, taking delivery of a smart new Francis Barnett Sports model equipped with a 172cc Villiers engine. On a shorter stop in Liverpool Hugh also visited the James family at Parkgate and spent a few days with them, although he still showed absolutely no aptitude for swimming. Hugh McAllister might have been a dashing young officer with great prospects, but predictably John and Gertie James were unimpressed.

**1928 - HILDA AND HER COUSIN "LITTLE" MARGERY BROOKS
ABOARD THE NEW FRANCIS BARNETT SPORTS**

Back at work it was business as usual. There was a series of four regular Liverpool to New York schedules to complete which ran up until just before Christmas. Carinthia then sailed on a Christmas and New Year Caribbean Cruise out of New York.

A major new adventure started on 12th January 1929 when the liner sailed from Manhattan's Pier 54 for an entirely new series of destinations on a marathon Round Africa Cruise. Taking in day stops at Funchal and Las Palmas during the Atlantic crossing, there were some very exotic ports to visit once Africa was reached. There were also day stops at Dakar, Senegal and Freetown, Sierra Leone. The long ocean voyage from there to Cape Town was broken with another brief day stop at St. Helena.

In anybody's view it was a long stretch of twenty five days from New York with just the five short day stops en route. Hilda managed to keep the guests sufficiently entertained, but after that length of time even she had begun to find it hard going. Finally they reached Cape Town for a six day layover, which allowed the guests plenty of shore time. There was an organised tour by train up to Victoria Falls, leaving the ship mostly empty as the majority of guests chose to go.

Hilda had been to Victoria Falls already and Hugh wasn't particularly interested, so they let that one go. Cape Town was a good place for Hilda to introduce Hugh to some old friends and also to get in some badly needed swimming training. Some of Hilda's acquaintances in the city planned a day out for the couple, hiking up the gorges to the top of Table Mountain for the best views of the city and a wonderful picnic.

Following another day stop in Port Elizabeth, Hilda and Hugh were once again entertained by the swimming fraternity on a four day layover at Durban. Hilda enjoyed a swim in the ocean, mindful of the ever present risk of sharks. Many of her friends and local club swimmers joined her for the day. Leaving Durban there was a brief stop in Madagascar before Carinthia called at Mombasa for another four days, allowing side trips to Nairobi and safari tours. Port Sudan was the last new destination before the cruise slipped through the Suez Canal into the Mediterranean and familiar ports.

During 1929 Carinthia once again visited the Mediterranean on a cruise from New York before taking in a couple of transatlantic schedules prior to the usual pair of Midnight Sun Cruises. The first of these kicked off from New York with a rapid turnaround in Southampton being made for the second. Although they were keeping it quiet until their families had been told, Carinthia's 29 year old Senior Wireless Officer had finally asked the 25 year old Cruise Hostess to marry him. It was seven years since they had first met, and there had been a very gradual and proper four year courtship aboard Carinthia as they sailed the globe together. Before finally making their engagement official, Hilda and Hugh made two more trips together from Liverpool to New York and back.

CHAPTER 24
PERFECT COUPLE

After breaking their news at home, Senior Wireless Officer Hugh McAllister and Cruise Hostess Hilda James made their official announcement at a massive party hosted by Cunard for them aboard Carinthia in New York. It was Hilda's final turn around in Manhattan after arriving there on 6th October.

Most of their friends had been waiting for this moment for a long while. There were Cunard crews and dignitaries present, together with many swimmers and hundreds of their other New York friends to congratulate them. They even discovered that some former Raymond-Whitcomb Club Members had wanted in on the act. After all, what would be the point of an engagement without a proper party? The very thought! The Swimming Star had captured her Officer at last and the party lasted all night. Prohibition? Very probably not!

After Carinthia arrived home in Liverpool Sir Percy Bates met the couple to offer his sincere congratulations and reluctantly accept Hilda James' resignation from Cunard. Like Bill Howcroft and AG Grenfell before him, he had known he would have to let her go sooner or later. He knew she would be in safe hands though, because that Wireless Office Hugh McAllister wasn't about to let her go for anybody.

At long last Hilda moved home to Parkgate, but took up residence in the self contained apartment at the Bath House where she could live sufficiently removed from her parents for comfort. In her own words she had to leave the sea because "In those days it just wasn't the done thing for an officer and his fiancée or wife to be on the ship together".

Hilda took Hugh to meet AG Grenfell and break their news. The Headmaster was delighted to hear that they were to be married and immediately broke out a bottle of champagne. He was even more astonished when Hilda asked if he would finally like to have her take up his old offer of 1924 and become the resident professional at Parkgate baths.

In the end Grenfell had been forced to wait patiently for a lot longer than Cunard's Sir Percy Bates, but the old man finally got his wish. The baths opened for their eighth season in 1930, and Hilda James was officially on hand to give swimming lessons, coach and entertain the crowds. As usual, the wily Grenfell advertised the fact widely, and business boomed.

Of course John and Gertie James didn't like the idea of Hilda getting married, even if it was to a respectable and highly regarded Cunard Officer. True to form, they had both spent some time complaining bitterly about their daughter's poor choice. By this time Hilda was wise to their games and no longer frightened of them, so after one tirade from the pair she simply told them to pack it in and grow up. They were so surprised that they both just stood and looked at her in open mouthed amazement. She had neatly killed two birds with one stone by finally challenging her father, and denying her mother any future rights to meddle in her affairs.

Her parents were largely ignored in the general excitement running up to the wedding. Left with instructions to organise a modest reception at the Bath House, they spent their time arguing and sniping at each other on the sidelines. The modern world had finally passed them by.

While Gertie was discussing catering arrangements for the reception with the couple, there was one particularly difficult moment when she nearly fell out with Hugh over alcohol. The Bath House was still dry of course, but her son-in-law elect pointed out that many of the senior Cunard management would be in attendance. At the very least a glass or two of champagne was called for under the circumstances. After being informed that she was not prepared to have alcohol in the house, Hugh bravely stood his ground and told her that the reception venue could easily be moved. After all, the very generous Sir Percy Bates had actually offered them Hinderton Hall for the purpose.

Gertie snapped angrily back at Hugh that if there had to be drinking then he had better organise it himself, and then went to wring her hands and wail at John about the Sins of the young. Satisfied that his future mother-in-law was not going to dictate to either himself or his fiancée, Hugh cheerfully organised supplies and glasses. He also quietly warned the guests, and apart from some very expensive champagne, there was by all accounts a wide variety of interesting hip flask manoeuvres during the reception. Eventually the party got quite loud.

Hilda Marjorie James was married to William Hugh McAllister at Mostyn House School Chapel on 4th September 1930 by a delighted AG Grenfell. As a qualified registrar he was allowed to officiate, but the service had to be secular. Under the circumstances that seemed to suit everybody concerned except the bride's mother, but by now nobody was paying her any attention.

MOSTYN HOUSE CHAPEL, PARKGATE, 4th SEPTEMBER 1930
MR AND MRS WILLIAM HUGH McALLISTER

CHAPTER 25
FROM PEACE TO WAR

Peace at the Bath House at Parkgate was shattered on Empire Day, May 24th 1931, when Hilda gave birth to Donald Hugh McAllister. Hugh missed all the excitement as he was away at work. Still fit and very athletic, Hilda had managed an easy enough birth, but a bit too rapidly for comfort. There had been a bit of a panic that the local midwife might not make it to the house in time but in the end she arrived just in time.

As the months passed quickly and he started walking, Don was doted on by the new grandparents. John James bought him an expensive pedal car as soon as he could walk, and living next door to the baths meant that there was always the shallow new pool for paddling and swimming. Don would happily follow his grandfather around at the pool "helping".

Grenfell and John had been working together on a plan to add another pool at Parkgate for years. With the baths bringing in so much trade it would get extremely busy around the weekends and holidays. Every available space in the water would be filled with bathers from as far away as Birkenhead, Wallasey, Liverpool and Chester. After a lot of thought they finally went for the cheapest workable solution, and attached a second pool on the beach side of the complex.

It was lower down at beach level and reached via a short flight of steps from the original complex. This aspect allowed it to be filled by tidal action without the need for a full second set of pumps. There were sluices and filters fitted to try and exclude fish. At 220' (67.05m) long, it was designed to be much shallower than the original pool. This encouraged families and younger guests to use it more as a play area, hopefully leaving the long pool mainly for swimmers and divers.

The plan was essentially sound, and when it opened in 1930 the crowds did start to spread out between both pools. The new tide pool did relieve the pressure on the facilities somewhat, but unfortunately the design wasn't entirely successful. The sea filters were apparently never as good as the original electrically powered equipment at the main pool, and early on the water would often be cloudy.

To bolster the staff, one of Hilda's young cousins and her family were employed on the busier weekends, with her mother in the tea shop and her father helping to marshal the frantically busy car park. They had to arrive early as Cousin Ethel's special job had to be completed by opening time.

189

Sometimes aided by Hilda, in fact anyone who wasn't busy doing something else, she would help her Uncle John to catch the eels which would somehow find their way in through the system. Still, it wasn't all bad news as the eels were quite profitable, being either sent to the tea shop for processing, or taken in a bucket to sell to one of the fresh fish outlets along Parkgate Parade. In time, the sea filters were fitted with proper meshing to keep the pesky creatures out once and for all. Delicious as the eels may have been, they were literally more trouble than they were worth.

The Great Depression took its toll on the ocean cruising market, and as traffic started to fall away Hugh finally moved on from Cunard. Without Hilda on board, most of the fun had gone out of it all anyway and he was glad of the change. In October 1932 he was once again head hunted, jumping at the chance to join International Marine Radio Corporation (IMRC) for a position initially split between working in London and Amsterdam. They were designing new and more modern radio equipment for ships, and by now Hugh had serious credibility as both a highly respected designer and pioneering operator in the field. It still meant being away from home a lot, but in the prevailing job market it was steady work and very well paid.

By the early 1930s, the River Dee had started to show signs of silting up along the Wirral shoreline and the baths found themselves in real trouble. The marsh grass "spartina" was rapidly invading the beaches, fixing the sand and turning more of the estuary into salt flats each year. Extensive piping was eventually laid at Parkgate to ensure the continued supply of seawater from the estuary to feed the main pool pump. As there began to be no tide water available for the new pool the system was also modified so that water flowed down from the main pool to the shallow pool, also alleviating some of the problems with water quality.

It all cost Mostyn House a fortune and the piping had to be extended further out after just a couple of years, but the writing was on the wall. After some success selling eels, John James and AG Grenfell attempted to stave off the inevitable with a new venture, acquiring a boat and briefly cashing in on the busy local shrimping trade. It helped briefly, but they didn't enjoy lasting success.

From the mid- 1930s onwards Parkgate baths suffered a sudden, and ultimately a terminal decline in popularity. Apart from ongoing problems with the shallow pool, there was serious competition from an absolutely spectacular new facility less than ten miles away in New Brighton on the far northern corner of the Wirral.

Opened in 1934, New Brighton baths consisted of an absolutely massive "D" shaped pool with a walk-in shallow area designed like a large curved beach. The entire complex was surrounded by a state of the art white ring building in the very latest art deco style, which acted both as a suntrap and windbreak. The surround also contained the changing and catering facilities, both of which were extensive. On opening, it was Europe's largest water arena with room for 4000 bathers plus upwards of 12,000 spectators.

To cater for the youngest visitors there was a tiled splash fountain in the form of a stepped pyramid designed for playing in, plus fun slides at both ends. For competition use the main part of the pool was 110 yards (100.58m) across, and opposite the beach area there was a deep diving basin with a very impressive set of high boards. Situated right on New Brighton Promenade and just a few hundred yards from both the Mersey ferries and the train station, it was easily accessible from Liverpool and Birkenhead. It was instantly a runaway success, and overnight customer numbers at Parkgate nosedived.

There was a reconnaissance trip by the James family to see what all the fuss was about, and hopefully work out what they would have to do to compete successfully. John had recently acquired a car for the first time, and so he drove Gertie, Hilda and three year old Don to New Brighton in his new Austin Seven. Arriving at the new baths they were greeted by the jaw-dropping facilities, and John immediately knew they were in serious trouble at Parkgate.

The family enjoyed a fantastic day out, but it was obvious that Parkgate had simply been eclipsed in every possible way. There was nothing they could do about it. At the end of the season Parkgate baths closed for the winter having had less than half the visitors of the previous year. AG Grenfell's dream was over, and sadly the Headmaster died at the end of the year.

Hugh was busy at IMRC with an important new contract. The recently launched Cunard White Star flagship RMS Queen Mary was being completed, and he was aboard as part of the technical crew building the radio office and installing the huge mass of equipment to give the ship four separate systems. This work was all taking place in Scotland on the River Clyde and as usual it meant more time spent away from home, but he was truly in his element. When the ship sailed on her maiden voyage she would carry the most up to date radio system yet possible.

Subsequently, Hugh participated in writing a major technical paper for the Institute of Electrical Engineers. Entitled "A Survey of Marine Radio Progress, With Special Reference to RMS Queen Mary", it caused a lot of excitement in the business. Because his technical education had been entirely practical

Hugh actually held no formal qualifications, yet he was a free-thinking innovator and had become a highly respected designer in the field. Based largely on this piece of work he was awarded an Associate Membership of the Institute, which was later upgraded to a full membership. After war work with the British Admiralty supporting the study and design of the early radar systems, Hugh's career would finally branch out into early guided missiles, designing navigation systems and tracking technology.

Hilda and Hugh decided to go into business with her brother Walter and between them they took a lease on a shop in Mackets Lane at Hunts Cross. It first opened as McAllister's shoe shop in about 1935, with Hilda and young Don moving from Parkgate to take up residence in the flat above. She brought in some extra money by becoming a swimming teacher back at Garston baths and delighted in renewing some old associations. She liked to be in the water with her class rather than shouting at them from the side, and quickly became a popular teacher as she remained true to form, always encouraging a bit of fun as well as learning. By the start of the war her sister Elsie was working at Hunts Cross primary school and living above the shop with their brother Walter, who by now was running it as a chandlery and hardware store, although it was still called McAllister's.

IMRC moved Hugh to a permanent position in London, prompting him to bring Hilda and Don to live in a rented house in Ashford, Middlesex during 1937. He had moved up from the installation team aboard Queen Mary to being lead designer of the next major radio office project for Cunard. Most of the work was being done in London, so he was finally able to settle properly with Hilda and Don for the first time. It gave all three of them a pleasant taste of life as a family unit. Hilda and Don swam at a local open air pool in Staines at The Lammas, a park alongside the River Thames.

In 1938 Hilda received a letter from Thelda Bleibtrey informing her of Charlotte Epstein's untimely death at the age of just 54. That greatly saddened Hilda as she had not visited New York for nearly ten years. She had begun to feel that her links with the swimmers there were gone. In fact Carinthia's departure from New York after their engagement party had brought Hilda to England for good. After being a regular globe trotter for so long, she would never travel abroad again.

With continued support from Mostyn House School, John James and his family struggled on as best they could over the next few seasons. The crowds were choosing to bathe at New Brighton, and the River Dee was deserting Parkgate. There was nothing more that could be done and while they kept going as long as they could, ultimately the fate of the baths was sealed. With war looming in Europe and continued technical problems finally rendering the shallow pool unavailable, Parkgate baths opened at Easter 1939 for what was to be the final season in John James' stewardship.

Following a highly successful tenure which had lasted over 16 years, John and Gertie finally left Parkgate at the end of the season and retired, buying a large house in Southport, Lancashire. After opening for a few brief weeks at Easter 1940, the baths were then closed for the duration of the war. There would be a brief swansong in 1946 when the main pool was reopened, but practically it was all over. There was another slow season or two before Parkgate finally lost its baths forever.

In the summer of 1939, Hugh was suddenly told to stop tinkering with his latest design, get the job finished pronto and pull it off the drawing board. He was instructed to personally take charge of installing it as rapidly and efficiently as possible aboard RMS Queen Elizabeth at Clydebank through the winter of 1939-40. When the war finally broke out, he decided to move his family away from the built up area in West London and out into the country at Biggin Hill in Kent, a decision which would inadvertently put them into even greater danger.

As spring approached in 1940, Queen Elizabeth was being made ready for her maiden voyage. A skeleton Cunard crew was aboard, testing out all the systems and readying the liner for sea trials, which had been widely reported to double as a move to Southampton for interior completion. On 3rd March, Hugh had spent a long day in the radio system's own generating room, testing equipment and tidying up some loose ends. He was looking forward to handing it all over to Cunard's own wireless officers and visiting Hilda and Don at Biggin Hill for a few days. He and Hilda had discovered they both missed Parkgate. The Dee Estuary was calling them back and they had made the decision to buy their own house there as soon as they could manage it. As a family they seem to have bounced around a bit so far and it would be really nice to have a proper home of their own.

During the day he had been listening to the great ship coming to life as the engines were running. In a week or two his work aboard her would be done. Cunard was planning to move her to Southampton and get her ready for service in the docks there. Hugh mulled over his career and their odd home life as he worked. It was ironic that here he was still employed on the Cunard ships after a twenty year association, although only half of that had been working for the Company itself with the rest being on contracts of one sort or another.

Hugh finally finished off for the day and closed up the generator room. There was a surprise waiting outside when he discovered that Queen Elizabeth was at sea. So much for engines running! It didn't take long to find out that there had been a bold plan to outwit the Germans, who had apparently been hoping to destroy the great liner before she could sail. Secret orders had been received and a skeleton crew sneaked aboard ready for the move, but for security reasons a group of day working contractors like Hugh had been completely left out of the loop.

Once out of the River Clyde, Captain Townley had opened his sealed orders, and the World's largest liner was already racing west on her way to New York. There was absolutely nothing that Hugh could do about it. He would be needed to complete the fitting out process aboard Queen Elizabeth in New York, and would not see his family again until the end of the year. By default Hugh McAllister was once again a transatlantic Cunard Wireless Officer.

And what of Hilda and Hugh's old ship, the first genuine Ocean Cruise Liner Carinthia? Cunard was once again going to war along with every other company in Great Britain, and like all the other ocean liners she was immediately requisitioned and assigned to military duty. In her case that meant having guns fitted and becoming an armed merchant cruiser, with her distinctive black and white colour scheme and orange-red funnel painted overall Navy grey.

Sadly, the fabulous Carinthia had a very brief Navy career. After being sent for modifications in August 1939, she was back at sea in her new guise as a warship by December. Carinthia was torpedoed by a German submarine in the Atlantic Ocean to the west of Ireland just six months later. Taken under tow towards the Harland and Wolff yard at Belfast for repairs, she valiantly stayed afloat for 36 hours but finally sank, sadly with the loss of four lives. The first Golden Age of Cruising was over, and Sir Percy Bates had lost his favourite ship.

Sir Percy would suffer a far greater loss in 1945 when his only son Edward was shot down and killed over Germany. The Cunard Deputy Chairman failed to arrive aboard Queen Elizabeth on 14th October 1946 for her maiden voyage. Having suffered a heart attack at Hinderton Hall just a couple of days previously, 66 year old Sir Percy died on the day she set sail.

Nine year old Don watched in awe with his mother as the dogfights unfolded over the famous airfield at Biggin Hill during the Battle of Britain in the summer of 1940. He would try to count the German bombers flying in to attack as he and Hilda walked out into the countryside to cower under hedgerows and wait out the raids with many others. Hugh was still away in New York supervising the final installation of Queen Elizabeth's wireless office, so at the beginning of September 1940 Hilda decided to take Don to join her parents living in Southport where it felt a bit safer.

Hilda should have known that Southport would be a major mistake, because she still didn't get along with her parents. Apart from that obvious difficulty, both her brothers were in residence with them in Park Road. Although the old Victorian house was large, it all made for some crowding. The James' had been methodically planning for war and there was also a large and now illegal food store housed in several secret rooms which had quietly been created by digging out into the local sandstone beyond the cellar walls. Jack and his family were occupying most of the ground floor of the house. Of course, Jack was far too frail for the draft.

On the other hand her younger brother Walter was fighting fit and had taken to hiding out in the extensive cellars. Having closed up the shop at Hunts Cross, he was planning to register as a conscientious objector if he was called up for service. In the meantime the family were supporting him as he lived quietly in the basement, planning to avoid the issue if at all possible. He supplied help to his father who was trying to feed them all out of a large kitchen garden. In fact Walter would indeed be called up, whereupon he would duly refuse to fight, quickly finding himself sent to work on the land as a regular farm hand.

Hilda quickly found that she couldn't stand the crowding combined with the atmosphere of secrecy and intrigue. To add to the problems Jack had completed his transformation into a wailing, God fearing bible thumper. Although he loved his uncle, Don was at once drawn to and terrified of the strange man. It seems highly likely that after his childhood accident Jack had suffered more lasting brain damage than was ever diagnosed, because over time he did develop a violent and unpredictable temper, later being sectioned on more than one occasion as a schizophrenic.

In a bid to protect their own sanity Hilda and young Don soon moved on again, this time back to The Wirral. She had begun feel herself being strongly attracted back to the beautiful Dee Estuary, so she found them a cottage to rent. It stood right on the sea front at Heswall, near to her cousins and a stroll of just a mile or so along the beach from the now closed up Parkgate baths. Although there was really nowhere nearby to swim, after all the moving about at least they felt safe enough from the air raids to finally settle there and see out the rest of the war.

195

CHAPTER 26
1980 - ENCORE!

Hilda McAllister had finally allowed herself to be chased out of the house sometimes. She had reluctantly gone across the road and joined a pensioners' community group at the local church hall. Since her heart attack four years previously in 1976 she had been living in New Brighton with Don and his family, and with no close friends left nearby she was bored a lot of the time these days. Her daughter-in-law Sheila had suggested that she go and meet the other local oldies. They had a kind of "show and tell" going on, and each week one or other of them would give a little talk or provide some form of entertainment for an hour or so.

When it was suggested that she take a turn one week and think of something to share she didn't really know what to do about it. Should she talk about swimming and breaking records? The old James family indoctrination of no self promotion vaguely bothered her for a day or two. Strictly no airs or graces allowed.

Then one evening, as she sat in her armchair waiting for something interesting to watch amid the junk and rubbish of modern television programming, she realised that they were no longer around to fret about it. What was more; she was thinking "To Hell with them all!" Hilda got out of the chair and knelt down to forage around under her bed, looking for a small cardboard box which had been hidden away in various dark corners for the best part of fifty years.

Having located the last few treasured medals that her mother hadn't managed to give away, the old lady sat and mulled over some of the episodes in her life that she might try and string together for a bit of a talk. Truth to tell there was an awful lot of it, and she would have to make it as brief as possible. That set her reminiscing about some of the strange coincidences and connections she had experienced along the way.

She found herself smiling about the time at Christmas 1962 when she and Hugh had been staying in Wallasey with Don and his family. Father and son had been playing billiards in the dining room, leaving the two women to talk. Something had started her and her daughter-in-law Sheila chatting about Cunard and the cruising days aboard Carinthia.

Sheila had told Hilda that her maternal grandfather had been a Master-at-Arms aboard the Cunarders and had always spoken fondly of the Scythia, one of Carinthia's sister ships. She added that he was a lovely, quiet man from the Outer Hebrides, an ex-policeman by the name of Archie MacDonald. Hilda had startled her as she suddenly shot out of her chair and run out of the room shouting "Hugh! It was Sergeant MacDonald! Hugh! Sergeant Mac was Sheila's Grandpa!" Oh yes, a lovely quiet man MacDonald might have been, but the couple were both laughing when they told Don and Sheila about the proper telling off he had once given them in Hong Kong when they arrived back at the ship late.

In the church hall the following week, the other pensioners sat and watched as Hilda McAllister stood before them and got herself ready to tell them a story. Oh, goody, she had laid out a few souvenirs on the table to show them.

"I haven't always been a McAllister of course . . . Hilda Marjorie James . . . Garston baths . . . Managed to hide in the lockers . . . 1920 Olympic Games . . . Pass the Silver Medal round and hold it . . . American Crawl . . . The speed you could swim . . . She said our whole team were cheats . . . I was eating a banana . . . Cunard paid . . . Aquitania . . . That was before the real skyscrapers of course . . . I broke two American Records in front of them all . . . You all remember the original Tarzan . . . Johnny was the most beautiful man but so shy . . . Gave me this tiny medal so I gave him one of mine . . . The pool at Parkgate was over a hundred yards long and we lived in the house next door . . . My coach said I would win three Gold Medals this time . . . Ma said I wasn't going to the Games . . . I shouted at Pa but he took his belt to me . . . Sir Percy Bates asked me if I would like a job on his new ship . . . Fancy meeting the same wireless officer three times in a row . . . When he looked at you, you stayed looked at! . . . Swam right round the ship . . . Nancy Astor was furious and wrote to me . . . Well, it was a very loud motorbike . . . We looped the loop! . . . Carinthia wasn't damaged but we just about lost every plate on board . . . Took me to the Taj Mahal and held my hand . . . Of course nobody would have suited Ma but I was going to marry him anyway . . . Got press-ganged on the Queen Elizabeth"

Not surprisingly, Hilda's talk ran well over the usual time. There was a brief silence when she had finished, and then the applause started. A few weeks later the Wallasey News suddenly got in touch. They wanted to publish an article about her story and sent a reporter to take her picture. A feature appeared entitled "From a little girl scared of the water, Hilda became the swimming star of the '20s". She was surprised but somehow mildly annoyed about the whole business, because when sharing her story she had naively expected that it would be kept in the group. Somebody must have started repeating it elsewhere and of course the word soon got out. Even as an old lady she didn't really believe it was all that interesting.

197

For the final time, Hilda was asked to make a guest appearance at a swimming gala. A surprise invitation arrived in the post from none other than her old friend and Garston team mate Austin Rawlinson MBE, who she hadn't seen in oh, it had to be at least forty years. Until the Wallasey News article, Austin had no idea that she was still alive, let alone living locally. The event had been organised to celebrate the life of another famous local swimmer, Ernie Warrington MBE, and was to be held on 4th October 1980 at Seacombe.

Well, Hilda thought to herself, would you believe it. The old salt water plunge pool at the Guinea Gap baths, eh? She reckoned that particular pool should really have been named after her because she had actually broken three of her six confirmed World Records there, the 150 yards in 1920 and '22 and then the 220 yards in 1923. There was no way Don and Sheila would ever allow her to swim at the gala though. Still, she was only 76 and the pacemaker seemed to be keeping her ticking along fine. She and Bill Howcroft had usually managed to fix things so she could do it her way without anybody realising how they had done it. Hilda sat and mulled over the possibilities . . .

Austin's invitation had originally been to appear at the gala as part of a parade around the side of the pool, a kind of victory lap on foot to introduce and honour several retired local swimmers of distinction. Hmph! Swimming pools were not designed for walking around, and after thinking about it long and hard, well, for at least ten seconds, Hilda had decided that she had an altogether more suitable idea.

Arriving at the baths accompanied by Don and Sheila, she was duly handed over to the organisers while the couple were shown to their seats poolside. A few days before, while trying to find a swimming costume fit to wear in the parade, she had casually asked her daughter-in-law if she thought there might be an opportunity for her to swim. Hilda had got back exactly what she expected when Sheila told her that she must be joking. It really wasn't a good idea for a heart attack patient with a pacemaker now, was it?

In fact Sheila knew her mother-in-law a lot better than that. She must have had an inkling about what might be about to happen, because as they arrived for the gala she had carefully said "Whatever else you do Hilda, for goodness' sake please don't try and dive"

David Wilkie was making a guest appearance at the gala, playing the exact role Hilda herself had done so many times some sixty years before. Hilda was as excited as a star struck teenager when she was introduced to the 200m Breast Stroke Gold Medal winner from the 1976 Montreal Olympics. Later in the evening after their respective appearances, the pair stood together outside the changing rooms and faced a battery of photographers. For several minutes the two former champions exchanged memories of past glories, much of it with Hilda tucked safely under the arm of an equally admiring Wilkie.

There are several photographs of that meeting in her collection and on the back of one, which clearly shows the pair swapping stories, she wrote "Hilda James, Olympics 1920. David Wilkie, Olympics 1976". Usually Hilda had to be heavily persuaded before she would talk about her amateur swimming career, but for months after that evening she simply couldn't stop herself telling everybody she met that she had been photographed with someone she was happy to describe as "a real champion". It was shortly after the Ernie Warrington gala that she finally began to make and keep notes about all the memories she had suddenly rediscovered.

During the gala programme the former swimmers duly took their walk around the pool, and each one received a polite round of applause as they were introduced, along with a list of their achievements. Austin Rawlinson was hosting the event himself and making the announcements.

Austin would tell me years later that from the moment she had walked in, Hilda had caused some consternation behind the scenes, because she clearly wasn't going to be content with just walking round the pool. In fact from the very moment Don and Sheila were safely out of sight she had started asking what time she was scheduled to be in the water and if not, why not? Of all people, Austin knew her well enough not to argue about it too much.

Austin had presided over most of the dozens of major galas held at Seacombe since the end of World War 2. He could never explain exactly why it seemed to be such a lucky pool, but he had been an official timekeeper at more record-breaking swims there over the years than anywhere else. In fact, so many records were broken there that it had been officially re-measured several times by the ASA, just to check that the length was correct. It was probably because of the salt water which affords swimmers that little bit of extra buoyancy but even so, most other salt water pools didn't have the same record-breaking history. Hilda had asserted many years before that it was just a special place, and Austin concurred with that sentiment.

After the retired swimmers' parade, Austin finally came to the announcement he had been mulling over all evening, how to introduce Hilda James. He surprised the audience by announcing that there was to be an extra item squeezed into the evening's already busy programme, one that he personally was really looking forward to.

4/10/80 WITH DAVID WILKIE AT GUINEA GAP BATHS, SEACOMBE, WIRRAL
WILKIE "DID YOU REALLY BREAK THREE WORLD RECORDS IN THIS VERY POOL?" JAMES "YES, BUT UNLIKE YOU I ONLY WON A SILVER OLYMPIC MEDAL!"

"Ladies and Gentlemen, it is now my great privilege to introduce to you a former World Champion, and one of the 1920 Antwerp Olympics Freestyle Relay Silver Medal winners. This remarkable lady was once the holder of the English Ladies' Freestyle Records at every possible distance from 100 yards to a mile. She has actually been causing quite a stir behind the scenes this evening, asking if we could find time for her to be allowed to entertain you and swim for a few minutes. As three of her amazing six confirmed World Records were actually set in this very pool during the early 1920s, I hope you would all agree that it would seem to be a reasonable request.

"I have known her since I was a kid living in the next street. She was one of my Garston team mates and training partners for many years, and I must say that in all my days I never met a braver or more determined competitor. Like me, she was a protégé of the club's pioneering and hugely successful coach, the late Bill Howcroft. She is appearing tonight with the express intention of showing you all how a swimming demonstration should really be done. Would you all please join me in welcoming truly one of my oldest friends? Ladies and Gentlemen, "The English Comet", Miss Hilda James".

Austin knew her well enough all right. He had correctly guessed about what might be about to follow, and he had been busy warning the folks backstage that they might want to stop and watch for a minute or two as they might just be in for a treat. As he made his speech, many of the competitors and officials were already sneaking out of the changing rooms to watch. By the time his announcement was over, there was beginning to be quite an air of anticipation.

Having consciously left the bored pensioner Hilda McAllister behind in the changing rooms along with the print dress and crocheted cardigan, the former Swimming Superstar Hilda James appeared by Her Pool to the expected smattering of polite applause. After all, most of these young people had never even heard of her. The diminutive old lady was dressed in a borrowed swimsuit and gave the outward appearance of being quite arthritic.

There were never that many indoor salt water pools, and Her Pool even had a particular smell of its own. She had taught both her grandsons to swim there some years before and had always felt nostalgic as the chlorinated salt water atmosphere met her whenever she walked into the building. Now as she walked to the pool itself, she was beginning to cast her mind way back to former glories.

She managed to step up and balance herself on a racing block for a few seconds as she carefully adopted a diving pose. Sheila held her breath. Having had a good look at the water though, Hilda apparently decided that a dive didn't look like such a brilliant idea after all. Stepping back down off the block and shaking her head sadly, she slowly walked round the pool to the nearest ladder and carefully climbed down it backwards. In the audience, Sheila quietly breathed a sigh of relief. For a minute she had thought her mother-in-law would ignore her advice and dive in, and frankly she wouldn't have been that surprised.

There was a ripple of amusement as Hilda dipped a toe in the cool water, screwed up her face and climbed back up a step or two while shaking her foot. Joining in the laughter, she finally slipped easily into the salt water and gently swam in a circle back to the steps with her head held high. The water felt great. Hilda was carefully lulling Sheila into a false sense of security by demonstrating the "Old Ladies' Breast Stroke" from her famous gala routine, following which she climbed back out smiling, to accept another polite round of applause.

Whatever Wallasey Council had tried to do about it over the years, the air was always cold in the building at the Guinea Gap baths. Even though the salt water was heated, somehow a chill breeze would find its way in from the River Mersey just outside the building, creeping clammily through the changing rooms and sneaking across the warm pool to make exposed shoulders shiver and pimple. As Hilda climbed up the ladder a race official was close at hand to offer her a large towel, lest the foolhardy pensioner catch a chill.

Never one to miss the opportunity for a spot of pantomime, the star looked at him in sheer disbelief, shook her head and testily waved the towel away. Seizing the moment, she suddenly sprang her surprise and visibly gave up on the creaky old lady persona, straightened her back and walked smartly back to the deep end wearing a huge grin.

Austin was grinning too, because even after all the intervening years he knew that face and its looks well enough to see that it had mischief written all over it. He could sense the vibe from the headstrong teenager lurking in there. He had announced that she would show them how to do it properly, and he could tell that they were jolly well going to get it.

Hang the blasted pacemaker! Hilda had decided that she didn't really care if it gave out now. She didn't actually think anybody would miss her that much. As had sometimes happened to her before, adrenaline got the better of common sense. The wave of nostalgia which she had started to feel on entering the building finally built up as she once again stepped up onto the block. Having finally got over herself she felt free to let a bit of emotion out. It was going to be just like the old days.

She carefully poised on the block ready for a proper racing dive. So let the fun begin. There was no starting pistol, but she didn't need one. Go! This time she was away. There was a collective gasp from the crowd, with Don and Sheila started to have real concerns as they watched the 76 year old thrash steadily down the pool and back, giving a proper two length demonstration of her old 6-beat American Crawl, complete with a passable tumble turn.

As one, the audience stood up and cheered, and for just a few moments she thought they sounded just like the old Garston faithful. As Hilda dived, time had slowed and she had literally felt herself falling back through all those years. She had left the block behind her in 1980, with plenty of time to realise that it was a reasonable dive before she finally hit the water, swimming as hard as she knew how in September 1922. By the end of her performance Hilda James was 18 again and had just demolished the 150 yards World Record, right here at Seacombe. Here in this very pool! "Encore!" She could hear them shouting. "Encore! More!"

As the echoes died away she fancied she could almost pick out Bill Howcroft's high pitched Lancashire accent ringing down from the rafters as he called out the times. She actually glanced towards the end of the pool to see if he was standing there, waving a stopwatch and grinning his approval at her, but as the sound faded he was gone forever. Elsie, Eppie, Johnny, Hugh, she thought of them all briefly but of course now they were all gone too. Instead there was her old pal Austin wiping his eyes as he stood to applaud with the others. Here she was back in the reality of 1980 and still performing. Only her and Austin left now, could it really be almost sixty years on?

It was Austin's reaction that finally got to her. There was suddenly an unexpected lump in Hilda's throat, and she might have left a tear or two of her own in the salty water as she floated on her back and quietly sculled out into the centre of the pool as slowly as she could manage, taking a few seconds to catch her breath. It was probably less than twenty seconds since she had finished swimming, but in that short space of time she had connected with so many memories. Bloody hell, what a remarkable life!

It's hard to get any degree of quiet in a swimming pool, but for once the audience were waiting in absolute silence, respectful as if they had an idea of what she might be thinking. So they wanted an encore, did they? Well, after all that excitement the old heart was still ticking . . . Hilda took one more deep breath and trod water as she slowly turned a full circle to wave her thanks before starting to play. There were just a few of the old tricks left that she and the pacemaker could still probably manage, "Duck Diving at The

Pond", "Porpoise", "Submarine", surprisingly the list went on. Eventually though, even the English Comet finally had to admit defeat, reluctantly climbing up the ladder one last time to gratefully accept the proffered towel.

With his eyes still brimming with tears of admiration and respect, Austin Rawlinson led a second long standing ovation for his oldest friend. He had always known it of course, but what a trooper! He couldn't bring himself to speak; in fact it was several minutes before he could control his emotions and attempt to make another announcement. Everybody waited patiently. Austin reckoned afterwards that the Guinea Gap baths had just witnessed something approaching true magic. There would probably not be a performance like it for at least another sixty years, if ever.

Hilda James had just brought the house down.

HILDA MARJORIE JAMES
27/4/1904 – 21/8/1982

APPENDIX 1
AUSTIN

When I originally started collecting data for this project in the early 1990s I was lucky enough to be invited to visit another famous Garston Olympic swimmer, the backstroke specialist and former British Record Holder Austin Rawlinson MBE. As another of Bill Howcroft's Garston Juniors from the same period as Hilda, I was to learn that Austin had known my Nana really well. After serving as president of the Garston Swimming Club for over 40 years, he eventually became Chairman of the ASA and was also their top historian. He laughed as he told me that it was just because he was the oldest one left.

It was a letter to Peter Hassall at the Amateur Swimming Association which led to my original contact with Austin as their historical expert. Austin carefully checked some of my collected data against his own (official ASA) records, and graciously pronounced my research fit for purpose. Only then was I invited to visit him at home in Garston, where he and Mrs. Rawlinson proceeded to spoil me with a very traditional afternoon tea. Austin sounded delighted that I was planning to write Hilda's life story, and even though he was 90 years old he had already told me on the phone that he was bursting with new information to add to my history.

Like a lovely old Scouse auntie, Mrs. Rawlinson told me that since I had spoken to Austin they had both been reminiscing about Hilda James and the other Garston Juniors of the period, as well as Bill Howcroft. She remembered Hilda as that amazing young swimmer who could win a race against anybody. She added that she and Austin had both been very fond of Hilda, and Garston had never seen anything like the excitement she could create, either before or since.

I learned that as a child Austin had actually lived just round the corner from the James family home in Moss Street. He and Hilda had been friends practically since they had learned to walk. She asked me if I knew that back when they had been young swimmers and team mates Austin had actually fancied Hilda for years, and she collapsed into a fit of the giggles as her husband blustered loudly about that in front of their guest. Finally she told me to make sure I stopped him when I'd had enough, because I'd soon find out that once I got him started he wouldn't half talk. Satisfied the she had the measure of her husband, Mrs. Rawlinson then dozed off peacefully in her armchair.

She was right too. Austin couldn't half talk, but what he had to say was worth so much to me. He started to tell me a seemingly limitless series of anecdotes that he had been preparing. He had been reminiscing for days and had made me various hand-written notes, detailing episodes that I had to be told about. Fortunately I had already been warned by Peter Hassall that Austin was a great raconteur, and I had arrived equipped with the very latest technology in the form of a portable cassette recorder. Soon enough my C90 cassette was full, and I struggled on by trying keep up making written notes. Once Austin was in the zone he was simply unstoppable.

A short winter afternoon turned to evening, and eventually Mrs. Rawlinson woke up to ask me if I had had enough of him rabbiting on yet? I promptly found myself being invited to stay for "a spot of supper", a very old Liverpool custom more usually offered to visiting relatives. In Scouse tradition she of course produced a lavish meal, by the end of which Austin had remembered a few more episodes for me to treasure. I stayed with the Rawlinsons far into the evening because the pair of them just wouldn't let me go.

Austin was probably at his most interesting and animated on the subject of the major Garston characters, many of whom I had previously known very little about. Of course as a teenager Austin had also known the James family much better than I ever did and for a lot longer too. He was fiercely proud of Hilda's achievements as one of his team mates, and he was fascinating on the eventual breakdown in the relationship between the star and her parents as her success grew and developed. I remembered my great grandparents John and Gertie James as very old people, but in talking to me Hilda had always and probably understandably left out a lot of detail about them on purpose.

It is also mainly through Austin that I learned so much about the amazing and complex character of the coach Bill Howcroft, and how instrumental he was in both Hilda's success and the triumphs of the Garston Club in general. What I had not known until that day was that Austin's anecdotes about Hilda were treasured by him through a long lifetime of respect and admiration. For years he had held a candle for my grandmother, and I actually found that quite touching. She was undoubtedly fond of him as a childhood friend and team mate, but beyond that she wasn't the slightest bit keen and nothing ever came of it.

Finally, he was able to throw some light onto one of the most intriguing threads in the story, the series of titanic clashes between Hilda and the Nottingham Club star Connie Jeans. He described Connie as another fine swimmer. In his considered opinion she was never as graceful as Hilda, but without doubt one of the strongest and most determined competitors on the circuit. The episodes concerning Connie and Hilda in the book were all written exactly as described to me by Austin. After all he was usually there to see what happened, and Peter Hassall had been correct in his assertion that the former ASA Chairman was equipped with a memory like a steel trap.

Of course raw history does not record anything other than a series of races and records which were hotly contested by the two swimmers over a seven year period, but Austin certainly had something emphatic to say about it. From the very first time they met and apparently after the briefest of spoken exchanges, the two women would take an intense and lasting dislike to each other. Don't I ever wish I knew exactly what was said?

Austin and I would exchange the occasional letter for years after my visit, in fact almost right up to his death in 2000, at the grand age of 98. I would write and ask him a question or two, and he would always reward me with a page or more of new information. More often than not he would follow up a few days later with a "My Dear Ian, I was thinking after I wrote to you, and that reminded me of the time . . ." That was actually how I learned that he had been one of the kids present when Hilda was chased off by the dog and lost her pinafore while scrumping apples for her friends. Without fail there would always be something or other interesting to tell me that I hadn't known, or he would share a piece of information that unexpectedly tied other events together.

The City of Liverpool rightly boasts a Sports Centre named in his honour. Austin Rawlinson was a gentleman and a real character, and I will always regret only ever meeting him on that one occasion.

208

APPENDIX 2
RESEARCH

I do not really consider myself a writer. This project was started as an attempt to learn more of Hilda's fascinating life. When my son Stuart was born in 1993 it became a mission to leave a record of his interesting great grandmother to go with Hilda's memorabilia collection, which he will eventually have to look after.

From the outset, the details I had about Hilda's early swimming years amounted to little beyond the technical records. Once I became interested, I had started with the collection of swimming certificates, newspaper cuttings and photographs, which had she had already given to me. Unfortunately, although the magnificent folder presented to her by Liverpool University still holds dozens of carefully collected news cuttings, they were not inserted in chronological order; in fact very few of them have sources or dates noted. It made for a lot of detective work.

Hilda (my Nana) would sometimes talk to me about her swimming and Cunard days, but even in later life she was somewhat reticent. As a child I was always interested in learning the details and I would often ask her about the many different aspects of her life. It took a lot of gentle persuasion before she finally opened up and shared it all with me, but very gradually she did begin to.

Between the ages of 10 and 12, I spent a lot of time staying with her and Hugh (my Grandpa) at Parkgate during the period from 1971 until his death in 1973. Hugh was very frail by then and slept a lot, so although he often participated in reminiscing for a while, Hilda and I were always left with plenty of time to talk. Thinking back, I am sure that that retiring to Parkgate had finally helped her to overcome the psychological difficulty of allowing somebody else to share her deepest thoughts about her past triumphs and successes. It was certainly there that she gave me the most information.

Often we would sit together on the old sea wall with a Pendleton's ice cream, or walk along the Parade to look at the Bath House and the green space where the pool had once stood. She would slowly start to tell me about the good times. I used to feel so sad when she spoiled it all by telling me some details about the price she had paid for her success, but it was only much later that I began to realise how privileged I had been to be allowed that deeply into her confidence.

Of the many chapters in her life, it seems strange that the five fabulous years spent cruising aboard Carinthia is the part that I probably still know least about. She never kept a proper journal, only starting to write about her life when she was in her seventies. I tried to encourage her to document as many facts and memories as she could. Sadly the project was one of those on and off tasks which are never properly finished, and when the dratted pacemaker suddenly quit in the summer of 1982 I was left with many fragments and partial recollections which needed to be pieced together.

Official archives and facts were much easier to pin down of course. For instance, I was able to access the ship's log for Carinthia during my initial research at the UK National Records Office at Kew, so the routes, ports of call and dates are all clearly defined. I started with that as a framework for the cruising section and have since added to it many of Hilda and Hugh's own recollections, plus a series of anecdotes collected from various other sources over more than thirty years. Some accounts exist regarding ports of call, a few passengers and crew members and so forth, but very little else. It has taken a great deal of work to construct a viable timeline for these events. I have added very little in the way of dramatisation.

Apart from a small amount of factual writing, Hilda's hand written notes were mostly presented in the form of several truncated attempts to write her life story as a work of fiction loosely based around the facts. Although I already had the folder and cuttings, and even after asking her to make these notes, it was not until after her death that I finally acquired them all. The names had been changed, not only to protect the innocent but, in some cases of course, the guilty too.

For example, in one version she had cast her role as that of a figure skater, but the home life, club details and events exactly matched reality. She had discovered that she was far too inhibited by her difficult upbringing to write of herself in the first person, I suppose it just didn't feel comfortable. I spent many years trawling through the tiny and rapidly fading soft pencil script filling several school exercise books. There were various crossings out, notes and almost indecipherable additions, but eventually I managed to get all the available details in the right order.

To add to the difficulty, as a great recycler she had written on left over scraps of paper, grocery bags, the backs of old letters and so on. There were lists which simply consisted of one word bullet points, some literally scribbled quickly on the insides of unfolded cigarette packets. Much of that data is now completely lost as the old paper has faded and literally fallen to dust. Even after deciphering the notes, so cryptic were some of the clues that it was often difficult to fathom out who she was referring to. It felt like trying to solve one of her famous treasure hunts aboard Carinthia, and I was often left unsure whether I had found the next clue or just another red herring. After a thirty year project, I suppose this book serves as the final prize.

I had managed to get some other research done in the pre-internet days, largely relying on letters to and from a range of surviving elderly relatives, together with various local and swimming historians. For matters relating to Garston, that meant turning to John Derbyshire of the Garston and District Historical Society, who kindly wrote to me many times with details to add and background information. Mostyn House historical expert Geoffrey Place supplied a lot of data on the subject of The Wirral and specifically the Parkgate baths.

I visited Liverpool University and checked some of the many Cunard records held there, as well as trawling through various Cunard archives held in the National Records Office at Kew. I also advertised in the local press on Merseyside, an exercise which resulted in a lot of interesting replies. A similar request for information in the Southampton newspapers produced another series of fascinating anecdotes from several of Hilda and Hugh's old Cunard colleagues.

AG Grenfell's niece, Dr. Bevyl Cowan wrote to me with an interesting account of life at the Parkgate baths in the early 1930s from the owner's point of view. She used to accompany her uncle to help empty the penny locks at the baths toilets on a Sunday evening. Aged about five, Bevyl learned to sort all the big old pennies into piles of twelve (one shilling) for him, receiving a very generous cut of one penny for every shilling. Her uncle told her that with all the costs that had to be met at the baths, plus the money spent on repairs, even though it was always busy the overall profit was mainly counted in the pennies from those toilets.

Hugh's much younger half brother, my Great Half-Uncle Douglas, was instrumental in furnishing me with enough data to write about his beloved Hughie. Douglas spent years sending me details above and beyond what I had learned from Hugh himself, and he also worked on a magnificent and extensive family tree. Douglas accomplished much of that when already in his late seventies. An energetic and enthusiastic man, in fact at well over 90 he still spurned his stair lift. Douglas preferred to rush the stairs and take them two at a time while complaining bitterly that he wasn't the man he used to be. He had researched his family tree the hard way, by travelling to remote churches to study parish records, often crawling about in overgrown graveyards to read the stones. Before the age of the internet he was a great letter writer, but being technically minded like Hugh he quickly got to grips with email. Without Douglas I would actually know very little about Hugh's early life.

211

Incredibly there is a piece of surviving Gaumont silent newsreel from the spring of 1927, showing Hilda giving a swimming demonstration at the Parkgate baths. It is headed "Ambitious Girl Swimmer – Miss Hilda James, ex- World Champion, who hopes to swim the Channel, gives a demonstration at Parkgate, Liverpool" (sic.) At the end of the brief 70 second clip, she and her sister Elsie are clearly shown performing some of their trick dives together in the natty hoop design costumes.

When I started researching the project, there were still people around who believed that Hilda James had swum the Channel, because they could remember she was going to. Because the press let her off lightly, the public had never actually been told that in fact she had withdrawn from the attempt. I do not own the rights to the film, but it can be viewed on the internet.

There is another piece of fascinating film on the internet. One of a series of training movies made in New York during 1932, it features Bill Howcroft commenting on Louis Handley's divers. It is a "talkie", with evidence of Howcroft's clear delivery, using his high pitched and rather refined Lancashire accent as described to me by Austin.

There are some items that I still wish were in the archive collection, but have never come to light. For instance, I would dearly love to have seen the original letter Hilda received from Lady Nancy Astor regarding the motorbike. In fact while doing some research with Hilda at Parkgate we searched her house high and low for it as she was certain that it still existed. Sadly it was gone.

Finally, as mentioned in the text Ma James gave away many of Hilda's hard won medals and trophies to individuals, swimming clubs and baths for display. Out of pure interest I would be absolutely delighted to learn of the whereabouts of any items bearing her name which still exist. Have you seen any in a museum or trophy cabinet?

If you have any comments, corrections or information to add, or would like to contact me for any reason please feel welcome to email me at;

ihmcallister@aol.com

Thank you for reading this book. If you have enjoyed it, please visit the website, or feel free to follow the facebook page. I am planning to gradually display more of Hilda James' photographs and cuttings using these platforms.

www.lostolympics.co.uk
www.facebook.com/lostolympics
@lostolympics

BIBLIOGRAPHY

Shipwrecks of the Cunard Line – Sam Warwick
Crawl stroke Swimming – Louis de B Handley with WJ Howcroft
The Romance of a Modern Liner – Captain EG Diggle RD RNR
Young Woman and The Sea – Glenn Stout

THANKS

I was encouraged along the way by several people who said "Why not write a book?" There was one particular conversation which finally kicked the project off. It took place during a cruise aboard the modern Cunard liner Queen Victoria in 2011. A Cunard historian himself, Victoria's Chief Engineer Ronnie Keir extracted a promise from me that I would get on with it. So for you, Chief, here it is.

Thank you to my Mother, Sheila McAllister, for editing. To modify one of your own favourites; "You can take the teacher out of the classroom, but you will never take the classroom out of the teacher!" Love and thanks to my wife and soul mate Simone for support, understanding and most of the coffee. To our Son, Stuart, my grateful thanks for various technical help. You three probably had to put up with the worst of it.

Thank you to Kate Bullock for long hours spent beta reading and for all the formatting suggestions. Sometimes it just all needs a different viewpoint.

And thanks to all those others who have contributed. Large or small, every single piece of information has made the whole project worthwhile. In no particular order;

Don McAllister, Douglas McAllister, Ross McAllister, Margery Wood (nee Brooks) Vivienne Carey, Anne Pearce, Ethel Hedger, Anne Riding, Tom James, Trevor James, Jean Reid.

Ron Warwick, Sam Warwick, Austin Rawlinson, Bevyl Cowan, Peter Hassall, Julie Dorado, John Derbyshire, Barbara Pell, Geoffrey Place, Amy Greir, Harry Lyon, Bernard Pettman.

Thanks to John Smale and emp3books.

Last of all, just as I finished writing the book I received a small parcel in the post. It contained a beautiful silver plated napkin ring from Carinthia, together with a hand-written italic script letter written using a fountain pen. It was not easy to read and looked like it had probably been hard work to write. There was no return address and I could only partially decipher the signature. I have decided to reproduce it here verbatim to serve as a thank you to the anonymous lady;

"Dear Mr. McAllister
I have been told by a friend that you are writing a book about the Garston swimmer Hilda James – and about time too may I say! Hilda worked with my great aunt when they were both aboard the Cunard liner "Carinthia" in the 1920's.
Because I am now 92 years of age and with nobody to leave my few souvenirs to, I have asked the staff in my retirement home to send this small item in the hope that it will find a place in your collection of Cunard memorabilia.
It is a small napkin ring that my aunt gave to me when I was a young girl one Christmas and I suspect that she should not have had it in the first place!
She was a hairdresser on the ship and said that she learned to swim because Hilda James would hold a party in the grand pool at night for the crew when the passengers were all in bed.
I remember the open air baths at Neston and I believe that the James were the owners. My father took me to Wallasey baths to see Hilda swim and she broke the World Record.
Yours Faithfully,

Wherever you are I wish I could reply to you personally. I have been left genuinely humbled by your kind wishes and generous gesture. Thank you so much.

215

Lightning Source UK Ltd.
Milton Keynes UK
UKOW06f1518091214

242883UK00003B/18/P